W9-CAH-134

The Sweeter Side of
Amy's Bread

The *Sweeter* Side of
AMY'S BREAD

Amy Scherber and Toy Kim Dupree

Photography by Aimée Herring

WILEY

John Wiley & Sons, Inc.

This book is printed on acid-free paper. ∞

Copyright © 2008 by Amy Scherber and Toy Kim Dupree. All rights reserved

Photography copyright © 2008 by Aimée Herring

Published by John Wiley & Sons, Inc., Hoboken, New Jersey

Published simultaneously in Canada

No part of this publication may be reproduced, stored in a retrieval system, or transmitted in any form or by any means, electronic, mechanical, photocopying, recording, scanning, or otherwise, except as permitted under Section 107 or 108 of the 1976 United States Copyright Act, without either the prior written permission of the Publisher, or authorization through payment of the appropriate per-copy fee to the Copyright Clearance Center, Inc., 222 Rosewood Drive, Danvers, MA 01923, (978) 750–8400, fax (978) 646–8600, or on the web at www.copyright.com. Requests to the Publisher for permission should be addressed to the Permissions Department, John Wiley & Sons, Inc., 111 River Street, Hoboken, NJ 07030, (201) 748–6011, fax (201) 748–6008, or online at http://www.wiley.com/go/permissions.

Limit of Liability/Disclaimer of Warranty: While the publisher and author have used their best efforts in preparing this book, they make no representations or warranties with respect to the accuracy or completeness of the contents of this book and specifically disclaim any implied warranties of merchantability or fitness for a particular purpose. No warranty may be created or extended by sales representatives or written sales materials. The advice and strategies contained herein may not be suitable for your situation. You should consult with a professional where appropriate. Neither the publisher nor author shall be liable for any loss of profit or any other commercial damages, including but not limited to special, incidental, consequential, or other damages.

For general information on our other products and services or for technical support, please contact our Customer Care Department within the United States at (800) 762–2974, outside the United States at (317) 572–3993 or fax (317) 572–4002.

Wiley also publishes its books in a variety of electronic formats. Some content that appears in print may not be available in electronic books. For more information about Wiley products, visit our web site at www.wiley.com.

Book design by Cassandra J. Pappas

Prop styling by Lauren Hunter

Library of Congress Cataloging-in-Publication Data:
Scherber, Amy.
    The sweeter side of Amy's Bread / Amy Scherber and Toy Kim Dupree; photography by Aimée Herring.
        p. cm.
    Includes index.
    ISBN 978–0–470–17074–8 (cloth: alk. paper)
  1. Bread. 2. Baking. 3. Amy's Bread (Bakery) I. Dupree, Toy Kim. II. Amy's Bread (Bakery) III. Title.
    TX769.S3968 2008
  641.8'15—dc22

                                                                007046845

Printed in China

10 9 8 7 6 5 4 3 2 1

To the amazing team of pastry bakers at our Hell's Kitchen location

(both during the day and overnight), who take pride in

crafting the flavors and textures to make

"the sweeter side" of Amy's Bread a reality.

T.K.D.

To my parents, Pat and Tony,

for their endless support and encouragement.

A.J.S.

Contents

Acknowledgments

First and foremost, thank you to our agent, Sharon Bowers, for believing in the bakery with her whole heart, and for encouraging us with her enthusiasm to make this book a reality. Thanks also to Angela Miller at The Miller Agency for her interest in and support for this project.

To Aimée Herring, our photographer, we are awed by your ability to capture the essence of the things we bake and the spirit of the bakery in two-dimensional photographs. Thanks also to Lauren Hunter, our prop stylist, and to our photographer's assistant, Katie Hawthorne. Their creativity and humor made our five long days of shooting photos a pleasure to endure.

We extend a huge thank you to our editor, Justin Schwartz, who used his patience and foresight to successfully guide two opinionated women bakers through the ins and outs of producing a beautiful cookbook. Thanks also to assistant editor Christine DiComo, copy editor Jenna Dolan, interior designer Cassandra Pappas, cover designer Suzanne Sunwoo, and promotional maven Gypsy Lovett, who were all part of our team at John Wiley & Sons, Inc.

Thanks also goes to Kerrie McDevitt, Jack Mo, Molly Killeen, and Jaimee Young, for keeping everything running smoothly at our Hell's Kitchen location while Toy was submerged in writing the book manuscript; to Ann Burgunder, David Chaffin, and the team of bakers at the Chelsea Market bakery, especially Jorge Grande, who continued to make beautiful bread and keep things on track while Amy was working on the book.

We are grateful to Jeffrey Klopatek for his careful, insightful recipe testing; to Jeannie and Alf Alvestad for letting Toy test mountains of cookies in their big beautiful home kitchen; to Pat and Tony Scherber for letting Amy set up a test kitchen at their lake house; and to all of them for willingly sampling each and every one of the test results. Gratitude also goes to Susie Chester from our Chelsea Market location, who was always happy to deliver emergency ingredients and supplies to Toy at home during the recipe-testing phase.

Finally, Amy wants to thank her husband Troy Rohne and her son Harry for their patience and tolerance during the book-writing process. They had to taste pan after pan of sweets, deal with bags of ingredients sitting everywhere, and put their summer vacation plans on hold to accommodate Amy's book-writing deadline.

Introduction

Step inside one of our three Amy's Bread retail cafés any morning of the week and you'll be greeted by the pleasing aroma of freshly brewed coffee, the fragrance of toasty bread, and the sweet smell of just-baked breakfast pastries. Your eyes will be drawn to the rows of golden brown loaves lining the shelves on the wall behind the retail counter. Oatmeal-flecked ovals of Whole Wheat Oat Pecan Bread lean cozily against glossy batards of Picholine Olive Bread sparkling with a sprinkling of coarse sea salt crystals; long, plump French Baguettes stand at attention beside slender Ficelles, crusty Filone, Organic Wheat Baguettes, and a fanciful assortment of mini loaves, to name but a few.

On the antique hand-painted front counter, wicker baskets overflow with nubby scones, fruit-filled muffins, golden biscuits, Irish Soda Bread, gooey Pecan Sticky Buns, twelve different kinds of rolls, thirteen varieties of bread twists, and focaccia disks with bright slices of tomato and fresh basil. At one end of the long counter are seemingly endless stacks of large, luscious-looking cookies studded with chocolate, raisins, dried cherries, oatmeal, and nuts. Squares of freshly baked brownies and blondies are displayed on trays beside rows of fanciful cupcakes swirled with icing and colored sprinkles in their brown-and-gold paper wrappers. Cake stands hold six different kinds of old-fashioned layer cakes, including Definitely Devil's Food, Red Velvet, and the much-in-demand Amy's Bread Pink Cake. A tray of handmade quiche encased in tender, buttery crusts suggests a savory option. Later, for the lunch crowd, there will be sandwiches with a wide variety of fillings

to showcase the versatility of our breads. It's a gorgeous and bountiful selection of freshly baked products, laid out not only to tempt customers but also to display with pride the fruits of our labor.

It wasn't always like this. When I first opened the doors of Amy's Bread in 1992, my dream was to create a small neighborhood bread bakery where people would come for their daily loaves. I envisioned a cozy, charming little place that offered the best handmade bread using the best ingredients available. I wanted my bread to be affordable for everyone, with healthy options for those looking for something beyond white bread. It seemed like the right time to introduce New Yorkers to exceptional, crusty, fragrant loaves that were hearth-baked just a few hours before, in the little kitchen right there behind the retail store. If they peered through the open doorway to the left of the retail counter, they would be able to see the bakers at work.

The opening menu included breads such as Country Sourdough, Organic Whole Wheat Walnut, Black Olive, and my signature bread, Semolina with Golden Raisins and Fennel. I was proud of these products, and of my goal to make the best bread New York City had ever tasted. That's why I chose the name Amy's Bread.

The original bakery was set in a long, narrow, 650-square-foot space in the middle of Hell's Kitchen. The store had been a fish market since the construction of the building in 1896, and it still had the original wood storefront with its extended bay window and carved trim and molding. The shop had been vacant for five years, the wooden front was sagging, and the glass was covered with graffiti. I had always imagined finding an old New York storefront—like the kind in old world bakeries or quaint boulangeries in France—and this old storefront was the last of its kind in

Hell's Kitchen, so it seemed like the perfect place to begin. The neighborhood had become rather seedy, but it certainly had potential.

With the help of friends and family, we renovated the space and opened our doors to the public. The neighborhood appreciated our bread, coming back often for more, and soon our original bakery space became too small. Within the first year, we expanded into the adjoining section of the ground floor to make a 1,300-square-foot space. Today it's home to our most popular retail café and the Amy's Bread pastry kitchen.

On opening day, I never imagined the wide variety of products we would be making sixteen years later, or the sheer volume of food our little bakery would be able to produce in one day—or that besides those crusty, rustic handmade loaves, Amy's Bread would be a cake bakery, a sandwich shop, a coffee bar, and a breakfast spot all rolled into one. Without a crystal ball, how could I have known that my narrow little shop on a quiet block in New York's Hell's Kitchen would have a perpetual line snaking out the door, or that Amy's Bread would become one of the most loved, respected, and acclaimed bakeries in Manhattan?

And would a crystal ball have shown me our bakery in the unique and fascinating Chelsea Market, now full of residents shopping for groceries, nannies with children, high school students giggling over their lunch, tourists sightseeing, business tenants working upstairs, and streams of visitors exploring this melting pot of food and activity? Who could have imagined that the empty warehouse I visited in 1995 would become such a dynamic place or that my bakery would feel so comfortably at home there? Would my cozy little corner café in the Village have been pictured in the crystal ball, filled with neighbors enjoying lunch in the daytime and slices of cake with cappuccino in the evening?

I would never have guessed that my bakery's reputation for products of outstanding quality and flavor would also draw so many celebrities to our three retail locations. One famous actor has friends from New York bring him an Amy's Bread Pink Cake every time they visit him in L.A., and many of the Broadway theaters order our cakes for birthdays and other celebrations.

Little did I know in 1992 that so many of the people who shopped at the bakery would eventually become "regulars" and wonderful friends who would come in every day to say hello and chat as they picked up their coffee and scones, or sit relaxing awhile at one of our café tables, enjoying a big slice of cake in the afternoon; or that my initial staff of 5 employees would grow to 145, and that many of those people would work with me for years to come—that they would become part of the bigger "family" of loyal employees that is the heart and soul of Amy's Bread.

Of course we've gone through growing pains over the years, as any small business does. We've worked through difficult times when business was slow, when cash flow was weak, when costs were rising, and when members of our staff misbehaved, but those struggles are inevitable in the evolution of a business. Today we feel lucky to have three locations, a terrific staff, and a steady stream of loyal customers who recognize the hard work we do each day.

If you visit one of our three retail cafés, you'll likely meet one of the dedicated managers who run our stores. They understand the spirit and passion that are so important to the bakery's mission—and they try to impart that spirit and passion to their employees and to our customers.

Each store has its unique personality based on the location and the staff. In Hell's Kitchen, where it's always busy, our manager and her team set the tone with a welcoming attitude and a sense of efficiency. The retail staff is encouraged to be independent, professional, and proud of what they do. Because this is our original location, many customers ask about the history of the bakery, and have lots of questions about all the products, too. Since this is also the home of our pastry kitchen, we get many last-minute cake orders here. Between the visitors, the cake orders, and the long line of regular customers who just need their daily coffee or French Baguette, it's a challenge to keep everyone happy, but the staff maintains a good attitude and tries to do their best.

In Chelsea Market, our retail managers and their staff handle the morning coffee rush from the many companies with offices upstairs. They regroup for the slam at lunch, and then move with the ebb and flow of the neighbors and tourists who stop in for their daily bread and snacks each afternoon. Their store is Bread Central. All the bread for the three Amy's Bread locations and our wholesale customers is baked in the kitchen at the Chelsea Market location, and as it comes out of the oven, they receive piles and piles to sell throughout the day. Devoted Amy's Bread customers know that the largest selection of the bakery's bread products can be found at this location.

Our Village store is always welcoming, with its fanciful window displays and seasonal décor. Our manager and his team offer a full selection of breads that can be paired with the sophisticated cheeses sold next door at Murray's Cheese. This location has become our "espresso bar," with more coffee drinks sold here than at our other two locations. Our manager also takes care of the local sweet tooth by offering a wider array, and larger supply, of cakes and cupcakes than we have at any other location.

In addition to our retail stores, we also have a thriving wholesale business. When we first opened, we acquired a few wholesale customers: restaurants willing to try bread from the new kid on the block. But we had no idea that Amy's Bread would become the midsize wholesale bakery that it is today. Among our three hundred–plus wholesale bread customers are upscale New York restaurants such as The Sea Grill, Union Square Cafe, River Café, Tavern on the Green, and Telepan, and notable retail food purveyors such as Dean and DeLuca and Zabar's. Our outstanding team of bread bakers, who work around the clock making bread by hand at our Chelsea Market location, takes great pride in knowing that their products are being showcased in some of New York's finest food establishments.

We're grateful to the other dedicated employees we've worked with for years who make our daily work life such a pleasure. The bakers in our pastry kitchen are always smiling and are willing to take on any new project they're given; our cookie decorators make each of their seasonal cookies a little work of art; and the longtime employees in the bread kitchen are very skilled and knowledgeable about the preparation of our daily bread. Bread bakers must adapt to changes in flour, changes in the weather, and big increases in production, and ours do a great job of making consistently beautiful bread from one day to the next. Our dynamic office team handles customer service, sales, bookkeeping, and the very necessary process of collections for our wholesale business; they're also a proud and professional group. We're glad to have a staff of dedicated delivery drivers, and a maintenance team that works behind the scenes to keep the place running smoothly every day

of the week. Without our terrific staff, Amy's Bread would not be what it is today.

As we've grown and expanded, we've stayed true to our original goal of preparing everything from scratch, by hand, and fresh every day. We're driven by relentless attention to detail and a passion for making the best-tasting, most attractive products we can make. We try to have fun while we work and put our hearts into everything we do. Providing a congenial workplace, where people are happy to spend their time and which they're proud to be a part of, helps make that possible. Our employees' happiness and pride comes through in the products we sell.

We believe in taking care of the environment and using green products and processes to help protect the earth for future generations. We also strongly believe in supporting our community, donating where and when we can. Each year, we donate bread and gift certificates to hundreds of local events. And every day, we donate our extra bread to City Harvest, where we rank among their top ten food donors each year.

It all began with my dream of starting my own business. My opening team comprised five women and one man. One of the original employees, Toy Dupree, has been part of the bakery since the day we opened, when she went from being a corporate executive developing computer software for a market research company to being a professional baker. She really wanted to bake bread, and was very excited to be part of a bakery startup, willing to do whatever it took to get the place going. In fact, for the first several weeks, she ran the retail store as our only salesperson, working alone to introduce our unique varieties of bread to all of our new customers. Later she became the head mixer, coming in early in the morning to make all the bread dough, and eventually, as the bakery's production staff grew, training others to mix beautiful dough. She has been involved in all the phases of running the bakery and has helped develop and improve many of the recipes for our selection of breads and sweets over the years. Today she is the executive pastry chef, overseeing "the sweeter side" of Amy's Bread. Together we co-authored our first cookbook, *Amy's Bread,* published in 1996. And now, once again, we have the privilege of sharing more of the bakery's recipes and tales of bakery life.

We've reproduced our bakery's recipes here as faithfully as we could, taking into consideration the limitations of home kitchen equipment and the ingredients available in the local grocery stores and health food markets. The focus is primarily on our Amy's Bread sweets, because that's the product line that has expanded the most since we wrote our first book, and those are the recipes requested most often by our customers throughout the country.

We hope this comprehensive selection of recipes will bring up memories of your visits to our bakery or, if you've never been there, will make you want to visit us one day very soon. Interspersed among the recipes are a few stories about a few of our loyal customers and some of the employees who've been with us for many years. We wish that we had the time and space to include stories about all of our customers and employees, but that would require a whole other book.

You won't need to buy a lot of new equipment in order to make the recipes found in this book. But there are a few essential tools used in our professional kitchen that will make your baking more successful. If there is one thing we think will improve your baking more than anything else, it's a scale. We recommend a small digital scale that weighs ingredients in grams and ounces. These scales are not expensive and are easy to use. In each recipe, we give the formula in grams, ounces, and volume. At the bakery, we use grams to measure all our ingredients, because it's easy and very accurate. With a handy digital scale in your kitchen, you can be a baking pro in no time.

The other bakery essential we can't live without is our sheet pans. In the professional kitchen they're known as half-sheet pans, and they're found in huge stacks in every pastry shop and bakery. Measuring 12 by 17 inches with 1-inch-high sides, these pans are a little heavier than most baking sheets, and they're made of aluminum, so they conduct heat well. We use them for absolutely everything. They must always be lined with a sheet of baking parchment before using, however, which makes them easy to clean. One of these pans will last a lifetime, and may become one of your favorite tools.

There are lots of cookbooks available that explain how to make cakes, bake muffins, or produce the perfect loaf of bread, but our intention is to share the way we make our products at Amy's Bread and to teach you some new techniques that work well for us and that we hope will take your baking to a higher level. We think the shapes and sizes, the textures, and the flavors of our products set them apart from many others. We use less sugar in our sweets, so the taste of the other ingredients shines through. We hope that as you try our recipes you discover the pleasure of baking sophisticated products that taste as good as they look.

We've been baking for New Yorkers since 1992, and we've loved every minute of it. We're happy to be part of our customers' daily lives as their local neighborhood bakery. We're not certain what the future will bring, but we hope that we'll be here to share our beautiful baked goods with you for many years to come. Thanks to all of our loyal friends, customers, families, and staff who've made Amy's Bread what it is today.

The Sweeter Side of
Amy's Bread

Scones, Soda Bread, and Biscuits

*U*nlocking the bakery door at 5:45 A.M., stepping into a dimly lit, clean, and peaceful kitchen is one of the things we enjoy most at our location in the Hell's Kitchen neighborhood of Manhattan. The night owl pastry team went home at 4:00 A.M. The first daytime pastry baker won't be in for another hour. The noisy commercial kitchen equipment is quiet now, taking a brief rest before starting up again with the daytime bakers. The speed racks, tucked neatly into their spaces against the walls, are filled with freshly baked breakfast pastries, perfuming the air with mouthwatering scents of warm butter, sugar, baked fruit, and toasted nuts. Soon the retail staff will be in to fill the café shelves with bread and pastries to tempt our customers when the doors are opened at 7:30. But for now we can savor the only quiet moments in the bakery's day and feel pride and satisfaction as we review the beautiful results of the work done by the overnight pastry crew.

Small breakfast pastries such as biscuits and scones are best if they are eaten just a few hours after they've come out of the oven. To be sure our customers have the opportunity to taste our breakfast pastries at their best, we bake them every night from 8:00 P.M. to 4:00 A.M. Those who work this shift in the bakery are known fondly as the "night owls." It takes a special kind of person to work the overnight shift successfully for any length of time. Amy's Bread is fortunate to have a lot of very special night owl bakers who've been with us for many years and who take great pride in making our products every night so our customers can enjoy having them freshly baked every day.

TIPS and TECHNIQUES

• When making the breakfast pastries in this chapter, mix the dough only until it is barely moistened—even leaving a few bits of dry flour remaining in the bottom of the bowl is preferable to overmixing. The Cherry Cream Scones are the only exception to this rule; that dough must be completely moistened before turning it out of the bowl.

• Be sure to use very cold butter. If you're mixing with a food processor, as these recipes suggest, freezing the butter for at least 30 minutes after it's been diced works exceptionally well. If you bake these pastries often, keep a heavy-duty plastic bag of diced ½-inch unsalted butter chunks in the freezer and just weigh out the amount you need when you're ready to mix the dough.

• It's important to cut the butter into tiny chunks that can be suspended in the dough instead of being rubbed into the flour. A food processor is the best way to do this, but if you don't have one, cut the butter into the flour with a pastry blender or two sharp knives. The little chunks of butter will melt during baking, creating a network of small air pockets that help to make a tender, light-textured pastry. If the butter is too warm and gets rubbed into the flour, the texture of the pastry will be heavy and doughy.

• Turbinado sugar (Sugar In The Raw) is a lovely golden brown color, the granules are larger than those of refined white sugar, and the flavor is more complex. If you can't find it, substitute regular granulated sugar.

• It's not absolutely necessary to use a 12 x 17-inch sheet pan for these recipes. Any baking sheet will do, but keep in mind that smaller pans will not hold as many pieces, and your pastries may brown more quickly on the bottom when lighter-weight pans are used.

• For most of these recipes, divide the dough into 2 portions before shaping it and cutting it into smaller pieces. The easiest way to do this is to weigh the entire dough mass by pouring it into a clean bowl that has been zeroed out on the scale. Divide the displayed weight by 2, and remove dough from the bowl until the readout on the scale is equal to half the total weight. You'll be left with 2 portions of dough that are equal in weight.

• All of these recipes were tested using a gas oven, with an oven thermometer to monitor the temperature. When only one pan was being used, it was often necessary to bake in the top third of the oven to get the tops of the pastries to brown nicely and to keep the bottoms from getting too dark. This would probably not be necessary in a standard electric oven or one with a convection option. It's best to pay close attention to the idiosyncrasies of your particular oven and adjust the baking temperatures and baking times as necessary.

Cherry Cream Scones

Yield: 12 large scones

Equipment: two 12 x 17-inch sheet pans

Our Cherry Cream Scones are one of the most popular breakfast choices every morning at the bakery. These deep golden wedges wake up your taste buds with bursts of sweet-tart cherries and the melting richness of heavy cream. A light sprinkling of raw sugar, deposited on top just before baking, adds a pleasing crunch with every bite. On alternate days we substitute imported dried blueberries for the cherries. You can use almost any dried fruit cut into bite-size chunks; even fresh cranberries will do because of their low moisture content. For these scones, we prefer fruits that are tart rather than sweet, because the tartness brings a nice balance to the buttery richness of the heavy cream.

INGREDIENTS	GRAMS	OUNCES	VOLUME
Unbleached all-purpose flour	510	18.0	3$\frac{1}{2}$ cups
Baking powder	20	0.70	1 tablespoon + 1 teaspoon
Kosher salt	1$\frac{1}{2}$ teaspoons	1$\frac{1}{2}$ teaspoons	1$\frac{1}{2}$ teaspoons
Light brown sugar	200	7.0	1 cup
Dried cherries	200	7.0	1$\frac{1}{4}$ cups
Heavy cream	630	22.22	2$\frac{2}{3}$ cups
Egg for egg wash	50	1.76	1 large
Turbinado sugar for sprinkling on top			

1. Position one rack in the top third of the oven, one rack in the bottom third of the oven, and preheat the oven to 400°F. Line the sheet pans with baking parchment.

2. In a large bowl, whisk together the flour, baking powder, and salt. Stir in the brown sugar until evenly distributed, then add the dried cherries and stir again for even distribution. Make a deep well in the center of the dry ingredients and pour the cream into the well. Stir with a rubber spatula or a wooden spoon until soft dough is formed. It should be completely moistened and soft enough to form easily into a disk that will hold its shape without spreading. If the dough seems stiff, add a little more cream to soften it.

3. Weigh the dough and divide it into 2 equal pieces—or divide it equally by eye if you don't have a scale. Gently shape each piece into a round disk about 2 inches thick. Using a dough scraper or a sharp knife dipped in flour, cut the disks in half and then cut each half into 3 wedges. You should have a total of 12 wedges when you've finished cutting. Try to cut the wedges as evenly as possible so they'll all bake at the same rate. Arrange 6 wedges on each prepared baking sheet, leaving as much space as possible between the pieces to allow for spreading. Remember to leave some space around the edge of the pan, too. In a small bowl, mix 1 egg with 1 teaspoon of water to make an egg wash. Brush the top of each scone generously with egg wash and sprinkle it lightly with turbinado sugar.

4. Place one pan on each oven rack and bake for 7 minutes. Reduce the oven temperature to 350°F and rotate the pans from top to bottom. Continue baking for another 10 minutes. Rotate the pans from top to bottom again and continue baking for 15 to 20 more minutes, or until the scones are dark golden brown and firm to the touch. A toothpick inserted in the center of a scone should come out clean. The oven may be turned down to 325°F if the scones are browning too quickly. Remove them from the pans to cool on a wire rack. Serve at room temperature. Store any leftovers in an airtight container. They're best if eaten within 2 days.

TIPS and TECHNIQUES

The dough for these scones should be soft and malleable, not stiff and dry. You may have to increase the amount of heavy cream to achieve the correct texture.

When baking, this soft dough tends to spread because of the high fat content. That's why we start with a hot oven, to set the outer crust, and then lower the temperature to finish the baking. It's important when shaping the dough that you make the disks thick rather than thin, to help control the spreading. Don't worry if you end up with Cherry Cream pancakes the first time you make them. They'll still taste wonderful. Next time try a slightly hotter oven temperature to start or make your disks a little thicker, or perhaps you'll have to do both of these things.

The finished scones should be a deep golden brown. Watch them closely as they bake, because they can brown too quickly if you haven't lowered the oven temperature enough.

If you're using an electric oven, you may have to rotate the pans more than twice to keep the scones on the lower rack from burning on the bottom before their tops can brown properly.

To use fresh cranberries instead of dried cherries, coarsely chop 2½ cups whole cranberries and mix them with 112 g/4 oz./½ cup light brown sugar. Let the cranberries macerate while preparing the other ingredients. Then add them as you would the dried cherries.

Oat Scones with Cranberries and Walnuts

꙳ Yield: 12 large scones
꙳ Equipment: two 12 x 17-inch sheet pans

We included the recipe for Oatmeal Scones in our first cookbook, *Amy's Bread,* but we love these rustic-looking golden breakfast pastries so much we decided that this book just wouldn't be complete without them, so we created an updated version of the recipe to use here. Our customers love them too; in fact they're the biggest-selling breakfast pastry item in our Hell's Kitchen retail café. One of our customers even took these scones to Russia. Her Russian friends were immediately hooked on them and insisted she bring them every time she visited.

These crunchy, free-form scones are fun to make, and with the endless possible combinations of fruits and nuts—bananas and pecans, figs and hazelnuts, golden raisins and walnuts, pears and almonds, to name a few that we use at the bakery— it's easy to create a new taste sensation every time you make them. In this recipe we use dried cranberries and toasted walnuts. We hope you'll enjoy making these as much as we do. Use your imagination to come up with some taste-tempting combinations of your own.

INGREDIENTS	GRAMS	OUNCES	VOLUME
Unbleached all-purpose flour	264	9.30	1¾ cups + 1 tablespoon
Whole wheat pastry flour	100	3.52	⅔ cup
Sugar	100	3.50	½ cup
Baking powder	1 tablespoon	1 tablespoon	1 tablespoon
Kosher salt	1¼ teaspoons	1¼ teaspoons	1¼ teaspoons
Cinnamon	1 teaspoon	1 teaspoon	1 teaspoon
Baking soda	¾ teaspoon	¾ teaspoon	¾ teaspoon
Unsalted butter, cold, ½-inch dice	272	9.60	1¼ cups
Old-fashioned rolled oats	204	7.20	2⅓ cups
Dried cranberries	125	4.40	⅞ cup
Walnuts, toasted, coarsely chopped	90	3.20	¾ cup
Buttermilk	340	12.0	1½ cups
Eggs	50	1.76	1 large
Turbinado sugar for sprinkling on top			

1. Position one rack in the top third of the oven, one rack in the bottom third of the oven, and preheat the oven to 400°F. Line the sheet pans with baking parchment.

2. In a food processor fitted with the metal blade, combine the 2 flours, sugar, baking powder, salt, cinnamon, and baking soda and process them for 5 seconds, until they

TIPS *and* TECHNIQUES

We always like to toast nuts before we use them—to enhance their flavor and give them a crunchier texture—but untoasted nuts can be used, too.

When substituting other fruits and nuts in this recipe, cut the fruit into bite-size chunks. Leave the nuts whole or chop them coarsely, as it suits your fancy. It's also safest, at least the first time around, to use ¾ cup of each fruit and nut, adjusting the amount in future batches to suit your taste if the balance isn't what you expected.

are just combined. Add the butter and process again for 10 to 15 seconds, until the mixture looks like coarse meal. The largest pieces of butter should be about the size of tiny peas. (If you don't have a food processor, mix the dry ingredients in a large bowl with a wire whisk and cut in the cold butter with a pastry blender or 2 knives.) The butter should be suspended in tiny granules throughout the flour, not rubbed into it to make a doughy mass. Transfer this mixture to a large bowl and stir in the oats, cranberries, and walnuts until they are evenly distributed.

3. In a small bowl, whisk together the buttermilk and egg. Remove ⅓ cup of this mixture and set it aside. Pour the remaining liquid over the dry ingredients and lightly and briefly stir them together, just until everything is barely moistened. It's fine if there is still a little bit of unmoistened flour in the bottom of the bowl. Don't overmix or your scones will be heavy and doughy. This dough won't be a single cohesive mass. It should look more like moistened clumps of flour and fruit.

4. Using your hands, drop free-form portions of dough about 3½ inches in diameter (120 g/4¼ oz. each) onto the prepared baking sheets. Evenly space 6 scones on each sheet. Don't try to press them down or squeeze them together—they should look like irregular mounds or clumps. Using a pastry brush, dab the reserved buttermilk/egg mixture generously all over the tops of the scones and sprinkle them lightly with turbinado sugar.

5. Place one pan on each oven rack and bake for 15 minutes. Reduce the oven temperature to 375°F and rotate the pans from top to bottom. Bake for 10 to 15 minutes longer, until the scones are a deep golden brown on both the top and bottom. A toothpick inserted in the center of a scone should come out clean. Remove the scones from the pans to cool on a wire rack. Serve slightly warm or at room temperature. Store any leftovers in an airtight container. They're best if eaten within 2 days.

Maple Syrup Breakfast Cakes with Cappuccino Glaze

☽ Yield: 12 small breakfast cakes
☾ Equipment: one 12 x 17-inch sheet pan

Our friend and fellow bakery owner Joanne Chang makes wonderful Oatmeal Maple Scones to sell at Flour Bakery in Boston. She was generous enough to share her recipe with us several years ago. As bakers do, we took Joanne's recipe and played with it to come up with a scone of our own that's sweetened with maple syrup. The coffee-flavored glaze offers a pleasing contrast to the rich combination of cream cheese and pecans. We like to call these "cakes" instead of scones, because they're frosted.

INGREDIENTS	GRAMS	OUNCES	VOLUME
Unbleached all-purpose flour	260	9.20	1¾ cups
Old-fashioned rolled oats	100	3.50	1⅛ cups
Baking powder	2 teaspoons	2 teaspoons	2 teaspoons
Kosher salt	¾ teaspoon	¾ teaspoon	¾ teaspoon
Baking soda	¼ teaspoon	¼ teaspoon	¼ teaspoon
Unsalted butter, ½-inch dice, cold or frozen	130	4.50	½ cup + 1 tablespoon
Cream cheese, ½-inch dice, cold or frozen	130	4.50	½ cup
Pecans, toasted, coarsely chopped (see page 242)	75	2.65	⅔ cup
Maple syrup	150	5.30	½ cup
Milk, whole	100	3.50	⅓ cup + 1 tablespoon
Eggs	50	1.76	1 large
Egg for egg wash	50	1.76	1 large
Glaze			
Instant coffee	½ teaspoon	½ teaspoon	½ teaspoon
Water	½ teaspoon	½ teaspoon	½ teaspoon
Vanilla extract	¼ teaspoon	¼ teaspoon	¼ teaspoon
Kosher salt	A pinch	A pinch	A pinch
Half-and-half	15	0.53	1 tablespoon
Confectioner's sugar	90	3.17	¾ cup

1. Preheat the oven to 400°F. Line the sheet pan with baking parchment.

2. In a food processor fitted with the metal blade, combine the flour, oats, baking powder, salt, and baking soda and process them for 5 seconds, until they are just combined. Add the butter and process again for 10 to 15 seconds or until the mixture

looks like coarse meal. The largest pieces of butter should be about the size of tiny peas. (If you don't have a food processor, mix the dry ingredients in a large bowl with a wire whisk and cut in the cold butter with a pastry blender or 2 knives.) The butter should be suspended in tiny granules throughout the flour, not rubbed into it to make a doughy mass. Transfer this mixture to a large bowl and stir in the cream cheese and pecans until they are evenly distributed.

3. In a medium bowl, whisk together the maple syrup, milk, and eggs. Make a deep well in the center of the dry ingredients and pour this mixture into the well. Stir with a rubber spatula or a wooden spoon just until the dry ingredients are moistened. The dough may look a little crumbly, but it should stick together easily when gently pressed. With floured hands, weigh the dough and divide it into 2 equal pieces—or divide it equally by eye if you don't have a scale. On a lightly floured work surface, gently shape each piece of dough into a ball then flatten it into a round disk about 1¼ inches thick. Try not to compress the dough too much. Using a floured dough cutter or a sharp knife, cut the disks in half, then divide each half into 3 wedges of equal size. You should have 12 wedges after cutting both disks. Arrange the wedges on the prepared sheet pan. In a small bowl, mix 1 egg with 1 teaspoon of water to make an egg wash. Brush the top of each scone generously with the egg wash.

4. Bake the scones in the center of the preheated oven for 12 minutes. Rotate the pan from front to back and continue baking for 8 to 10 more minutes, or until the scones are golden brown and feel firm on the top when touched lightly. If the bottoms of the scones are getting too brown, move the oven rack up one level for the last few minutes of baking. It's okay if the scones' bottoms are dark, as long as they're not black. A toothpick inserted in the center of a scone should come out clean. Transfer the scones to a wire rack to cool completely before glazing.

5. To make the glaze, in a small bowl, combine the instant coffee, water, vanilla, and salt, swirling or stirring it until the coffee has dissolved. Add the half-and-half next and, finally, the confectioner's sugar, stirring vigorously with a small whisk until the glaze is completely smooth. Use the small whisk to drizzle a generous zigzag pattern of glaze on the top of each scone. If possible, allow the glaze to dry before serving the scones. Store any remaining scones in a single layer in an airtight container. They're best if eaten within 2 days.

> ### TIPS *and* TECHNIQUES
>
> To make measuring maple syrup easier if you're using volume measurements, coat the inside of the measuring cup with vegetable oil, and the syrup will slip right out of the cup.

Savory Cheese and Scallion Scones

Yield: 12 small scones
Equipment: one 12 x 17-inch sheet pan

We didn't feel our scone menu was complete until we had at least one savory scone to offer our retail customers. This is as close as we could come to making a cheese and scallion omelet into a scone. The mouthwatering scents that fill the kitchen while these are baking will make you want to eat them as soon as you pull them from the oven. Crusty on the outside, tender on the inside, they make delicious mini breakfast sandwiches if you split them and fill them with a slice of honey-glazed ham.

INGREDIENTS	GRAMS	OUNCES	VOLUME
Unbleached all-purpose flour	270	9.50	1⅞ cups
Old-fashioned rolled oats	90	3.17	1 cup
Baking powder	2 teaspoons	2 teaspoons	2 teaspoons
Kosher salt	1 teaspoon	1 teaspoon	1 teaspoon
Baking soda	¼ teaspoon	¼ teaspoon	¼ teaspoon
Unsalted butter, ½-inch dice, cold or frozen	130	4.50	½ cup + 1 tablespoon
Feta cheese, crumbled	145	5.10	1¼ cups
Scallions, green and white parts, chopped	75	2.65	¾ cup
Parmesan, finely shredded	40	1.46	⅔ cup
Buttermilk	225	8.0	1 cup
Eggs	50	1.76	1 large
Honey	25	0.88	⅛ cup
Egg for egg wash	50	1.76	1 large

1. Preheat the oven to 400°F. Line the sheet pan with baking parchment.

2. In a food processor fitted with the metal blade, combine the flour, oats, baking powder, salt, and baking soda and process them for 5 seconds, until they are just combined. Add the butter and process again for 10 to 15 seconds or until the mixture looks like coarse meal. The largest pieces of butter should be about the size of tiny peas. (If you don't have a food processor, mix the dry ingredients in a large bowl with a wire whisk and cut in the cold butter with a pastry blender or 2 knives.) The butter should be

TIPS and TECHNIQUES

To make measuring honey easier if you're using volume measurements, coat the inside of the measuring cup with vegetable oil, and the honey will slip right out of the cup.

suspended in tiny granules throughout the flour, not rubbed into it to make a doughy mass. Transfer this mixture to a large bowl and stir in the feta, scallions, and Parmesan until they are evenly distributed.

3. In a medium bowl, whisk together the buttermilk, egg, and honey. Make a deep well in the center of the dry ingredients and pour this mixture into the well. Stir with a rubber spatula or a wooden spoon just until the dry ingredients are moistened. The dough may look a little crumbly, but it should stick together easily when gently pressed. With floured hands, weigh the dough and divide it into 2 equal pieces—or divide it equally by eye if you don't have a scale. On a lightly floured work surface, gently shape each piece of dough into a ball then flatten it into a round disk about 1¼ inches thick. Try not to compress the dough too much. Using a floured dough cutter or a sharp knife, cut the disks in half, then divide each half into 3 wedges of equal size. You should have 12 wedges after cutting both disks. Arrange the wedges on the prepared sheet pan. In a small bowl, mix 1 egg with 1 teaspoon of water to make an egg wash. Brush the top of each scone generously with the egg wash.

4. Bake the scones in the center of the preheated oven for 14 minutes. Rotate the pan from front to back and continue baking for 12 to 14 more minutes, or until the scones are golden brown and feel firm on the top when touched lightly. If the bottoms of the scones are getting too brown, move the oven rack up one level for the last few minutes of baking. It's okay if the scones' bottoms are dark, as long as they're not black. A toothpick inserted in the center of a scone should come out clean. Transfer the scones to a wire rack. Serve slightly warm or at room temperature. Store any leftovers in an airtight container. They're best if eaten within 2 days.

Irish Soda Bread

Yield: 2 loaves, each scored into 5 pieces
Equipment: one 12 x 17-inch sheet pan

Susan Testa is one of the five women who helped us open the bakery more than sixteen years ago. Her primary job was to mix all the bread dough every day, but she also generously shared some of her family's favorite recipes to help us expand our line of breakfast items. This authentic soda bread recipe came to Susan from her Irish grandmother, Tillie McCormack, who hailed from County Mayo. Susan no longer works at Amy's Bread, but we've maintained a lasting friendship and we still use her grandmother's recipe to make our Irish Soda Bread.

We make a few loaves every day to sell in our retail cafés, but on St. Patrick's Day every available rack in the kitchen is covered with Irish Soda Bread. The first St. Paddy's Day after we opened the bakery, our soda bread sales were lagging, so Amy hung a huge sign in the window that read, "We Have Irish Soda Bread!" After that, we'd hear the squealing of brakes as delivery vans speeding down Ninth Avenue made an unplanned detour to Amy's Bread to pick up a few dozen last-minute Irish Soda Bread loaves. That sign is now in our window every year on March 17.

INGREDIENTS	GRAMS	OUNCES	VOLUME
Buttermilk	460	16.20	2 cups
Eggs	50	1.76	1 large
Baking soda	1¼ teaspoons	1¼ teaspoons	1¼ teaspoons
Unbleached all-purpose flour	550	19.40	3¾ cups
Sugar	60	2.10	⅓ cup
Baking powder	1 teaspoon	1 teaspoon	1 teaspoon
Kosher salt	1 teaspoon	1 teaspoon	1 teaspoon
Unsalted butter, ½-inch dice, cold or frozen	50	1.76	¼ cup
Dark raisins	170	6.0	1¼ cups
Caraway seeds	8	.28	1 tablespoon

1. Preheat the oven to 400°F. Line the sheet pan with baking parchment.

2. In a medium bowl, whisk together the buttermilk, eggs, and baking soda and set it aside while preparing the other ingredients, to let the chemical reaction work.

3. In a food processor fitted with the metal blade, combine the flour, sugar, baking powder, and salt and process them for 5 seconds, just until they are combined. Add the butter and process again for 15 to 20 seconds, until the mixture looks like coarse meal. The largest pieces of butter should be about the size of tiny peas. (If you don't

have a food processor, mix the dry ingredients in a large bowl with a wire whisk and cut in the cold butter with a pastry blender or 2 knives.) The butter should be suspended in tiny granules throughout the flour, not rubbed into it to make a doughy mass. Transfer this mixture to a large bowl. If any large chunks of butter remain, break them up with your hands until they're pea size, then stir in the raisins and caraway seeds until they are evenly distributed.

4. Make a deep well in the center of the dry ingredients and pour the buttermilk mixture into the well. Stir with a rubber spatula or a wooden spoon just until the dry ingredients look like a shaggy mass. This dough will be very wet but should be firm enough to hold its shape after the loaves have been formed. With floured hands, weigh the dough and divide it into 2 equal pieces—or divide it equally by eye if you don't have a scale. On a floured work surface, gently shape each piece into a rough-textured round about 5 inches in diameter. It should be more like a shaggy pile of dough than smooth, compacted round ball. Be warned, your hands are going to be a gloppy mess. Place the rounds on the prepared sheet pan, leaving several inches between each loaf and around the edges of the pan to allow for spreading. Clean your hands. Then, using a floured dough scraper or a sharp knife, deeply score each round into 5 wedges, cutting all the way down to the pan. Try to cut the wedges as evenly as possible. Sprinkle the tops of the loaves with a little unbleached flour to give them a rustic look.

5. Bake the loaves in the center of the preheated oven for 20 minutes. Reduce the oven temperature to 375°F and rotate the pan from front to back. Continue baking for 15 to 20 more minutes, until the loaves are golden brown on both the top and bottom. A toothpick inserted in the center of a loaf should come out clean. Remove the loaves from the pans to cool on a wire rack. Serve slightly warm or at room temperature. Store any leftovers in an airtight container. They're best if eaten within 2 days.

TIPS *and* TECHNIQUES

This is a very dense, heavy loaf, so it's important to mix the baking soda with the liquids as your first step, to start the chemical reaction between the buttermilk and soda before they're combined with the dry ingredients. Be sure to mix them in a bowl that is large enough to allow for the buttermilk mixture to increase slightly in volume.

This dense bread is sometimes tricky to bake just right. It should be crunchy on the outside and moist, not doughy, on the inside. If the loaves are underbaked, they'll be doughy; if they're overbaked, they'll be too hard and dry and the flavor will be diminished. Don't be discouraged if it takes you a couple of tries to get a perfectly baked loaf. Our professional bakers go through the same learning curve. When you get it right, the delicious results are totally worth the effort.

Irish Soda Bread and Whole Wheat
Irish Soda Bread (page 18)

Whole Wheat Irish Soda Bread

Yield: 2 loaves, each scored into 5 pieces
Equipment: one 12 x 17-inch sheet pan

Amy created this recipe for our customers who wanted more whole grain breakfast pastry choices. These moist, chewy wedges flavored with a hint of molasses are so deliciously satisfying that they've become a big favorite with many of our customers who used to buy our regular Irish Soda Bread, and with those who never bought soda bread at all. Eaten plain or with a little dab of unsalted butter and a steaming cup of tea or coffee, they're a delightful way to start your day. They're also great for a healthy midafternoon snack.

INGREDIENTS	GRAMS	OUNCES	VOLUME
Buttermilk	380	13.40	1⅔ cups
Eggs	50	1.76	1 large
Molasses	25	0.88	1 tablespoon + 1 teaspoon
Baking soda	1 teaspoon	1 teaspoon	1 teaspoon
Coarse organic whole wheat flour	250	8.82	1⅔ cups
Whole wheat pastry flour	210	7.40	1⅓ cups
Sugar	50	1.76	¼ cup
Kosher salt	1 teaspoon	1 teaspoon	1 teaspoon
Baking powder	¾ teaspoon	¾ teaspoon	¾ teaspoon
Unsalted butter, ½-inch dice, cold or frozen	70	2.5	⅓ cup
Dark raisins	145	5.10	1⅛ cups
Caraway seeds	8	0.28	1 tablespoon

1. Preheat the oven to 400°F. Line the sheet pan with baking parchment.

2. In a medium bowl, whisk together the buttermilk, egg, molasses, and baking soda and set it aside while preparing the other ingredients, to let the chemical reaction work.

3. In a food processor fitted with the metal blade, combine the flours, sugar, salt, and baking powder and process them for 5 seconds until they are just combined. Add the butter and process again for 15 to 20 seconds, until the mixture looks like coarse meal. The largest pieces of butter should be about the size of tiny peas. (If you don't have a food processor, mix the dry ingredients in a large bowl with a wire whisk and cut in the cold butter with a pastry blender or 2 knives.) The butter should be suspended in tiny granules throughout the flour, not mixed into it to make a doughy mass. Transfer this mixture to a large bowl and stir in the raisins and caraway seeds until they are evenly distributed.

4. Make a deep well in the center of the dry ingredients and pour the buttermilk mixture into the well. Stir with a rubber spatula or a wooden spoon just until the dry ingredients are barely moistened. This dough will be very wet but will firm up slightly as the coarse grain begins to absorb the liquid. With floured hands, weigh the dough and divide it into 2 equal pieces—or divide it equally by eye if you don't have a scale. Be warned, your hands are going to be a gloppy mess. Don't try to shape this very wet dough on the table. Keeping your hands well floured, place each portion of the dough directly onto the prepared sheet pan shaped into a rough-textured round about 5 inches in diameter. It should be more like a loose pile of dough than a compacted round ball. Leave several inches between each loaf and around the edges of the pan to allow for spreading. Clean your hands. Then, using a floured dough scraper or a sharp knife, deeply score each round into 5 wedges, cutting all the way down to the pan. Dip your cutter in flour before each cut. Try to cut the wedges as evenly as possible. Sprinkle the tops of the loaves with a little whole wheat flour to give them a rustic look.

5. Bake the loaves in the center of the preheated oven for 20 minutes. Rotate the pan from front to back and continue baking for 15 to 18 more minutes, until the loaves are firm to the touch and a toothpick inserted in the center of the loaves comes out clean. Remove the loaves from the pans to cool on a wire rack. Serve slightly warm or at room temperature. Store any leftovers in an airtight container. They're best if eaten within 2 days.

TIPS and TECHNIQUES

This is a very dense, heavy loaf, so it's important to mix the baking soda with the liquids as your first step, to start the chemical reaction between the buttermilk and soda before they're combined with the dry ingredients. Be sure to mix them in a bowl that is large enough to allow for the buttermilk mixture to increase slightly in volume.

To make measuring molasses easier if you're using volume measurements, coat the inside of the measuring spoon with vegetable oil, and the molasses will slip right out of the spoon.

If you can't find coarse whole wheat flour, substitute 160 g/5.6 oz./1 cup of regular whole wheat flour plus 90 g/3.10 oz./1 cup of old-fashioned rolled oats. If you're not using a food processor you'll need to grind the rolled oats very briefly in a blender to break up the flakes. Don't grind them into flour; just break them into smaller pieces.

This dense bread is sometimes tricky to bake just right. It should be crunchy on the outside and moist, not doughy, on the inside. If the loaves are underbaked, they'll be doughy, if they're overbaked, they'll be too hard and dry and the flavor will be diminished. Don't be discouraged if it takes you a couple of tries to get a perfectly baked loaf. Our professional bakers go through the same learning curve. When you get it right, the delicious results are totally worth the effort.

Country Biscuits, Cheese Biscuits (page 23), and Whole Wheat Biscuits (page 25)

Country Biscuits

Yield: 1 dozen 3-inch biscuits (using a cutter 2½ inches in diameter)
Equipment: one 12 x 17-inch sheet pan

Biscuits with butter and honey or jam conjure up fond breakfast memories from childhood, when we used to eat them piping hot from the oven. Little did we know while enjoying this wonderful treat as children what a challenge it would be to make a really good biscuit.

There are baking powder biscuits, buttermilk biscuits, and beaten biscuits. Biscuits can be made with butter, lard, or vegetable shortening. The dough can be kneaded like bread dough, rolled like pie dough, or barely mixed and dropped by spoonfuls, and can be dry or wet. Biscuits are baked at between 350° and 500°F. The possibilities are endless. And at the bakery, we've tried at least a dozen of them. But there was always one overriding goal—the biscuits had to be moist and flavorful enough to taste appealing even after they had been out of the oven all day. We're happy to say we finally accomplished that goal.

Our biscuit dough is very wet, must be gently kneaded, uses vegetable shortening to accommodate our vegetarian customers, and bakes in a very hot oven. These biscuits can be eaten warm from the oven or at room temperature at the end of the day. We hope you'll enjoy them as much as our Amy's Bread customers do.

INGREDIENTS	GRAMS	OUNCES	VOLUME
Unbleached all-purpose flour	400	14.10	3½ cups
Baking powder	27	0.95	1 tablespoon + 2½ teaspoons
Kosher salt	2½ teaspoons	2½ teaspoons	2½ teaspoons
Vegetable shortening	84	3.0	⅓ cup + 1 tablespoon
Milk, whole	395	14.0	1⅔ cups
Unsalted butter, melted	56	2.0	¼ cup

1. Preheat the oven to 475°F. Line the sheet pan with baking parchment.

2. In a large bowl, whisk together the flour, baking powder, and salt. Using your hands or a pastry blender, work the shortening into the dry ingredients until the largest pieces remaining are the size of tiny peas. Make a deep well in the center of the dry ingredients and pour the milk into the well. Stir with a rubber spatula or a wooden spoon just until the dry ingredients are moistened. This dough should be very wet.

3. Pour the dough out onto a floured work surface. With floured hands, very gently knead the dough by folding it in half—pull the top edge down toward you until it meets the bottom edge; give it a ¼ turn to the left, and fold it in half again. Fold and turn the dough a total of 8 times. Do not press down too hard. If the dough is sticking

to the table, use a dough scraper to help lift it. Keep the work surface lightly floured. When you've finished the turns, you should have a moist, cohesive dough mass; it should not be too tight and compact. Sprinkle the top of the dough with flour and press it lightly into a 9-inch circle about ¾ inch thick. Using a floured 2½-inch round cutter, cut as many pieces as you can from the circle of dough. Dip the cutter into flour frequently to keep it from sticking to the dough. Place the cut biscuits on the prepared baking pan, leaving about an inch between each biscuit and around the edges of the pan to allow for spreading. Gently gather the dough scraps together into a ball and press them into a circle ¾ inch thick. Cut more biscuits. Repeat this process until all the dough has been shaped into biscuits. You will notice that the dough gets tighter and tighter each time you reuse the scraps, so the last biscuits you cut may not rise as nicely during baking as the first ones. You'll have to shape the last biscuit by hand, pressing together any remaining scraps into a disk ¾ inch thick. Use a pastry brush to baste the top of each biscuit generously with melted butter.

4. Bake the biscuits in the center of the preheated oven for 8 minutes. Rotate the pan from front to back and continue baking for 6 to 8 more minutes, or until the biscuits are golden brown on both the top and bottom. A toothpick inserted in the center of a biscuit should come out clean. Remove the biscuits from the pans to cool on a wire rack. Serve slightly warm or at room temperature. Store any leftovers in an airtight container. They're best if eaten within 2 days.

TIPS *and* TECHNIQUES

Don't be tempted to knead more flour into the wet dough when you're giving it turns. It's better to use a dough scraper to help you lift the dough if it's sticking and then lightly flour the work surface. Wetter dough makes lighter, more flavorful biscuits that won't dry out by the end of the day.

If possible, use a thin metal biscuit cutter that has a fairly sharp edge. Using a dull biscuit cutter seals the sides of the biscuits as they're being cut, keeping them from rising as much when they're baking. Keep the cutter floured so it won't stick to the dough and seal the edges.

Don't twist the biscuit cutter as you press it down into the dough. A twisting motion will also seal the biscuit edges and prevent the biscuits from rising nicely during baking.

We baked our test biscuits in the top third of a 500°F gas oven, but baking at that temperature in an electric oven would probably burn the biscuits. If you have a convection oven, try baking at 450°F for a total of 12 minutes.

Cheese Biscuits

Yield: 1 dozen 3-inch biscuits (using a cutter 2½ inches in diameter)
Equipment: one 12 x 17-inch sheet pan

These biscuits are made with a generous portion of sharp cheddar cheese and a little Parmesan thrown in to give them an irresistible fragrance and flavor. We use yellow cheddar cheese because it makes it easier to distinguish the Cheese Biscuits from the plain Country Biscuits in the retail café, but sharp white cheddar works just as well, if you prefer to use cheese that hasn't been colored. Try different kinds of cheddar with this recipe to see which one you like the best. On the weekends in the retail cafés, we offer Ham and Cheese Biscuits as a special treat for brunch.

INGREDIENTS	GRAMS	OUNCES	VOLUME
Unbleached all-purpose flour	420	14.80	3 cups
Baking powder	20	0.70	1 tablespoon + 1 teaspoon
Kosher salt	2½ teaspoons	2½ teaspoons	2½ teaspoons
Vegetable shortening	75	3.0	⅓ cup + 1 tablespoon
Sharp cheddar cheese, grated medium	120	4.23	1½ cups
Parmesan, grated fine	55	2.0	1 scant cup
Milk, whole	425	15.0	1¾ cups
Unsalted butter, melted	56	2.0	¼ cup

1. Preheat the oven to 475°F. Line the sheet pan with baking parchment.

2. In a large bowl, whisk together the flour, baking powder, and salt. Using your hands or a pastry blender, cut in the shortening until the largest pieces remaining are the size of small peas. Stir in both cheeses until they are evenly distributed. Make a deep well in the center of the dry ingredients and pour the milk into the well. Stir with a rubber spatula or a wooden spoon just until the dry ingredients are barely moistened. This dough should be very wet.

3. Pour the dough out onto a floured work surface. With floured hands, very gently knead the dough by folding it in half—pull the top edge down toward you until it meets the bottom edge; give it a ¼ turn to the left and fold it in half again. Fold and turn the dough a total of 8 times. Do not press down too hard. If the dough is sticking to the table, use a dough scraper to help you lift it. Keep the work surface lightly floured. When you've finished the turns, you should have a moist, cohesive dough mass; it should not be too tight and compact. Sprinkle the top of the dough with flour and press it lightly into a 9-inch circle about ¾ inch thick. Using a floured 2⅝-inch

round cutter, cut as many pieces as you can from the circle of dough. Dip the cutter into flour frequently to keep it from sticking to the dough. Place the cut biscuits on the prepared sheet pan, leaving about an inch between each biscuit and around the edges of the pan to allow for spreading. Gently gather the dough scraps together into a ball and press them again into a circle ¾ inch thick. Cut more biscuits. Repeat this process until all the dough has been shaped into biscuits. You will notice that the dough gets tighter and tighter each time you reuse the scraps, so the last biscuits you cut may not rise as nicely during baking as the first ones. You'll have to shape the last biscuit by hand, pressing together any remaining scraps into a disk ¾ inch thick. Use a pastry brush to baste the top of each biscuit generously with melted butter.

4. Bake the biscuits in the center of the preheated oven for 8 minutes. Rotate the pan from front to back and continue baking for 6 to 8 more minutes, until the biscuits are golden brown on both the top and bottom. A toothpick inserted in the center of a biscuit should come out dry. Remove the biscuits from the pans to cool on a wire rack. Serve slightly warm or at room temperature. Store any leftovers in an airtight container. They're best if eaten within 2 days.

TIPS and TECHNIQUES

Don't be tempted to knead more flour into the wet dough when you're giving it turns. It's better to use a dough scraper to help you lift the dough if it's sticking and then lightly re-flour the work surface. Wetter dough makes lighter, more flavorful biscuits that won't dry out by the end of the day.

If possible, use a thin metal biscuit cutter that has a fairly sharp edge. Using a dull biscuit cutter seals the sides of the biscuits as they're being cut, keeping them from rising as much when they're baking. Keep the cutter floured so it won't stick to the dough and seal the edges.

Don't twist the biscuit cutter as you press it down into the dough. A twisting motion will also seal the biscuit edges and prevent the biscuits from rising nicely during baking.

We baked our test biscuits in the top third of a 500°F gas oven, but baking at that temperature in an electric oven would probably burn the biscuits. If you have a convection oven, try baking at 450°F for a total of 12 minutes.

Whole Wheat Biscuits

We thought making a good biscuit using only whole wheat flour was going to be next to impossible, but we knew our customers would buy such a biscuit if we could figure out a way to do it. We started putting together formulas for the nighttime pastry crew to try. After several attempts, we were very close to having a product that made us happy. The flavor balance was right, but the texture still needed some work. We adjusted the ratio of regular to coarse whole wheat flour a little and left it for the night owls to try again. It was a busy night for the bakers, and they were a little rushed trying to squeeze a new product test into their production. They misread the recipe and used whole wheat pastry flour instead of the regular whole wheat flour. It was a magical mistake—the texture of the biscuits turned out to be exactly what we were looking for, and as an added bonus, the biscuit's buttery flavor was also enhanced.

A month after we started selling the new biscuit in our retail cafés, one of our Chelsea Market customers told Amy he'd just eaten one of our organic whole wheat biscuits and had loved it. "It was so amazing. It was the best thing I've ever eaten." We hope you'll feel that way, too, when you try this recipe in your own kitchen.

INGREDIENTS	GRAMS	OUNCES	VOLUME
Whole wheat pastry flour	345	12.20	2⅓ cups
Coarse whole wheat flour	175	6.17	1⅛ cups
Baking powder	34	1.20	2 tablespoons + 1 teaspoon
Kosher salt	12	0.42	1 tablespoon + ½ teaspoon
Turbinado sugar	1¼ teaspoons	1¼ teaspoons	1¼ teaspoons
Unsalted butter, ½-inch dice, cold	140	5.0	⅝ cup
Milk, whole	510	18.0	2⅛ cups
Unsalted butter, melted	56	2.0	¼ cup

1. Preheat the oven to 425°F. Line the sheet pan with baking parchment.

2. In a food processor fitted with the metal blade, combine the flours, baking powder, salt, and sugar and process them for 5 seconds, just until they are combined. Add the butter and process again for 10 to 15 seconds or until the mixture looks like coarse meal. The largest pieces of butter should be about the size of tiny peas. (If you don't have a food processor, mix the dry ingredients in a large bowl with a wire whisk and cut in the butter with a pastry blender or 2 knives.) The butter should be suspended in tiny granules throughout the flour, not mixed into it to make a doughy mass. Make

a deep well in the center of the dry ingredients and pour the milk into the well. Stir with a rubber spatula or a wooden spoon just until the dry ingredients are barely moistened. This dough should be fairly wet.

TIPS and TECHNIQUES

If you can't find coarse whole wheat flour, substitute 114 g/ 4 oz./⅝ cup of regular whole wheat flour plus 60 g/2.10 oz./ ⅝ cup old-fashioned rolled oats. Some of the buttery flavor will be diminished, but the biscuit's texture is almost the same. If you're not using a food processor you'll need to grind the rolled oats very briefly in a blender to break up the flakes. Don't grind them into flour; just break them into smaller pieces.

3. Pour the dough out onto a floured work surface. With floured hands, very gently knead the dough by folding it in half—pull the top edge down toward you until it meets the bottom edge; give it a ¼ turn to the left and fold it in half again. Fold and turn the dough a total of 8 times. Do not press down too hard. If the dough is sticking to the table, use a dough scraper to help you lift it. Keep the work surface lightly floured. When you've finished the turns, you should have a moist, cohesive dough mass; it should not be too tight and compact. Sprinkle the top of the dough with flour and press it lightly into a 9-inch circle about ¾ inch thick. Using a floured 2½-inch round cutter, cut as many pieces as you can from the circle of dough. Dip the cutter into flour frequently to keep it from sticking to the dough. Place the cut biscuits on the prepared sheet pan, leaving about an inch between each biscuit and around the edges of the pan to allow for spreading. Gently gather the dough scraps together into a ball and press them into a circle ¾ inch thick. Cut more biscuits. Repeat this process until all the dough has been shaped into biscuits. You will notice that the dough gets tighter and tighter each time you reuse the scraps, so the last biscuits you cut may not rise as nicely during baking as the first ones. You'll have to shape the last biscuit by pressing together any remaining scraps into disk ¾ inch thick. Use a pastry brush to baste the top of each biscuit generously with melted butter.

4. Bake the biscuits in the center of the preheated oven for 9 minutes. Rotate the pan from front to back and continue baking for 8 to 10 more minutes, until the biscuits are golden brown on both the top and bottom. A toothpick inserted in the center of a biscuit should come out dry. Remove the biscuits from the pans to cool on a wire rack. Serve slightly warm or at room temperature. Store any leftovers in an airtight container. They're best if eaten within 2 days.

Alice B. Chernich

The Whole Wheat Biscuits were Alice's idea. Alice B. Chernich was the first customer to walk through the door of Amy's Bread on opening day more than sixteen years ago. She took her time scrutinizing the array of bread products our fledgling bakery in Manhattan's Hell's Kitchen neighborhood was offering and, in a disappointed tone, asked, "Don't you have anything without raisins?" Toy, who was working behind the retail counter at the time, thought, "Oh boy. Is this what running a bakery is going to be like? We'll probably never see this little woman again." Amazingly enough, Alice was also the first customer to walk through the door of our Hell's Kitchen location years later, on the day of the bakery's fifteenth anniversary. She and her friend Walter Dunn join us for breakfast almost every day, and often we see them for lunch or a late afternoon snack as well. Resident of the Hell's Kitchen neighborhood for many years, Alice is a member of the self-help program Fountain House and of the Forty-seventh Street Block Association. She is a petite woman who knows what she likes, and when it comes to the quality and consistency of our products, she certainly keeps us on our toes. If one of her favorites isn't up to snuff, Alice is not shy about letting us know, but she also tells us when something's exceptionally good.

One morning Alice, sitting at her usual table, asked Toy, "Your biscuits are really good, but why don't you make a whole wheat biscuit?" "I don't know if it's possible to make a biscuit using one hundred percent whole wheat flour without having it resemble a hockey puck made out of sawdust, Alice," was Toy's initial response. But the idea stuck. Toy knew that Alice wasn't the only customer interested in eating more whole grain products, and she thought it might be fun to see if she could come up with a whole wheat biscuit just as good as the biscuits made with unbleached flour. It took a few tries, and a fortuitous mistake, but Amy's Bread now has a 100 percent whole wheat biscuit on its menu—and there's no danger that it will ever be mistaken for a hockey puck. Thanks, Alice, we never would have done it without your nudging.

Quickbreads and Muffins

When we opened the bakery in 1992, we offered twelve kinds of beautiful, handmade breads. Our sweetest items were simple rolls containing raisins and nuts, such as our Whole Wheat Oat Pecan and Golden Raisin rolls. But these dinner rolls simply weren't enough for our customers. They wanted "real" breakfast items, such as muffins and quickbreads—baked goods that weren't sourdough- or yeast-based.

Our goal was to please our customers and give them what they wanted, so we added quickbreads early on, and they complemented our menu perfectly. They were a lifesaver in our petite first New York kitchen. We could make them in the afternoon, when the oven and worktable were free, and serve them the next morning. If wrapped tightly in plastic film, they would stay fresh and tasty for 2 days or more. Besides that, they could be made with different grains, nuts, and fruits, so the selection could change often, to keep things interesting.

We usually use seasonal ingredients in our quickbreads, which provides us a chance to show off the first rhubarb of spring, fresh blueberries in the summer, and pumpkin with cranberries right at Halloween. Our Date Nut Quickbread with Cream Cheese is a very popular winter sandwich. Paired with an aromatic cup of coffee, it's a rich, satisfying treat on a cold and blustery day.

When we expanded to our second location, around our fourth anniversary, we finally had enough room in the kitchen to make muffins. While developing our selection, we found that muffins made elsewhere in the city were disappointing and didn't show off the potential of muffins carefully made with top-quality ingredients. The ones we tried were too oily or far too dry; they were extremely sweet; they were enormous; and they often tasted unnatural. We were determined to create a selection of muffins that were delicious, tender, healthful, and moderately proportioned so that they would be a sensible breakfast option or afternoon snack.

Most of our muffins are made with ingredients that are available all year round, and our selection at the bakery changes every day. Our two most popular muffin choices are French Blueberry, and Zucchini, Carrot, Apple. Both muffins are moist and flavorful, with plenty of fruit inside. Another muffin with a large following is the Banana Bran with Toasted Walnuts, something Amy created for those looking for more fiber and lots of flavor. We include the recipes for all the muffins and quickbreads our customers love most, so they can re-create them in their own kitchens.

TIPS *and* TECHNIQUES

All the recipes in this chapter are easy to follow, and can be completed relatively quickly. We offer here a few tips for making perfect muffins and quickbreads.

• Be very careful not to overmix the batter. Stir it just until it's barely combined. A light, delicate hand with stirring gives you a tender and airy finished product. As you are scooping the batter into the muffin cups, try to scoop from the edge of the bowl instead of dragging the scoop across the batter repeatedly. This will keep the batter from being overworked.

• Cut the fruit in even, medium-size pieces so you get some fruit in almost every bite. If the fruit is cut too small, its flavor will be lost in the batter; cut too big, the pieces will be few and far between.

• When measuring the flour for muffins and quickbreads, we use the dip-and-sweep method (see page 103). We recommend unbleached all-purpose flour that is not too high in protein, about 11.5 percent. This will give you a tender product that still holds up to the addition of the fruit and nuts found in most of these recipes.

• We tested all our recipes in a conventional oven, but if we had a choice, we would use a convection oven for baking muffins and quickbreads. With convection, the muffins and quickbreads rise more, brown better, and develop a firmer top, which is a pleasing characteristic for muffins. If you use a convection oven, you will have to adjust the baking times accordingly. Baking times will be shorter than the times given here.

• We love to eat our muffins warm from the oven, but they can be enjoyed for the next day or two if wrapped tightly in plastic after they have cooled. The quickbreads last even longer, and will be moist and delicious for several days if wrapped in plastic and stored in the refrigerator.

Date Nut Bread with Cream Cheese

Yield: two 9 x 5-inch loaves
Equipment: two 9 x 5-inch loaf pans

When we introduced this quickbread several years ago, we were surprised by the number of comments we got from New Yorkers who loved date nut bread. Apparently this was a New York favorite with a big following. When Amy was developing the recipe, her goal was to make a quickbread with the perfect balance of toasty nuts and moist, sweet dates with a batter holding it together that was not overly sweet. This version seemed just right. We like to spread two thin slices with softened cream cheese to make a sandwich. The rich, savory cream cheese offsets the sweetness of the dates and makes this quickbread absolutely irresistible.

INGREDIENTS	GRAMS	OUNCES	VOLUME
Dates, diced	350	12.35	3 cups
Boiling water	680	24	3 cups
Light brown sugar	220	7.76	1 cup
Sugar	110	3.88	½ cup + 1 tablespoon
Vegetable oil	57	2	6 tablespoons
Eggs	100	3.52	2 large
Unbleached all-purpose flour	615	21.69	4¼ cups
Baking powder	30	1.23	2 tablespoons + 1 teaspoon
Kosher salt	12	0.35	1 tablespoon + 1 teaspoon
Walnut pieces, toasted (see page 242)	230	8.11	2 cups
Cream cheese (for spreading on slices)	283	10	1¼ 8-oz. packages

1. Position one rack in the middle of the oven, and preheat the oven to 350°F. Grease the loaf pans.

2. In a medium bowl, cover the date pieces with the boiling water and set aside.

3. In another bowl, combine the brown sugar, sugar, oil, and eggs.

4. In a separate bowl, add the flour, baking powder and salt and whisk together. Pour the sugar mixture and the date mixture onto the dry ingredients and fold together until almost mixed. Add the walnuts and stir until just combined.

5. Pour the batter gently and evenly into the 2 prepared loaf pans. Bake for 55 to 65 minutes, or until a toothpick inserted in the middle of the loaf comes out clean. Do not overbake.

6. Cool the loaves in the pans for 15 minutes, then turn them out and place on a wire rack to cool completely. This bread has a crunchy crust and stays fresh for several days. Enjoy it soon after baking and avoid wrapping it in plastic film until one day later, to preserve the crunchy crust. Store the loaves at room temperature unwrapped or refrigerate after wrapping. This bread freezes well wrapped in plastic film and then foil.

7. Serve each slice with an ounce of cream cheese for a delicious and satisfying treat.

Pumpkin Walnut Cranberry Quickbread

Yield: two 9 x 5-inch loaves
Equipment: two 9 x 5-inch loaf pans

We started making this bread as a breakfast treat for the Thanksgiving holiday, but our customers loved it so much they begged us to make it more often. Now, as soon as the weather starts to turn cool and fresh cranberries are available, we include this on the bakery quickbread menu. It is very popular around Halloween. The richly colored orange-gold slices scattered with dark red cranberries add a tempting touch of fall to any breakfast table. We use a combination of fresh cranberries and toasted walnuts, but if cranberries aren't in season or you want to omit the nuts, simply increase the amount of either to suit your personal taste. The muffins we make from this recipe are also a big favorite—so moist and delicious you won't need to eat them with any additional butter. To make muffins instead of loaves, grease 18 muffin cups or line them with muffin papers, and divide the batter evenly among the cups. Bake at 350°F for 25 to 30 minutes, or until a toothpick inserted in the center of a muffin comes out clean.

INGREDIENTS	GRAMS	OUNCES	VOLUME
Unsalted butter, melted	285	10	1¼ cups
Eggs, lightly beaten	250	8.8	5 large
Pumpkin puree	624	22	2⅔ cups
Sugar	500	17.65	2½ cups
Orange zest	-	-	Zest of 1 small orange
Water	198	7	⅞ cup
Unbleached all-purpose flour	600	21.16	4⅛ cups
Cinnamon	2 teaspoons	2 teaspoons	2 teaspoons
Nutmeg	1¼ teaspoons	1¼ teaspoons	1¼ teaspoons
Baking soda	2¾ teaspoons	2¾ teaspoons	2¾ teaspoons
Kosher salt	1 tablespoon	1 tablespoon	1 tablespoon
Cranberries	200	7.05	2 cups
Walnut pieces, toasted (see page 242)	150	5.3	1⅓ cups
Turbinado sugar	-	-	Enough to sprinkle on top of loaves

1. Position one rack in the top third of the oven, and preheat the oven to 350°F. Grease the loaf pans.

2. In a large mixing bowl, combine the butter, cooled slightly, with the eggs. Whisk in the pumpkin puree and sugar. Stir the orange zest into the water then add to the pumpkin mixture and whisk to combine.

3. In a separate bowl, add the flour, cinnamon, nutmeg, baking soda, and salt and whisk together.

4. Pour the dry ingredients onto the liquid ingredients and fold in gently until almost combined, then add the cranberries and walnuts. Finish with a few gentle strokes to combine without overmixing.

5. Divide the batter evenly between the 2 prepared loaf pans. Sprinkle the top of each loaf lightly with the turbinado sugar, about 1 tablespoon per loaf, to form a crystal crust. Bake for 55 to 65 minutes, or until a toothpick comes out clean when inserted in the middle of a loaf.

6. Cool the loaves in the pans for 15 minutes, then carefully turn them out of the pans and place the loaves on a wire rack until completely cooled. Wrap in plastic film and store in the refrigerator. These loaves keep well for 3 to 4 days, and freeze well if wrapped in plastic and then foil.

Banana Blueberry Quickbread

Yield: two 9 x 5-inch loaves
Equipment: two 9 x 5-inch loaf pans

Long before Amy became a professional baker, she loved baking for friends and family. One friend liked Amy's baking so much, she recommended Amy for a job as a private cook for a family. To her surprise, she was hired, and had to create a repertoire of breakfast, lunch, and dinner menus. A clear favorite for breakfast or a snack was her quickbread, so she came up with new ones every week. Starting with a base of liquid and dry ingredients, she simply changed the flour, fruit, or nuts to make each loaf unique. When we added sweets to the bakery menu, this quickbread was right at the top of the list. To this day, the Banana Blueberry is one of our most popular bakery treats.

INGREDIENTS	GRAMS	OUNCES	VOLUME
Eggs, lightly beaten	250	8.8	5 large
Vegetable oil	198	7	7/8 cup
Milk, whole	312	11	1¼ cups + 2 tablespoons
Old-fashioned rolled oats	148	5.22	1¾ cups
Unbleached all-purpose flour	600	21.16	4⅛ cups
Sugar	250	8.8	1¼ cups
Baking powder	23	0.81	1 tablespoon + 2 teaspoons
Kosher salt	11	0.39	1 tablespoon + ½ teaspoon
Baking soda	¼ teaspoon	¼ teaspoon	¼ teaspoon
Ripe bananas, coarsely mashed	455	16	2 cups
Fresh blueberries	375	13.22	3 cups

1. Position one rack in the middle of the oven, and preheat the oven to 375°F. Grease the loaf pans.

2. In a large mixing bowl, combine the eggs, oil, and ¼ cup plus 2 tablespoons of the milk with a whisk and set aside.

3. Pour the remaining 1 cup of milk over the oats and let them soak for 5 minutes.

4. In a large mixing bowl, add the flour, sugar, baking powder, salt and baking soda and whisk together.

5. Pour the egg mixture onto the dry ingredients and stir until partially moistened, then add the oat mixture and bananas. Gently fold together until nearly mixed, add the blueberries, and fold a few more times until all the ingredients are just moistened.

6. Divide the batter evenly into the 2 prepared loaf pans. Bake for 10 minutes, then reduce the oven temperature to 350°F and bake for 45 to 55 more minutes, or until a toothpick comes out clean when inserted in the middle of a loaf and the top springs back when touched lightly with a finger.

7. Let the loaves cool in the pans for 15 minutes, then turn out of the pans and place on a wire rack until completely cooled. This quickbread tastes great when it's freshly baked, or keeps well for up to 5 days wrapped tightly in plastic film and stored in the refrigerator. It also freezes well if wrapped in plastic, then in foil.

Rhubarb Quickbread with Crumb Topping

⟳ Yield: two 9 x 5-inch loaves
⟳ Equipment: two 9 x 5-inch loaf pans

Being born and raised in Minnesota, Amy has always loved rhubarb. Her grandmother and her aunts had prolific rhubarb plants in their yards, and the coming of spring meant bags of their rhubarb would be piled around the kitchen waiting to be made into pies, sauce, and quickbread. Starting at an early age, Amy had rhubarb sauce for breakfast when her mom had an abundant supply. Her resourceful relatives exchanged recipes for rhubarb cakes, bars, coffee cake, meringue-covered desserts, and more.

At the bakery we use rhubarb in this delicious quickbread. The disappointing thing about being in New York City is that we have to buy our rhubarb—it doesn't just appear in our kitchen by the bagful. And the stalks we get never have the pretty, deep pink color that is found in the Minnesota variety. Nevertheless, this quickbread always tastes great—it's sweet and tart and it most definitely says, "It's spring!"

INGREDIENTS	GRAMS	OUNCES	VOLUME
Fresh rhubarb	600	21.16	3½ cups
Streusel Topping			
Old-fashioned rolled oats	43	1.51	½ cup
Unbleached all-purpose flour	50	1.76	⅓ cup
Light brown sugar	75	2.64	⅓ cup
Kosher salt	½ teaspoon	½ teaspoon	½ teaspoon
Unsalted butter, cold, diced	55	1.94	¼ cup
To Continue			
Eggs	300	10.58	6 large
Unsalted butter, melted	280	9.9	1¼ cups
Sugar	400	14.11	2 cups
Milk, whole	240	8.47	1 cup + 1 tablespoon
Vanilla extract	12	0.40	1 tablespoon
Old-fashioned rolled oats	127	4.48	1½ cups
Unbleached all-purpose flour	610	21.52	4¼ cups
Baking powder	13	0.45	1 tablespoon
Kosher salt	2 teaspoons	2 teaspoons	2 teaspoons
Cinnamon	½ teaspoon	½ teaspoon	½ teaspoon
Nutmeg	¼ teaspoon	¼ teaspoon	¼ teaspoon
Cloves	¼ teaspoon	¼ teaspoon	¼ teaspoon
Golden raisins	105	3.75	¾ cup

1. Position one rack in the middle of the oven, and preheat the oven to 350°F. Grease the loaf pans.

2. Wash, dry, and trim the rhubarb and cut in small pieces about ½ inch long. If the stalks are wide, split them in half before cutting. You should have about 3½ cups.

3. To prepare the streusel topping: In a bowl, combine the oats, flour, brown sugar, and salt, then add the cold butter and rub together with fingertips to create small pea-size pieces of topping. Work quickly so the butter stays cold and firm. Place in the refrigerator while you continue with the recipe.

4. In a medium bowl, whisk together the eggs, melted butter, sugar, milk, and vanilla extract. Stir in the rolled oats and let soak for several minutes to moisten. In a large bowl, add the flour, baking powder, salt, cinnamon, nutmeg, and cloves, and whisk together.

5. Add the wet ingredients to the dry and fold in gently until almost moistened. Add the raisins and the diced rhubarb to the batter and fold in gently until just combined.

6. Divide the batter evenly between the 2 prepared loaf pans. Sprinkle half of the streusel topping down the middle of each loaf. Bake for 55 to 65 minutes, rotating the pans once after 20 minutes. A toothpick inserted in the center of a loaf should come out clean, and the top of the loaves should be golden brown.

7. Allow the loaves to cool in the pans on wire racks for 15 minutes, then turn out of the pans and place directly on a wire rack to cool completely, or the slices will crumble when cut.

8. Serve the slices of this quickbread with a little butter, and whatever you don't use on the first day, wrap in plastic film and store in the refrigerator.

Lemon Poppy Seed Muffins

Yield: 12 muffins
Equipment: standard 12-cup muffin pan

Agood Lemon Poppy Seed Muffin is a real treat. The best ones are made with creamed butter and sugar and are more like a delicate cake than a typical muffin. Our version includes sour cream in the batter, which provides an extra level of richness and moisture. If you are careful to cream the butter and sugar until they are light and fluffy before adding the eggs and other ingredients, you will come out with the perfect muffin that combines sweetness, tangy lemon, and tiny poppy seeds suspended in a tender cake that melts in your mouth. We top ours with a glaze made of lemon juice and sugar to add a little sweet and tart balance to the finished product. Be very careful not to overbake this muffin, or it will seem dry, even though it is filled with rich ingredients.

INGREDIENTS	GRAMS	OUNCES	VOLUME
Unsalted butter, at room temperature	225	8	1 cup (2 sticks)
Sugar	330	11.64	1½ cups + 1 tablespoon
Eggs	250	8.81	5 large
Poppy seeds	40	1.41	⅓ cup
Lemon zest, grated	15	0.53	2 tablespoons + ½ teaspoon
Lemon juice	25	0.88	2 tablespoons + ½ teaspoon
Vanilla extract	12	0.42	1 tablespoon
Unbleached all-purpose flour	465	16.40	3¼ cups
Baking soda	¾ teaspoon	¾ teaspoon	¾ teaspoon
Baking powder	¾ teaspoon	¾ teaspoon	¾ teaspoon
Kosher salt	¾ teaspoon	¾ teaspoon	¾ teaspoon
Sour cream, full-fat	235	8.29	1 cup + 2 tablespoons
Glaze			
Lemon juice	50	1.76	¼ cup
Sugar	55	2	¼ cup

1. Position one rack in the middle of the oven, and preheat the oven to 350°F. Grease 12 muffin cups or line 12 muffin cups with muffin papers.

2. In a stand mixer with the whisk attachment or with a handheld mixer, cream the butter and sugar until light and fluffy, about 3 minutes. Gradually add the eggs, and mix until fully combined.

3. In a small bowl, combine the poppy seeds, lemon zest, the lemon juice, and the vanilla extract. Add to the butter mixture and mix until well combined.

4. In a separate bowl, add the flour, baking soda, baking powder, and salt and whisk together. Add half of the dry ingredients to the butter mixture and mix slowly until almost combined. Add the sour cream, and mix until almost combined. Finally add the remaining dry ingredients and mix just until barely moistened. Be very careful not to overmix this batter.

5. Gently scoop the batter into the prepared muffin cups. Bake in a preheated oven for 16 minutes, rotating the pan from front to back halfway through the baking time. Bake for 3 to 5 more minutes, or until a toothpick inserted in the center of a muffin comes out clean. Watch the muffins carefully and do not overbake!

6. While the muffins are baking, in a small bowl, combine the lemon juice and sugar to make a glaze. Just as the muffins are removed from the oven, brush the lemon glaze generously over each one to moisten. Allow the muffins to cool in the pan for 10 minutes, then remove them from the pan and place on a wire rack to finish cooling. Serve these muffins warm from the oven or within 8 hours after baking. Wrap the remaining muffins in plastic film to keep them moist.

French Blueberry Muffins and
Banana Bran and Toasted
Walnut Muffins (page 49)

French Blueberry Muffins

Yield: 12 muffins
Equipment: standard 12-cup muffin pan

As far as muffins go, French Blueberry Muffins are our "bestsellers." They're tender and delicious, with plenty of tart blueberries throughout each muffin and a hint of lemon to heighten the flavor. Why do we call them French when blueberry muffins are the most all-American item on our menu? The answer: we use wild blueberries from France during nine months of the year, when local berries aren't available. These *myrtilles sauvages* are small, tart, and very flavorful—like wild blueberries from Maine.

INGREDIENTS	GRAMS	OUNCES	VOLUME
Unbleached all-purpose flour	450	15.87	3¼ cups
Sugar	265	9.34	1⅓ cups
Baking powder	15	0.53	1 tablespoon
Kosher salt	1¾ teaspoons	1¾ teaspoons	1¾ teaspoons
Unsalted butter, melted	227	8	1 cup
Eggs	150	5.29	3 large
Milk, whole	295	10.4	1¼ cups
Lemon zest, grated	1½ teaspoons	1½ teaspoons	1½ teaspoons
Blueberries, fresh or frozen	1⅔ cups	1⅔ cups	1⅔ cups

1. Position one rack in the middle of the oven, and preheat the oven to 375°F. Grease 12 muffin cups or line 12 muffin cups with muffin papers.

2. In a large bowl, add the flour, sugar, baking powder, and salt and whisk together.

3. In a separate bowl, whisk together the melted butter, eggs, milk, and lemon zest. Add the wet ingredients to the dry and fold in gently until 90 percent moistened.

4. Fold the blueberries into the batter until just combined. (Tip: Keep the blueberries frozen until the moment you fold them into the batter.) Do not fold in too much after you add the berries or the color will spread through the entire batter, creating blue muffins.

5. Gently scoop the batter evenly into 12 muffin cups. Bake for 10 minutes, then rotate the pan and reduce the oven temperature to 350°F. Bake for 10 to 14 more minutes more, or until a toothpick inserted in the center of a muffin comes out clean. The tops should be golden brown.

6. Allow the muffins to cool in the pan for 10 minutes, then remove from the pan and place on a wire rack to cool completely. Enjoy these muffins while still warm or serve them within 12 hours for the moistest muffins. Wrap any remaining muffins in plastic film to serve later.

Lemon Poppy Seed Muffins (page 42) and
Zucchini, Carrot, and Apple Muffins

Zucchini, Carrot, and Apple Muffins

Yield: 12 large muffins
Equipment: standard 12-cup muffin pan

Zucchini, Carrot, and Apple Muffins are loaded with fruit, vegetables, and toasted walnuts, and they're completely satisfying for breakfast or a snack. Although many of these ingredients could be combined to make a flavorful salad, we mix them into muffins that taste great and contain a healthy dose of plant fiber, too. These muffins provide a wonderful way to enjoy the bounty of the harvest at the end of summer, when zucchini is abundant, carrots are fresh and sweet, and apples are just coming into season.

INGREDIENTS	GRAMS	OUNCES	VOLUME
Unbleached all-purpose flour	435	15.34	3 cups
Sugar	227	8	1⅛ cups
Sweetened coconut	60	2.12	½ cup + 2 tablespoons
Cinnamon	2½ teaspoons	2½ teaspoons	2½ teaspoons
Baking soda	2¼ teaspoons	2¼ teaspoons	2¼ teaspoons
Kosher salt	1 teaspoon	1 teaspoon	1 teaspoon
Baking powder	¾ teaspoon	¾ teaspoon	¾ teaspoon
Carrots, peeled and grated	340	12	3 cups
Zucchini, grated	255	9	2 cups
Granny Smith apples, grated	255	9	2 cups
Eggs	200	7	4 large
Vegetable oil	120	4.23	½ cup + 1 tablespoon
Vanilla extract	2½ teaspoons	2½ teaspoons	2½ teaspoons
Walnut pieces, toasted (see page 242)	85	3	¾ cup

1. Position one rack in the middle of the oven, and preheat the oven to 400°F. Grease 12 muffin cups or line 12 muffin cups with muffin papers.

2. In a large mixing bowl, add the flour, sugar, coconut, cinnamon, baking soda, salt, and baking powder and whisk together.

3. In a medium mixing bowl, add the carrots, zucchini, and apples and gently toss together.

4. In a medium bowl, whisk together the eggs, oil, and vanilla. Pour the liquid egg mixture over the grated vegetables and fruit and fold in gently to combine.

Zucchini, Carrot, and Apple Muffins (*continued*)

5. Place the dry ingredients onto the wet ingredients and fold in until almost fully moistened, then add the walnuts and fold in gently until just combined. The batter will be very thick and hard to stir. Be careful not to overmix it.

6. Scoop the batter gently with a large spoon or measuring cup and divide evenly among the 12 muffin cups. Bake for 10 minutes, then rotate the pan and reduce the temperature to 350°F. Bake for 22 to 25 minutes more, or until a toothpick inserted in the center of a muffin comes out clean.

7. Leave the muffins in the pan for 10 minutes, then remove from the pan and place on a wire rack to cool completely. Serve the muffins the same day, and after 12 hours wrap any remaining muffins in plastic film to keep fresh.

Banana Bran and Toasted Walnut Muffins

Yield: 12 muffins
Equipment: standard 12-cup muffin pan

We created this muffin to add a high-fiber alternative to our menu that also tastes great. It has a crunchy top and a moist, delicious crumb. The secret to success with this muffin is to use bananas that are very ripe and fragrant. They add liquid and sweetness to the batter and make these muffins irresistible. We also toast our walnuts before folding them in, to give the muffins a deeper flavor. Even if you think you don't like bran muffins, these will change your mind.

INGREDIENTS	GRAMS	OUNCES	VOLUME
Unbleached all-purpose flour	312	11	2⅛ cups
Wheat bran	160	5.64	2¼ cups
Baking soda	2 teaspoons	2 teaspoons	2 teaspoons
Kosher salt	1¾ teaspoons	1¾ teaspoons	1¾ teaspoons
Mashed ripe banana	500	17.64	2½ cups
Unsalted butter, at room temperature	250	8.82	1 cup + 2 tablespoons
Eggs	100	3.52	2 large
Brown sugar, packed	200	7	1 cup
Walnut pieces, toasted (see page 242)	150	5.29	1⅓ cups
Sliced ripe banana	150	5.29	1 cup

1. Position one rack in the middle of the oven, and preheat the oven to 350°F. Grease 12 muffin cups or line 12 muffin cups with muffin papers.

2. In a large bowl, add the flour, wheat bran, baking soda, and salt and whisk together.

3. In another bowl with a mixer, beat the mashed banana and the softened butter until mixed. Don't worry if the mixture looks lumpy and curdled. Add the eggs and brown sugar to the banana mixture and mix until completely combined.

4. By hand, gently fold the dry ingredients into the banana mixture and stir just until combined, then gently fold in the walnut pieces and sliced banana.

5. Gently scoop the batter into 12 muffin cups, being careful not to overwork the batter. Bake for 23 to 25 minutes, or until a toothpick inserted in the center of a muffin comes out clean and the muffin top is medium brown.

6. Cool in the pan for 5 minutes, then remove the muffins from the pan and place on a wire rack to cool completely. Serve within 8 hours to enjoy the crunchy tops on these muffins, and wrap the remainder in plastic film to keep fresh.

Ann Burgunder

One of the biggest fans of the Amy's Bread Banana Bran Muffin is Ann Burgunder, the bakery's business manager. We're glad to know that when we bake these muffins every Thursday, we have a loyal taster who will make sure they're still up to snuff. Ann is one of the three top managers at Amy's Bread. She arrived at the bakery around our first anniversary, as a new graduate of the Natural Gourmet Cooking School, hoping to work as an intern to learn more about bread baking. Ann was a career changer with an MSW degree who had worked with the Fordham-Tremont Community Mental Health Center in the Bronx, securing funding for, and then managing and growing the staff and scope of, their community-based services. She later moved into the arena of hospital management consulting.

After her internship with us during the summer and fall, she was hired as a full-time baker, shaping bread, becoming a mixer, and even taking her turn baking bread on the night shift. It wasn't long before we realized that Ann was exceptionally skilled at organizing and creating systems, and slowly she got involved in the business side, in addition to continuing her baking. As the bakery grew, more and more of Ann's talent was needed in the office, and she became the organizational force behind the business operations at Amy's Bread. She helped to establish our computer systems for production and finance and has been one of the key managers involved with each move and expansion.

Ann is very involved in the world of bread baking: she is on the board of directors of the Bread Bakers Guild of America, and has been one of the main organizers of Camp Bread, a stimulating educational event for artisanal bread bakers. Ann is also the bakery's champion of celebrations. She loves to pay special attention to employees for their important occasions such as birthdays, new babies, anniversaries, and farewells. She's also the only person at Amy's Bread who can accessorize the bakery uniform—jeans and an Amy's Bread T-shirt—with one of her many scarves and a pair of earrings and look like she's just walked out of the pages of *Vogue.* She is very passionate about the bakery and has put her heart into making it a great place for people to work.

Corn Muffins and Their Variations

Yield: 12 muffins
Equipment: standard 12-cup muffin pan

Throughout the bakery we use coarse-ground cornmeal in all our baking. It is the coating on our famous Semolina Raisin and Fennel Bread, and it's the main ingredient in our cornmeal muffins. We like coarse cornmeal because it has a full flavor and a definitive crunch. The other ingredient that sets our corn muffins apart is creamed corn. The sweet corn flavor and extra moisture from creamed corn make these muffins say, "corn," in every bite. We like to vary the ingredients in the muffins, using jalapeños when we need a spicy kick, blueberries when the best New Jersey berries are in season, and tart whole cranberries when autumn arrives. When adding tart berries, you need a little extra sugar to round out their flavor. If you don't have berries or peppers on hand, just make the muffins without them. They'll still taste great.

INGREDIENTS	GRAMS	OUNCES	VOLUME
Unbleached all-purpose flour	400	14.11	2¾ cups
Coarse cornmeal	255	9	1½ cups
Sugar	100	3.53	½ cup
Kosher salt	2½ teaspoons	2½ teaspoons	2½ teaspoons
Baking powder	1½ teaspoons	1½ teaspoons	1½ teaspoons
Baking soda	1½ teaspoons	1½ teaspoons	1½ teaspoons
Buttermilk	445	15.70	2 cups
Eggs	100	3.53	2 large
Creamed corn	410	14.46	1½ heaping cups
Unsalted butter, melted	115	4	½ cup
Ingredients to fold in			
Canned jalapeños, drained and cut into ¼-inch dice *or*	55	2	⅓ cup
Cranberries *or*	1½ cups	1½ cups	1½ cups
Blueberries	1½ cups	1½ cups	1½ cups
Sugar to toss with berries	50	1.76	¼ cup

1. Position one rack in the middle of the oven, and preheat the oven to 400°F. Grease 12 muffin cups or line 12 muffin cups with muffin papers.

2. In a large bowl, add the flour, cornmeal, sugar, salt, baking powder, and baking soda and whisk together.

3. In a separate bowl, whisk together the buttermilk, eggs, creamed corn, and butter.

Gently fold the wet ingredients into the dry ingredients and stir until almost moistened. Add the jalapeños or fruit and sugar and stir gently until just combined.

4. Scoop the muffin batter evenly into 12 muffin cups. The cups will be quite full and almost running over if you have added peppers or fruit. Bake for 10 minutes. Rotate the pan from front to back, reduce the temperature to 350°F, and bake 18 to 23 more minutes or until a toothpick inserted in the center of a muffin comes out clean.

5. Cool the muffins in the pan for 10 minutes, then remove from the pan and place on a wire rack to cool completely. Serve within 6 to 8 hours to enjoy these muffins at their freshest, and wrap the remainder in plastic film to store them.

Lowfat Applesauce Doughnuts

Yield: 12 "doughnuts"
Equipment: 2 mini Bundt pans (6 "cups" each)

How can a doughnut be low in fat when it's usually fried in hot oil? These little treats are baked, not fried. We call them doughnuts because, like our chocolate doughnuts, they're baked in miniature Bundt molds that have cute, round shapes and holes in the middle. One of the many fads that have passed since we opened in 1992, the lowfat craze inspired us to create something with great taste and texture that also had only 4 grams of fat per serving. Applesauce, apple juice, and maple syrup provide moisture and flavor for these doughnuts. The apple flavor is enhanced by a combination of five spices that keep your taste buds singing. Although most of our customers no longer ask about the fat content of our breakfast items, these are still extremely popular because their flavor is so pleasing.

INGREDIENTS	GRAMS	OUNCES	VOLUME
Unbleached all-purpose flour	365	112.87	2½ cups
Baking powder	1½ teaspoons	1½ teaspoons	1½ teaspoons
Kosher salt	1 teaspoon	1 teaspoon	1 teaspoon
Baking soda	¾ teaspoon	¾ teaspoon	¾ teaspoon
Cinnamon	½ teaspoon	½ teaspoon	½ teaspoon
Ginger	½ teaspoon	½ teaspoon	½ teaspoon
Mace	½ teaspoon	½ teaspoon	½ teaspoon
Nutmeg	¼ teaspoon	¼ teaspoon	¼ teaspoon
Allspice	¼ teaspoon	¼ teaspoon	¼ teaspoon
Applesauce	265	9.35	1 cup
Dark brown sugar	145	5.11	¾ cup, firmly packed
Eggs	100	3.52	2 large
Apple juice	115	4	½ cup
Buttermilk (nonfat)	85	3	⅓ cup
Maple syrup	115	4	⅓ cup
Unsalted butter, melted	40	1.41	3 tablespoons
Vanilla extract	1 teaspoon	1 teaspoon	1 teaspoon
Superfine sugar for coating pans			

1. Position one rack in the middle of the oven, and preheat the oven to 350°F. Prepare the pans. Spray evenly with nonstick spray and coat with plenty of superfine sugar, if available; otherwise use regular granulated sugar. Shake out the excess.

2. In a large mixing bowl, add the flour, baking powder, salt, baking soda, cinnamon, ginger, mace, nutmeg, and allspice and whisk together.

3. In a medium mixing bowl, add the applesauce, brown sugar, eggs, apple juice, buttermilk, syrup, butter, and vanilla and mix well with a whisk to combine.

4. Add the wet ingredients to the dry and whisk together just until the batter is smooth.

5. Divide the batter evenly among the prepared pans, using approximately ⅓ cup per doughnut. Bake for 10 minutes, rotating the pans from front to back after 5 minutes. The doughnuts are done if they spring back when touched lightly on the top. Their tops should not be browned.

6. Let the pans cool for 5 minutes, then turn the doughnuts out and place them on a wire rack to cool. Enjoy them warm from the oven or eat them within 6 to 8 hours. Wrap the remaining doughnuts in plastic film to keep fresh.

TIPS and TECHNIQUES

If the miniature Bundt pans aren't sprayed and sugared enough, the doughnuts will stick to the pan, but don't use so much spray that it puddles in the bottom of the cup, or you'll have big lumps of sugar that either fall out of the pan when you shake out the excess, leaving "bald" spots in the coating, or sit unappealingly on the tops of the finished doughnuts.

Not Lowfat Chocolate Doughnuts

✑ Yield: 1 dozen "doughnuts"
✑ Equipment: 2 mini Bundt pans (6 "cups" each)

These sinful little chocolate gems are called doughnuts only because they have a hole in the middle. Like our Lowfat Applesauce Doughnuts, they're actually a miniature version of the Bundt cake. Originally we were trying to make a lowfat product to sell as an alternative to our popular Lowfat Applesauce Doughnuts. And we did succeed in creating a perfectly delicious lowfat chocolate doughnut that had great texture and taste and only 5 grams of fat per serving. For some unknown reason, though, our customers just didn't buy them. Ever curious about the whims of those we serve, we revised the recipe to plump up those fat grams and put the doughnuts back on the retail counter with at sign that read, "Not Lowfat Chocolate Doughnuts." Did they sell? Yes, they did! It seems that, at least in the minds of our Amy's Bread customers, chocolate and fat just go together. Here's our quick and easy current recipe, with every gram of fat faithfully included.

INGREDIENTS	GRAMS	OUNCES	VOLUME
Unbleached all-purpose flour	300	10.58	2 cups + 1 tablespoon
Baking powder	1½ teaspoons	1½ teaspoons	1½ teaspoons
Baking soda	½ teaspoon	½ teaspoon	½ teaspoon
Kosher salt	½ teaspoon	½ teaspoon	½ teaspoon
Sugar	220	7.76	1⅛ cups
Valrhona cocoa powder	50	1.76	½ cup
Bittersweet chocolate, grated	50	1.76	¼ cup + 3 tablespoons
Very hot water	170	6	¾ cup
Unsalted butter, melted	60	2.12	¼ cup + 1 tablespoon
Buttermilk, room temperature	290	10.23	1¼ cups
Eggs, room temperature	100	3.53	2 large
Vanilla extract	1 teaspoon	1 teaspoon	1 teaspoon
Superfine sugar for coating pans			

1. Position one rack in the middle of the oven, and preheat the oven to 350°F. Prepare the pans. Spray the cups evenly with nonstick spray and coat with plenty of superfine sugar, if available; otherwise use regular granulated sugar. Shake out the excess.

2. In a medium bowl, add the flour, baking powder, baking soda, and salt and whisk together.

3. In a medium mixing bowl, combine the sugar, cocoa powder and grated chocolate. Pour in the water and whisk until the mixture is smooth and the chocolate has melted completely. Add the butter, buttermilk, eggs, and vanilla and whisk until well combined.

4. Add the dry ingredients to the chocolate mixture and stir until moistened. The batter should not be lumpy. Distribute it evenly among the 12 prepared miniature bundt pans (about 100 g/3½ oz. per doughnut). Bake for 10 minutes, rotating the pans from front to back after 5 minutes. The tops should spring back when touched lightly and a toothpick inserted into the center of a doughnut should come out with a few moist crumbs.

5. Let cool for 5 minutes in the pan, then turn out onto a wire rack to cool. These doughnuts are moist and delicious for several hours after baking. After 6 to 8 hours, wrap the remainder in plastic film to maintain freshness.

TIPS and TECHNIQUES

All ingredients should be at room temperature to prevent the melted butter from solidifying when the ingredients are combined.

If the pans aren't sprayed and sugared enough, the doughnuts will stick to the pan. Don't use so much spray that it puddles in the bottom of the cup, or you'll have big lumps of sugar that either fall out of the pan when you shake out the excess, leaving "bald" spots in the coating, or sit unappealingly on the tops of the finished doughnuts.

Yeasted Breakfast Breads

Warm butter and brown sugar, yeasted bread baking in the oven, cinnamon, toasted nuts—the aromas are intoxicating. Walk through our Hell's Kitchen bakery at 3:00 A.M. any day of the week and you'll be overwhelmed by the sweet, irresistible aroma of yeasted breakfast breads just coming out of the oven. When people read the word *yeast* in a recipe, they panic, expecting an arduous and time-consuming process. This selection of recipes should help to allay any such fears. Our yeast-leavened breakfast breads are delicious and rather quick to make. Most of the dough can be kneaded by hand in 5 to 10 minutes. Kneading bread by hand is great fun for kids, and all of these recipes yield a final product that both kids and adults will love, making your baking project all the more appealing for everyone involved.

Cinnamon Raisin Twists are the fastest and easiest. We took the idea of a round cinnamon roll, created our own soft and tender dough, and shaped it into our signature shape, the twist. We've become famous for our bread twists, in all flavors, and the Cinnamon Raisin Twist is our sweetest and richest. We offer it only three days a week, and devoted fans have the schedule memorized. The dough is fragrant with cinnamon, full of plump raisins, and the twists are glazed with a drizzle of confectioner's sugar icing.

Another very popular breakfast bread is our Pecan Sticky Bun. Who can resist a yeasted white roll swirled with butter and cinnamon-sugar and topped with delicious brown-sugar-and-butter caramel and lots of toasted pecans? We offer two versions here, one made with a simple lean dough, and the other made with an enriched dough, both with plenty of gooey caramel topping.

Almond Brioche Toast is another impressive yet simple recipe that makes a great breakfast, snack or a delicious dessert. If you make the almond topping in advance, and have a loaf of brioche on hand, you can whip up a freshly baked batch in 30 minutes from start to finish.

Cinnamon Challah Knots—our challah dough rolled in cinnamon-sugar—are sweet, simple delights. And for chocolate lovers, we share two bread recipes: our Chocoholic Twists and our Soft Brioche Rolls with Melting Chocolate Centers. Both incorporate lots of chocolate into tender, enriched dough. Chocolate isn't just for dessert. It makes a great breakfast, too!

TIPS and TECHNIQUES

- Most of the bread dough in this chapter can be kneaded by hand. We give instructions for hand-kneading, but an electric mixer can also be used. To mix in an electric stand mixer, place the ingredients in the bowl of the mixer following the steps given in the recipe. Using a dough hook, mix on low speed to bring the ingredients together, then switch to medium speed to knead the dough for about 3 minutes, to begin to develop some structure. Switch to medium-high, not the highest speed, to knead the dough for 2 to 3 minutes, until it begins to get stretchier and more supple. Turn off the mixer and let the dough rest 10 minutes, then mix again at medium-high speed for 1 to 2 minutes. The dough should *not* pull away completely from the sides of the bowl and slap the bowl, but instead should feel smooth and elastic. These doughs are more delicate and do not require strong kneading. They will continue to develop strength during the rising process.

Cinnamon Raisin Twists

Yield: 12 twists
Equipment: two 12 x 17-inch sheet pans

Our Cinnamon Raisin Twists have a strong following, particularly among runners. For years we made them only twice a week, on Tuesdays and Thursdays. One year, a week before the New York City Marathon, a longtime customer who had relocated outside of New York called Amy and begged her to make Cinnamon Raisin Twists on the Saturday before the marathon. The customer would be in town with a large group of other runners and they could think of nothing better to carboload on than our delicious icing-glazed twists. Amy explained that we didn't really have the staff to make one more product that night, but being a runner herself, she got into the spirit and added the twists to the Friday night bake. On Marathon Saturday, we posted a sign in our window that read, "Welcome, Runners! We have Cinnamon Raisin Twists!" Our runner friends were very grateful, and soon we decided to add Cinnamon Twists to our selection every Saturday morning.

If you haven't had much experience baking yeasted breads, this recipe is a lot of fun and an easy way to start. The dough is silky, bouncy, and enjoyable to knead, and it doesn't take very long to rise.

INGREDIENTS	GRAMS	OUNCES	VOLUME
Milk, whole	326	11.5	1¼ cups + 3 tablespoons
Unsalted butter, cold	57	2	¼ cup
Eggs	50	1.76	1 large
Raisins	275	9.7	1⅔ cups
Very warm water (105° to 115°F)	70	2.47	¼ cup + 1 tablespoon
Active dry yeast	1 packet	1 packet	2¼ teaspoons
Sugar	50 grams + ½ teaspoon	1.76 ounces + ½ teaspoon	¼ cup + ½ teaspoon
Unbleached bread flour	560	19.75	3¾ cups + 3 tablespoons
Kosher salt	2½ teaspoons	2½ teaspoons	2½ teaspoons
Cinnamon	1 teaspoon	1 teaspoon	1 teaspoon
Unsalted butter, softened	57	2	¼ cup
Light brown sugar	45	1.59	¼ cup
Egg for egg wash	50	1.76	1 large
Confectioner's sugar	120	4.23	1 cup
Milk	28	1	2 tablespoons

1. In a small saucepan over low heat, warm the milk until it just begins to bubble around the edges. Remove it from the heat and add the cold butter to cool it. Add the egg to the cooled milk and whisk to combine.

2. If the raisins are dry and hard, soak them in just enough warm water to cover for a few minutes. Drain the raisins after soaking.

3. Place the water, yeast, and ½ teaspoon of the sugar in a measuring cup and stir with a fork to dissolve the yeast. Let stand for 3 minutes. Add the yeast mixture to the milk mixture.

4. In a large mixing bowl, add the flour, the remaining sugar, and the salt and cinnamon and whisk together. Pour the liquid ingredients onto the dry ingredients and mix with your hands or a wooden spoon until the dough gathers into a shaggy mass. Move the dough to a very lightly floured surface and knead for 5 minutes. This is soft, moist dough; if it seems stiff and hard to knead, add extra water, 1 tablespoon at a time, until the dough softens. Don't be tempted to use a lot of flour during the kneading. Leave the dough sticky and use a plastic scraper to lift it off the work surface. Gently shape the dough into a loose ball, place it in a lightly oiled bowl, cover it with plastic wrap, and let it rest for 20 minutes so it can relax. It should already look smooth at this point.

5. Gently dump the rested dough onto a lightly floured work surface and pat it to stretch it into a rectangle. Place the drained raisins evenly on the dough, all the way to the edges, and roll it up, then fold in the ends to form a ball. Knead the dough again for 2 to 3 more minutes, until it becomes smooth, supple, and elastic. The raisins will pop out at first, but eventually they will stay in the dough. Shape the dough into a loose ball, place it in a lightly oiled bowl, and turn the dough to coat it with oil. Cover the bowl with plastic and let the dough rise at room temperature (75° to 77°F) until it has doubled in volume, 1 to 1½ hours. A hole poked into the dough with a finger should stay indented. The dough should hold its shape and not collapse.

6. When the dough has doubled, gently pour it out of the bowl onto a lightly floured work surface. Flatten the dough by patting and stretching it with your fingertips to form a 10 x 13-inch rectangle, with the short sides running across the top and bottom of the rectangle, working gently so you don't tear the dough. The dough should stretch easily at this point, but if it resists, let it rest for 5 minutes before resuming stretching.

Spread the softened butter evenly over the dough. Sprinkle a thin layer of brown sugar evenly over the butter. Starting with the upper edge of the dough, fold the top third down and the bottom third up, like a business letter, so you have 3 equal layers. All corners and edges should meet evenly. Pat this new rectangle with your fingertips to flatten it and to seal it around the edges. Place it on a lightly oiled sheet pan or work surface and cover it with plastic wrap. Let it rise for about 30 minutes, or until the dough is soft and slightly puffy. It should now be about 13 inches long and 5½ inches wide. While the dough is rising, line the two 12 x 17-inch sheet pans with baking parchment.

7. Using a dough cutter with a metal blade or a long, sharp knife, make small indentations in the dough, marking 12 even twists each approximately 1 inch wide, along the length of the rectangle. Then cut the dough all the way through at each mark. Lift a strip of dough, give it a gentle twist by moving your hands one turn in opposite directions, and lay it on one end of the prepared pan, about 2 inches from the edge of the pan. Don't stretch it to lengthen it. These twists should be plump and about 6½ inches long. Repeat the twisting procedure with the remaining strips of dough, laying 6 twists side by side on each pan, in a straight, even row with about ⅛ inch between each. Cover the twists with plastic wrap and let them rise at room temperature (75° to 77°F) for 30 to 45 minutes, or until nearly doubled in volume. They will look very plump and puffy when fully risen.

8. About 20 minutes before baking, preheat the oven to 425°F and position two racks in the center of the oven. In a small bowl, mix 1 egg with 1 teaspoon of water to make an egg wash. Brush the twists with the egg wash, coating them evenly on the top and sides. Bake for 10 minutes, rotate the pans from top to bottom, and reduce the oven temperature to 350°F. Continue baking for another 12 to 17 minutes. If your oven has a convection option, switch it to convection for the last 5 minutes of baking, to improve the browning of the crust. Watch the twists carefully during the last few minutes. They can become dark very quickly. They should be golden brown but still slightly soft.

9. Immediately slide the twists off the baking pans and onto a wire rack to cool. After they have cooled, prepare a glaze made from the confectioner's sugar and milk. Using a whisk or a large spoon with a pointed tip, drizzle the glaze back and forth over the twists to coat them with icing. The icing should drip over the edges and make the twists look very tempting. Serve them immediately or within 5 to 6 hours to enjoy them at their freshest. Store the remaining twists wrapped in plastic or foil at room temperature. Reheat the leftovers in a toaster oven to refresh them.

Pecan Sticky Buns, the Original Version Revisited

Yield: 12 buns

Equipment: one 9 x 13 x 2-inch nonstick metal or glass baking pan; one 12 x 17-inch
sheet pan or similar size cookie sheet to catch the dripping caramel

One of the most fascinating things about working in a bakery is you get a front-row seat to watch the ebb and flow of what's hot and what's not in the marketplace of food lovers.

In our first *Amy's Bread* cookbook we included the recipe for Pecan Sticky Buns based on the caramel rolls Amy's mother used to make at home in Minnesota. The dough is "lean," with no additional eggs, milk, butter, or sugar incorporated into it. All of the butter and sugar goes into the swirl in the middle of the roll and the topping. The buns are baked pull-apart style, in a rectangular pan, so the caramel and nuts stay primarily on the top—a crunchy-sweet garnish to decorate and enhance the hearty chunks of delicious bread. Our customers loved them, spreading the buns with lots of soft butter as if they were rolls. We sold dozens of them every day in our retail stores. But gradually we saw our customers' tastes change. The quality of the sticky buns remained the same, but the number of them being sold declined. Out of curiosity, we decided to test a sticky bun version that was a little smaller, that was made from dough that was a little richer, and that was baked individually in oversized muffin pans so the syrupy caramel and toasted nuts would enrobe each tender bun when it was tipped out, upside down, onto the sheet pan to cool.

Customer reaction was exactly what we anticipated. The customers who were still buying the original buns detested the newer version, but the new buns were flying off the retail counter. Obviously we were appealing to a different kind of sticky bun palate. Now we make both versions, but offer them on alternate days. We're proud of both recipes and include both here so you can try each one and decide if you belong in the "simple, lean dough" camp or the "richer, gooier" camp.

INGREDIENTS	GRAMS	OUNCES	VOLUME
Very warm water (105° to 115°F)	56	2	¼ cup
Active dry yeast	1¾ teaspoons	1¾ teaspoons	1¾ teaspoons
Warm water (90°F)	354	12.5	1½ cups + 1 tablespoon
Unbleached bread flour	312	11	2 cups
Unbleached all-purpose flour	232	8.18	1⅔ cups
Kosher salt	1¾ teaspoons	1¾ teaspoons	1¾ teaspoons
Dark brown sugar, firmly packed	227	8	1⅛ cups
Unsalted butter	198	7	1 cup minus 2 tablespoons
Pecan pieces, toasted (see page 242)	115	4.05	1 cup

Unsalted butter, softened	86	3.03	6 tablespoons
Sugar	66	2.32	⅓ cup
Cinnamon	¾ teaspoon	¾ teaspoon	¾ teaspoon

1. Combine the very warm water and the yeast in a large bowl and stir to dissolve the yeast. Let stand for 3 minutes. Add the warm water, the flours, and salt to the yeast mixture and mix with your hands or a wooden spoon until it gathers into a shaggy mass. Move the dough to a lightly floured surface and knead for 5 minutes. Do not knead extra flour into the dough. Instead, use a plastic scraper to loosen the dough from the work surface. This is soft, moist dough; if it seems too stiff and hard to knead, add extra warm water, 1 tablespoon at a time, until the dough softens. Gently shape the dough into a loose ball, place it in a lightly oiled bowl, cover it with plastic wrap, and let it rest for 20 minutes so the dough can relax. It will still be slightly shaggy at this point.

2. Knead the dough again for 1 to 2 more minutes, until it becomes smooth, supple, and elastic, but not too firm. Shape the dough into a loose ball, place it in a lightly oiled bowl, and turn the dough to coat it with oil. Cover the bowl with plastic and let the dough rise at room temperature (75° to 77°F) until it has doubled in volume, 1½ to 2 hours. A hole poked into the dough with a finger should stay indented. The dough should hold its shape and not collapse.

3. While the dough is rising, combine the brown sugar and butter in a small saucepan. Over low heat, stirring occasionally, warm the butter and sugar until the butter has melted and the sugar is completely moistened and starting to melt (it won't be dissolved). Whisk the mixture until it looks silky and a little lighter in color. Remove the saucepan from the heat and pour the caramel into a 9 x 13-inch baking pan, tilting the pan slightly so the mixture spreads evenly over the bottom. Sprinkle the toasted pecans over the warm caramel all the way to the corners of the pan and press them down slightly. After the caramel has cooled a little, use 1 tablespoon of the softened butter to grease the sides of the baking pan. Set the pan aside.

4. In a small bowl add the sugar and cinnamon and stir until it is evenly mixed. Set aside.

5. When the dough has doubled in volume, gently pour it out of the bowl onto a lightly floured work surface. Flatten the dough by patting and stretching it with your fingers to form a 13 x 10-inch rectangle, with the long sides running across the top and bottom of the rectangle. Work gently so you don't tear the dough. The dough should stretch easily at this point, but if it resists, let it rest for 5 minutes before resuming stretching. Check to be sure the dough isn't sticking to the work surface, adding flour to the table if necessary.

6. Spread the remaining softened butter evenly over the dough. Sprinkle the cinnamon-and-sugar mixture generously and evenly over the butter. Starting with the bottom edge, roll up the dough jelly-roll fashion into a long log; if the dough sticks to the table as you're rolling, use a plastic scraper to loosen it. Pinch the dough gently but firmly along the seam to seal it.

7. Cut the log of dough into 12 equal pieces. It's easiest if you mark the log first, to show where you're going to make the cuts—a slight indentation with a knife's edge will do—then use a sharp serrated knife or a metal dough cutter to cut completely through the log. Lay the pieces cut side down on the top of the cooled caramel in the baking pan, 3 rolls across and 4 rolls down. Let the dough rise, covered with oiled plastic wrap, at room temperature until it has almost doubled in volume, 1 to 1¼ hours. The rolls should fill the pan and rise to the top.

8. About 20 minutes before baking, position a rack in the center of the oven and preheat the oven to 375°F. Line a 12 x 17-inch sheet pan with baking parchment and put the pan of sticky buns on this lined sheet pan. Bake for 10 minutes, then reduce the temperature to 350°F and bake for 20 to 30 minutes longer, until the tops of the buns are golden brown and firm. It's important to bake the buns long enough so the dough is cooked all the way through and the caramel topping can be seen bubbling around the inside edges of the pan.

9. Set the baking pan of buns on a wire rack to cool for 3 minutes. Then quickly but carefully turn the baking pan upside down and release the sticky buns onto a large, flat heatproof plate. Immediately scrape out any hot caramel and pecans remaining in the bottom of the baking pan and spread it on the tops of the buns, filling in any bare spots. Let cool until just warm before serving. (Clean the pan by soaking it in very hot water to dissolve the caramel.) Store any leftover rolls at room temperature, covered with foil or plastic, and reheat them in a toaster oven before serving.

TIPS *and* TECHNIQUES

The recipe in our original cookbook made a larger batch of bread dough with less caramel. In this version the dough has been reduced so that each roll is only 2 inches tall and coated with a generous helping of caramel and nuts. Our sticky bun dough is fairly forgiving, and can be made with just bread flour or with only all-purpose flour, if either one is all you have on hand. We have suggested using a combination of both bread flour and unbleached all-purpose flour to make the bread dough chewier and more resilient but still tender. If you use only bread flour you will get denser, heavier dough, and with only all-purpose flour, your rolls will be slightly flatter and more porous. Both ways will work, though.

Pecan Sticky Buns, New Version

Yield: 12 large buns or 16 small buns

Equipment: two 6-cup nonstick giant muffin pans; two 12 x 17-inch sheet pans to catch the dripping caramel

This is the richer, sweeter version of our Pecan Sticky Buns. We think of this as an "East Coast" version as compared to our original Midwestern-style sticky buns.

INGREDIENTS	GRAMS	OUNCES	VOLUME
Very warm water (105° to 115°F)	56	2	¼ cup
Active dry yeast	1 packet	1 packet	2¼ teaspoons
Warm water (90°F)	397	14	1¾ cups
Unsalted butter, melted	46	1.62	3 tablespoons + 1½ teaspoons
Unbleached bread flour	312	11	2 cups
Unbleached all-purpose flour	290	10.23	2 cups
Sugar	60	2.11	⅓ cup
Kosher salt	14	0.5	1 tablespoon + ½ teaspoon
Dark brown sugar, firmly packed	254	8.96	1¼ cups
Unsalted butter	126	4.44	½ cup + 1 tablespoon
Dark corn syrup	44	1.55	⅛ cup
Pecan pieces, toasted (see page 242)	115	4.05	1 cup
Sugar	72	2.53	⅓ cup + 1 tablespoon
Cinnamon	1 teaspoon	1 teaspoon	1 teaspoon
Unsalted butter, softened	56	2	4 tablespoons

1. Combine the very warm water and yeast in a large mixing bowl and stir to dissolve the yeast. Let stand for 3 minutes. Add the remaining warm water and the melted butter to the yeast mixture and whisk together.

2. In a medium bowl, add the flours, sugar, and salt and whisk together. With your hands or a wooden spoon, mix the dry ingredients into the yeast mixture until the dough gathers into a shaggy mass. Move the dough to a lightly floured surface and knead for 5 minutes. Do not knead extra flour into the dough. Instead, use a plastic scraper to loosen the dough from the work surface. This is soft, moist dough. If it seems too stiff and hard to knead, add extra warm water, 1 tablespoon at a time, until the dough softens. Gently shape the dough into a loose ball, place it in a lightly oiled bowl, cover it with plastic wrap, and let it rest for 20 minutes so the dough can relax.

3. Gently knead the dough for 1 to 2 more minutes, until it becomes smooth, supple, and elastic. Shape the dough into a loose ball, place it in a lightly oiled bowl, and turn the dough to coat it with oil. Cover the bowl and let the dough rise at room temperature (75° to 77°F) until it has doubled in volume, 1½ to 2 hours. A hole poked into the dough with a finger should stay indented. The dough should hold its shape and not collapse.

4. While the dough is rising, combine the brown sugar, the next measure of butter, and the corn syrup in a small saucepan over low heat, stirring occasionally, until the butter has melted and the sugar is completely moistened and beginning to melt (it won't be dissolved). Whisk the mixture until it looks silky and a little lighter in color. Remove it from the heat.

5. Spray the muffin cups lightly with nonstick cooking spray or grease them with softened butter, then apportion an equal amount of the caramel into the bottom of each cup (approximately 35 g/1.23 oz. for the giant muffin cups). Sprinkle 2 teaspoons of the toasted pecans over the warm caramel in each cup and press them down slightly.

6. In a small bowl add the sugar and cinnamon and stir until evenly mixed.

7. When the dough has doubled in volume, gently pour it out of the bowl onto a lightly floured work surface. Flatten the dough by patting and stretching it with your fingers to form a 13 x 10-inch rectangle, with the long sides across the top and bottom of the rectangle. Work gently so you don't tear the dough. The dough should stretch easily at this point, but if it resists, let it rest for 5 minutes before resuming stretching. Check to be sure the dough isn't sticking to the work surface, adding flour to the table if necessary.

8. Spread the remaining softened butter evenly over the dough, all the way to the edges. Sprinkle the cinnamon-and-sugar mixture generously and evenly over the butter. Starting with the bottom edge, roll up the dough jelly-roll fashion into a long log; if the dough sticks to the table as you're rolling, use a dough scraper to loosen it gently. Pinch gently but firmly along the seam to seal it. If necessary, gently roll the dough back and forth to make a nice uniform log.

9. Cut the log of dough into 12 equal pieces. It's easiest if you mark the log first to show where you're going to make the cuts—a slight indentation with a knife's edge will do—then use a sharp serrated knife or a metal dough cutter to cut completely through the log. Lay one piece of dough, cut side down, on the top of the cooled caramel in each muffin cup. Let the rolls rise, uncovered, at room temperature until the dough has almost doubled in volume, about 1 to 1¼ hours. The rolls should fill the pan and rise almost to the top of each cup.

10. About 20 minutes before baking, position two racks in the center of the oven with enough space between them for the muffin pans, and preheat the oven to 375°F.

11. Line two 12 x 17-inch sheet pans with baking parchment and put one muffin pan of sticky buns on each prepared sheet pan. Bake for 10 minutes, then reduce the oven temperature to 350°F and bake for 15 to 20 minutes longer, until the tops of the buns are golden brown. It's important to bake the buns long enough so the dough is cooked all the way through and the caramel topping develops properly.

12. Set the muffin pans of buns on a wire rack to cool for 1 minute. Then quickly but carefully turn each muffin pan upside down onto a parchment-lined sheet pan. Leaving the muffin pan in place, let it rest for another minute so the hot caramel can run down around the sides of each bun. Gently lift off the muffin pans to release the sticky buns. Immediately scrape out any hot caramel and pecans remaining in the bottoms of the cups and spread it on the tops of the buns, filling in any bare spots. Let cool until just warm before serving. (Clean the muffin pans by soaking in very hot water to dissolve the caramel.) Store any leftover rolls covered with foil or plastic at room temperature, and reheat them in a toaster oven before serving.

TIPS *and* TECHNIQUES

This recipe calls for dark corn syrup and dark brown sugar. Both ingredients contribute to a darker, deeper-flavored caramel that flows nicely to cover the individual buns. If you have only light corn syrup or light brown sugar, either can be substituted. Your caramel topping will be lighter in color and have a milder flavor but will still taste delicious.

To use regular-size muffin pans instead of the giant ones, spray 16 regular-size muffin cups with nonstick cooking spray. Use 26.0 g/0.93 oz. caramel and 1½ teaspoons pecans in each cup. In step 9, cut the log of dough into 16 equal pieces, put 1 piece in each prepared muffin cup, and bake as indicated.

Almond Brioche Toast

Yield: **9 slices of toast**
Equipment: two 12 x 17-inch sheet pans

In France, cost-conscious bakery owners came up with this deliciously creative way to make use of day-old croissants and brioche loaves. At Amy's Bread, our Almond Brioche Toast has become so popular we can't make enough of it using only our leftover broiche. Instead, the pastry kitchen has a standing order for Brioche Pan Loaves delivered fresh every day from our Chelsea Market location. Maybe that's why our version of this treat is exceptionally moist and tender, infused with the delicate sweet flavor of almond syrup and buttery almond cream.

The best thing about Almond Brioche Toast is that it's incredibly easy to prepare, and it makes you look like a baking pro when you serve it to your guests. At the bakery, we make our almond cream with pre-ground blanched almond meal, sometimes known as almond flour. When making large batches for our retail cafés, it takes too long to grind enough whole almonds in a food processor, and we prefer the finer texture of the almond cream made with ground meal. Look for it in specialty gourmet food stores and health food shops. The only disadvantage to the meal is that it loses its freshness very quickly, so once the package is opened, be sure to refrigerate it or freeze it in an airtight container. You can make your own almond meal with whole natural almonds, which have the skins on them. Using natural almonds will give your almond cream a little darker color and a slightly deeper flavor. With a batch as small as this, it isn't hard to grind your own almond meal.

Any brioche, plain croissant, or even challah can be used for this recipe. Traditional "pan-shaped" loaves are best because, when sliced, they give you more surface for the luscious almond cream.

INGREDIENTS	GRAMS	OUNCES	VOLUME
Almond Syrup			
Water	113	4	½ cup
Sugar	100	3.52	½ cup
Almond extract	½ teaspoon	½ teaspoon	½ teaspoon
Almond Cream			
Natural whole almonds or almond meal	84	2.96	Heaping ½ cup of whole almonds or ½ cup meal
Confectioner's sugar	55	1.94	½ cup
Unsalted butter, room temperature	173	6.1	¾ cup
Sugar	150	5.29	¾ cup

Eggs, room temperature, slightly beaten	150	5.29	3 large
Almond extract	1¼ teaspoons	1¼ teaspoons	1¼ teaspoons
Toast			
Brioche loaf, about 10 x 5 inches	1 large loaf	1 large loaf	1 large loaf
Sliced almonds	54	1.90	9 tablespoons

1. To make the almond syrup: In a small heavy-duty saucepan, bring the water and sugar to a boil over medium-high heat to dissolve the sugar, stirring occasionally. Remove from the heat and allow the syrup to cool for 15 minutes.

2. Pour the syrup into a container with a tight-fitting lid and allow it to cool completely, then add the almond extract, and stir briefly. Cover and refrigerate the syrup until ready to use. It lasts for several weeks when refrigerated.

3. To make the almond cream: If using whole almonds, place them with the confectioner's sugar in a food processor or mini-chopper fitted with a steel blade. Grind until the almonds make a powder, but not until they become a paste. If using almond meal, stir the confectioner's sugar and the meal together with a fork to combine them and to break up any lumps of sugar.

4. With a mixer fitted with a whisk or beaters, cream the butter and granulated sugar at medium-high speed until it's light and fluffy, about 2 minutes. Add the almond meal mixture to the creamed butter and mix just to combine. Add the eggs and the almond extract to the creamed butter and mix on medium-high speed until light and fluffy, about 2 minutes. Be careful not to overmix, or the cream will break down, developing a thin, runny texture. If this happens, you'll need to chill the broken cream thoroughly to thicken it a little, and then use it directly from the refrigerator while it's still cold.

5. Transfer the almond cream to an airtight container with a lid and chill it for at least 1 hour before using it. It will keep for about a week in the refrigerator.

6. To make Almond Brioche Toast: Preheat the oven to 400°F and line two 12 x 17-inch sheet pans with baking parchment. Trim a thin slice of crust from each end of a brioche pan loaf and cut the loaf into 9 slices, each ¾ inch thick. Place 4 slices on one prepared pan, and 5 slices on the other.

7. With a pastry brush, moisten the top side of each slice of bread lightly with the almond syrup, making sure to get some syrup around the outer edges of the slice. If your bread is more than a day old, you may need to be more generous with the syrup. Place about 65 g/2.3 oz. (4 tablespoons) almond cream in the center of each slice of bread. Leaving a thick pile of cream in the middle of the slice, use a small metal spatula or knife to spread out a thin layer of the cream so it comes to within ¼ inch of the edges. Sprinkle the center of each slice of toast with 1 tablespoon of the sliced almonds.

8. Bake for 6 minutes, then reduce the oven temperature to 350°F and rotate the sheet pans from top to bottom. Bake for 6 to 7 more minutes, or just until the topping becomes light brown and puffy and the toast is golden. Don't overbake, or the toast will be too dry.

9. Remove the pans from the oven and immediately transfer the toast slices to a wire rack to cool. These can be eaten while still warm, or cooled to room temperature, but they should be eaten the same day they're baked.

TIPS and TECHNIQUES

The almond syrup and the almond cream can be made several days ahead and refrigerated in airtight containers. The almond cream works best when it is cold and firm, so make and refrigerate it for at least 1 hour before you plan to make the Almond Brioche Toast.

To make the lightest, fluffiest almond cream, make sure your butter is at a cool room temperature so it's not too soft. Almond cream should be mixed with an electric mixer fitted with a whisk or beaters to obtain a consistency that is light and well aerated. We suggest slicing the bread into ¾-inch-thick slices, to support a nice thick layer of topping. The almond cream should be used cold from the refrigerator, and when it's placed on the bread, it should be left in a thick mound in the center of the slice. If spread too far to the edges, it will drip off the slices during baking, leaving all the delicious topping on the sheet pan. As soon as the toasted slices come out of the oven, they must be transferred to a wire rack to cool. If left on the sheet pan, they will steam on the bottom and become soggy, losing their appealing toasted dryness.

If you make this recipe with leftover croissants, split them in half lengthwise and remove the tops. Moisten the cut sides of the bottom halves with almond syrup, spread on the almond cream, and top with sliced almonds. Bake for 8 minutes without the tops, and then replace the tops and bake for 4 more minutes.

Chocoholic Twists

Yield: 12 twists
Equipment: one 12 x 17-inch sheet pan

Bread twists are one of our signature products at Amy's Bread. We've been making them since we first opened our doors. Created from many of our bread doughs, they're a good alternative to a roll or bagel. Our first twists were made from Country Sourdough, with fillings such as Parmesan, fresh rosemary, or black olives. Once we mastered the savory twists, we turned our thoughts to chocolate.

Bread and chocolate is a well-loved pair. Many French friends of ours remember their favorite after-school snack from childhood: a hunk of a baguette sliced open and filled with a bar of chocolate to make a sandwich. We started our pairing with chopped chocolate and Country Sourdough, and over the years our Chocolate Sourdough Twists developed a strong following. But many customers wanted something slightly sweeter and more tender. For them, Amy created the Chocoholic Twist, made with chopped bittersweet chocolate rolled into tender-rich challah dough. When the dough is cut into strips, twisted, and baked, the chocolate displays itself in tempting spirals around the plump golden twists. Once you master the technique of "twisting," you'll want to double the recipe. The soft melting chocolate tucked into golden challah is totally addictive.

INGREDIENTS	GRAMS	OUNCES	VOLUME
Amy's Challah dough (see page 81)	860	30.33	1 recipe
Bittersweet chocolate, chopped medium-fine	198	7	1⅓ cups
Egg for egg wash	50	1.76	1 large

1. Prepare the recipe for Amy's Challah through step 3. After the dough has had its first rise, gently dump it onto a lightly floured work surface. Gently deflate it and pat it into a rectangle approximately 8½ x 11 inches, with the short sides at the top and bottom of the rectangle. Sprinkle chopped chocolate onto the dough, making sure to coat the entire surface all the way to the edges. Gently press the chocolate into the dough. Fold the top third down and the bottom third up, like a business letter, so you have 3 equal layers. All corners and edges should meet evenly. Pat this new rectangle gently with your fingertips to flatten it slightly and seal it around the edges so the chocolate stays inside. Place it on a lightly oiled sheet pan or work surface and cover it with plastic wrap. Let it rise for about 50 minutes, or until the dough is soft and slightly puffy. While the dough is rising, line a 12 x 17-inch sheet pan with baking parchment.

2. Using a dough cutter with a metal blade or a long, sharp knife, trim a little bit off each end of the rectangle to remove any dough that is not filled with chocolate and to make the edges straight. The rectangle should be about 13 inches long. If it's too short, stretch it gently to lengthen it. Using the dough cutter or the knife, make a gentle indentation in the dough, marking 12 even twists, each approximately 1 inch wide along the length of the rectangle. Then cut the dough all the way through at each mark.

3. Lift a strip of dough, give it a gentle twist by moving your hands one turn in opposite directions, and lay it on one end of the prepared sheet pan. Don't stretch it to lengthen it. These twists should be plump and about 6 to 7 inches long. Repeat the twisting procedure with the remaining strips of dough, laying them side by side down the length of the sheet pan in straight, even rows, with the long sides of the twists lightly touching.

4. In a small bowl, mix 1 egg with 1 teaspoon of water to make an egg wash. Brush the twists evenly with egg wash and reserve the remainder for later. Cover the twists with plastic wrap and let them rise at room temperature (75° to 77°F) for 60 to 75 minutes, or until nearly double in volume.

5. About 20 minutes before baking, preheat the oven to 375°F and position one rack in the center of the oven.

6. When the twists are ready to bake, lightly brush them again with the egg wash. Bake for 10 minutes, rotate the sheet pan from front to back, and reduce the oven temperature to 350°F. Continue baking for another 12 to 17 minutes. If your oven has the convection option, switch it to convection for the last 5 minutes of baking, to improve the browning of the crust. Watch the twists carefully during the last few minutes. They should be golden brown but still slightly soft.

7. Immediately slide the row of twists off the sheet pan and onto a wire rack to cool. They're best eaten slightly warm from the oven, when the chocolate is still soft and melted, or completely cooled and then reheated in a toaster oven, to make the outside crisp and the chocolate soft.

TIPS and TECHNIQUES

We have suggested using bittersweet chocolate in the recipe, but semisweet chocolate tastes great, too. Any kind of good-quality sweetened chocolate can be used. Just choose a bar of whatever kind suits you best, chop it into medium-fine pieces, and roll it into the dough. Try different kinds to find your favorite.

Cinnamon Challah Knots and Chocoholic Twists (page 76)

Cinnamon Challah Knots

Yield: 9 knots
Equipment: two 12 x 17-inch sheet pans

Cinnamon Challah Knots were an invention that came from the wholesale side of Amy's Bread. Our sales team requested that we make a bread for restaurant and café customers who wanted something sweet for their brunch-time bread basket. It had to be made in our bread kitchen instead of our pastry kitchen, so we could deliver it with our other wholesale orders. Since we make a huge batch of challah every day, why not add another shape made from the same dough? We took a small piece of dough, shaped it into a long rope, and dipped it in melted butter, then rolled it in cinnamon-sugar. To make a nice-looking shape, we tied it into a knot and set it on a parchment-lined sheet pan to rise. We baked it for a short time in our bread oven, and the result was a yummy, sweet roll with a natural glaze that formed as the cinnamon-sugar melted during baking. The customers loved it. Now it can be found at brunch in restaurants all over New York, as well as on the breakfast menu in corporate dining rooms around town. We think it's a lot of fun to tie the dough in knots. It is very easy but looks as if it takes a special skill to make that unique shape.

INGREDIENTS	GRAMS	OUNCES	VOLUME
Amy's Challah dough (see page 81)	860	30.33	1 recipe
Unsalted butter, melted	85	3	6 tablespoons
Sugar	113	4	⅓ cup
Cinnamon	½ teaspoon	½ teaspoon	½ teaspoon

1. Line two 12 x 17-inch sheet pans with baking parchment.

2. Prepare the recipe for Amy's Challah through step 3. After the dough has had its first rise, gently dump it onto a lightly floured surface. Divide the dough into 9 equal pieces, about 95 g/3.35 oz. each. Shape each piece of dough into a rope about 12 inches long. To form a rope, pat the dough piece and stretch it into a rectangle with the long sides running across the top and bottom edge of the rectangle. Fold the top edge down and the bottom edge up, then, working from one end to the other, fold the dough over itself down the length of the rectangle and seal the seam with the heel of your hand to form a cylinder, like forming a baguette. Now roll the cylinder back and forth under cupped hands to elongate it into a thinner rope, about 1 inch in diameter, and taper the ends slightly. When a piece of dough resists rolling, let it rest for 5 minutes or so while you shape the other pieces.

3. Place the melted butter in a medium bowl. In another medium bowl, add the sugar

and cinnamon and whisk together. Dip each rope of dough in the butter and then roll each rope in the sugar mixture. Gently tie the rope into a knot, being careful not to shake off too much sugar off. Place 4 knots on one prepared sheet pan and 5 on the other, leaving about 3 inches between them. Let the knots rise at room temperature (75° to 78°F) for about 1 hour, or until they have nearly doubled in volume.

4. About 20 minutes before baking, preheat the oven to 425°F and position 2 racks so there is enough space between them to allow for the height of the knots.

5. Bake for 10 minutes, then rotate the pans from top to bottom and reduce the temperature to 350°F. Bake the knots for 15 to 18 more minutes, or until they are golden brown but still slightly soft. Place the knots on a wire rack to cool. Serve them within 6 to 8 hours to enjoy them at their freshest.

Amy's Challah

Yield: 900 g/2 lbs. dough, enough to make 12 Chocoholic Twists, or 9 Challah Knots,
or 18 dinner rolls, or 10 sandwich rolls, or 1 braid and 1 round snail-shaped loaf
Equipment: two 12 x 17-inch sheet pans, or one 9 x 13-inch pan

In the early days of the bakery, we made challah every Friday to sell in our retail stores. Our customers looked forward to taking home a braided challah to eat for dinner on Friday evening, when challah is traditionally shared for the Jewish Sabbath. The dough contains no milk or butter but gets its richness from vegetable oil and eggs.

After years of Friday challah, we started thinking about the dough and how nice it would be if it were made into dinner rolls. When we tested the idea, our staff loved the taste of the rolls—they were soft and tender and reminded them of the rolls they ate as kids. They reminded us of Parker house rolls, so we added them to our product selection for wholesale and retail.

Next came the burger craze. All the high-end restaurants around New York added a deluxe burger to their bar menu, and they needed a deluxe bun to go with it. How about challah as a burger bun? It worked great! It was not too sweet, not too rich, and absorbed the juices from the burger the way a good burger bun should. Our Soft Sandwich Rolls can now be found on burgers and pulled pork sandwiches all over the city.

As you can see, this dough is very versatile. It can be used to make many things besides braided challah. Today it is so popular at the bakery that it has become one of the largest batches of dough we make. Here we give instructions for how to mix this dough by hand because it is easy to knead and it's fun to get your hands in it. Instructions for using a mixer are in the Tips and Techniques at the beginning of this chapter (see page 59).

INGREDIENTS	GRAMS	OUNCES	VOLUME
Very warm water (105° to 115°F)	57	2	¼ cup
Active dry yeast	1½ teaspoons	1½ teaspoons	1½ teaspoons
Warm water (90°F)	227	8	1 cup
Canola oil or other vegetable oil	54	1.90	4 tablespoons
Eggs	50	1.76	1 large
Sugar	44	1.55	3 tablespoons + 1 teaspoon
Egg yolk	1 large	1 large	1 large
Unbleached bread flour	351	12.38	2½ cups
Unbleached all-purpose flour	145	5.11	1 cup
Kosher salt	1 tablespoon	1 tablespoon	1 tablespoon
Egg for egg wash	50	1.76	1 large

1. In a measuring cup, combine the very warm water and the yeast, stirring to dissolve the yeast. Let stand for 3 minutes. In a large bowl, add the warm water, oil, egg, sugar, and egg yolk and whisk together. Add the yeast mixture and whisk again.

2. In a large bowl add the flours and the salt and whisk together. Add the liquid ingredients to the flour mixture and stir with your fingers or a wooden spoon until the dough gathers into a sticky mass. When all of the flour is incorporated, move the dough to a lightly floured surface and knead it for 5 minutes. The dough should be sticky and wet. If it feels stiff or dry, knead in additional cool water, 1 tablespoon at a time. Put the dough in a lightly oiled bowl, cover the bowl with plastic wrap, and let it rest for 20 minutes.

3. Return the dough to a very lightly floured work surface and knead it for 5 more minutes. The dough will go from being sticky to smooth and will become supple and stretchy. It should be soft, not firm. Check the temperature of the dough. It should be between 78° and 80°F. Place the dough in a clean, lightly oiled bowl and turn the dough to coat it with oil. Cover the bowl with plastic wrap and allow the dough to rise at room temperature (75° to 77°F) for 1½ to 2 hours, or until it doubles in volume. A hole poked into the dough with a finger should hold its shape, and should not bounce back.

4. Dividing and shaping: To make soft dinner rolls, lightly oil the sides of a 9 x 13-inch pan. Cut the dough into 18 equal pieces, 50 g/1.76 oz. each. Shape each roll tightly into a round ball and place the rolls side by side, slightly touching, 4 across and 5 down the length of the pan, with only 2 rolls in the last row. Cover the pan with oiled plastic wrap. For sandwich rolls, line two 12 x 17-inch sheet pans with baking parchment. Divide the dough into 10 equal pieces, 90 g/3.17 oz. each. Shape each piece of dough tightly into a round roll, and place 5 rolls on each prepared pan, leaving a few inches between each roll. Cover the pans with oiled plastic wrap and press down on each roll to make them wider. To make a braid, divide the dough into 3 pieces, 175 g/6.17 oz. each and 1 piece 375 g/13.22 oz. Roll the 3 smaller dough pieces into ropes, 17 inches long, and the other larger piece into a rope 20 inches long. Taper the ends on all the ropes. Take the 3 small ropes, press their tips together, and braid the 3 strands from one end to the other, then seal the 3 ropes together on the other end. Line two 12 x 17-inch sheet pans with baking parchment. Place the braid on a prepared sheet pan. With the other rope, hold the tip of the rope in the center of the prepared sheet pan and form a coil or snail starting at the center and coiling the dough around itself from inside to outside. Cover the dough with oiled plastic wrap.

5. For any of these shapes, let the dough rise at room temperature for 45 to 60 minutes or until nearly doubled in volume. About 20 minutes before the dough is ready to bake, preheat the oven to 425°F and position 2 racks in the center of the oven.

6. In a small bowl, mix 1 egg with 1 teaspoon of water to make an egg wash. Gently brush the tops and sides of each roll or loaf with egg wash, coating them evenly all the way around. Place the pans on the center racks in the oven and bake for 10 minutes. Rotate the pans from top to bottom, and reduce the oven temperature to 350°F. Continue baking the rolls or loaves for 10 to 12 more minutes. If your oven has a convection option, switch it to convection for the last 5 minutes of baking, to improve the browning of the crust. Watch the rolls carefully during the last few minutes. They can become dark very quickly. They should be golden brown but still slightly soft.

7. Place the pans of rolls or loaves on a wire rack to cool before serving. This bread is best eaten a few hours after it was baked.

Various shapes and products that come from one batch

BREAD SHAPE	GRAMS PER PIECE	OUNCES PER PIECE	NUMBER OF PIECES PER BATCH
Twist dough	900	31.74	1 rectangle of 12 twists
Challah knot	100	3.52	9 knots
Soft dinner rolls	50	1.76	18 dinner rolls
Soft sandwich rolls	90	3.17	10 sandwich rolls
Braided challah plus	525 + 375	18.51 + 13.22	1 braid + 1 small snail shape

Soft Brioche Rolls with Melting Chocolate Centers

Yield: 12 muffin-shaped rolls

Equipment: standard 12-cup muffin pan; one 12 x 17-inch sheet pan to catch the melting chocolate

This is an unusual recipe that has surprising results. It's made from an extremely wet brioche dough that can be mixed only with a heavy-duty electric mixer. The dough is kneaded for several minutes, and for the longest time it just looks like batter—as though it will never come together. Then, all of a sudden, the batter becomes stretchy dough and gathers into a ball. After mixing, you need to let it rest and rise before using it. It can be placed in a container and stored overnight in the refrigerator, to be used the next day; and it will even last for 2 days if kept well chilled.

To make the rolls, the dough is cut into small pieces and flattened into disks. Then each disk is placed in a muffin cup. The disks are topped with a spoonful of firm chocolate ganache, which is covered with another piece of dough and sealed around the edges. After a brief rise, the little "muffins" are placed in the oven to bake. Soon they puff up, turn golden, and become beautiful little rolls. And the best thing is that they're filled with a melting pool of luxurious chocolate. To make them deluxe, use a top-quality semisweet or bittersweet chocolate bar for the chocolate filling. To keep it simple, make the filling with ordinary chocolate chips. Whatever you choose, you'll be amazed by the chocolate surprise inside these simple-looking golden brown rolls.

INGREDIENTS	GRAMS	OUNCES	VOLUME
Very warm water (105° to 115°F)	56	2	¼ cup
Active dry yeast	2 teaspoons	2 teaspoons	2 teaspoons
Unsalted butter, softened	235	8.29	1 cup + 2 teaspoons
Sugar	70	2.47	⅓ cup
Kosher salt	10	0.35	1 tablespoon + ½ teaspoon
Eggs, at room temperature	225	7.94	4½ large
Milk, whole, at room temperature	170	6	¾ cup
Unbleached all-purpose flour	460	16.22	3¼ cups
Bittersweet chocolate, chopped	170	6	1 cup
Heavy cream	170	6	¾ cup
Egg for egg wash	50	1.76	1 large

1. Combine the very warm water and the yeast in a measuring cup and stir to dissolve the yeast. Let stand for 3 minutes. Using an electric stand mixer with a paddle attachment, cream the butter, sugar, and salt on medium speed for about 2 minutes, until the mixture is light and fluffy. Add the yeast mixture, eggs, milk, and half the flour. Beat together to combine, scraping the sides and the bottom of the bowl as needed. Add the remaining flour slowly, then beat it again on medium-high speed for 10 to 13 minutes, or until the dough is satiny and it gathers up onto the paddle in a mass, pulling away from the sides and the bottom of the bowl. Depending on the power of your mixer, it may take longer for the dough to gather on the paddle. The finished dough will be like soft batter but should gather into a loose ball and peel easily off the paddle of the mixer.

2. Let the dough rise at room temperature (75° to 78°F) until it has nearly doubled in volume, about 1½ hours. Stir the dough down and place it in an oiled container large enough to hold it if it doubles in volume. Cover it with plastic and store it in the refrigerator overnight. After one hour in the refrigerator you may need to push the dough down again to slow its rise and keep it from rising outside the container.

3. To make the chocolate filling (ganache), place the chocolate in a medium heatproof bowl. Warm the cream to a simmer and pour it over the chocolate, whisking all the while to melt the chocolate completely. Place the warm ganache into a container with a tight-fitting lid and refrigerate it overnight.

4. The next day, prepare a muffin pan by greasing it with softened butter, or by lining each cup with a muffin paper. Line a 12 x 17-inch sheet pan with baking parchment and place the muffin pan on top of the sheet pan. Using lots of flour to keep the dough from sticking, dump the cold dough onto the work surface and pat it into a long, narrow rectangle. Roll it into a log about 3 inches in diameter and 20 inches long. Starting at the top left corner, use your fingertips to roll it over onto itself about 1 inch all the way down the rectangle and press down on the seam to seal it. Then roll it over 1 more inch and seal the seam, and roll it again to close the final seam and to make a tight log. Cut the log into 24 equal pieces about 45 g/1.6 oz. each. Pat 12 dough pieces into disks and place 1 disk in the bottom of each muffin cup. Place 28 g/1 oz./ 1 rounded tablespoon of cold chocolate ganache filling in the center of the dough disk in each muffin cup, making sure the chocolate does not touch the sides of the cups. Cover the chocolate with another flattened dough disk and press it gently around the edges to seal the dough over the chocolate. Try to seal the two disks of dough well or the chocolate will drip out of the roll during baking.

5. In a small bowl, mix 1 egg with 1 teaspoon of water to make an egg wash. Brush each roll with egg wash, coating the top evenly. Cover the muffin pan with oiled plastic wrap and allow the dough to rise at room temperature (75° to 77°F) for 45 to 60 minutes, or until doubled in volume.

6. About 20 minutes before baking, preheat the oven to 400°F.

7. Brush the tops of each roll again with egg wash. Bake for 10 minutes, then rotate the muffin pan from front to back and reduce the oven temperature to 350°F. Bake for 8 to 10 more minutes, or until the rolls are medium golden brown and puffed up like balloons. Place the muffin pan on a wire rack to cool. After 20 minutes remove the rolls from the muffin pans and place them directly on the wire rack to continue cooling. Serve them while still warm from the oven.

Professional Bakers Baking at Home

Amy and Toy live in New York City, home to the smallest kitchens in the country. You might assume that as professional bakers, they would both have huge, beautiful kitchens, filled with the latest equipment, in which to work. But even a decent kitchen in New York may be no bigger than a walk-in closet, and Amy's and Toy's are no different. To begin with, their kitchen countertops are only three feet long and two feet deep. Toy's postage-stamp counter has room for only a blender and a toaster. When she's testing recipes, those items are relegated to the top of her bedroom dresser while the KitchenAid mixer and food processor take turns coming out of the closet. Amy has a narrow old gas oven that can accommodate only a sheet pan slid in lengthwise but not sideways. Toy has a full-size oven but the thermostat is faulty. An oven thermometer is mandatory because she never knows what the actual temperature will be when she sets the oven dial.

Both women have standard-size refrigerators (though Toy's fridge door won't open all the way because it is impeded by the sink cabinet), but when they're filled with testing ingredients, there's no space for personal food items. Good thing New York is a city where you can pick up the phone and order takeout anything for dinner! And of course there's no room for a dishwasher, or storage space for the large variety of pans or the multitude of dry ingredients such as sugars, flours, nuts, and raisins both bakers require. In spite of it all, they have faithfully tested all of their recipes at home, perching mixing bowls on top of the stove, the trash can, or a stool, and squeezing sheet pans, butter and eggs, and dry ingredients onto window sills and the dining table, or in boxes and bags on the living room floor.

When the baking is done, with a sink full of dirty mixing bowls and sheet pans, and flour and sticky stuff decorating the kitchen floor, both Amy and Toy wonder where their bakery maintenance team is when they really need them. And neither woman can wait to return to the bakery kitchens to do her baking, with loads of counter space, hundreds of baking pans, good ventilation, fabulous ovens, and plenty of help with the dishes.

Quiche

When we think of the savory pastries made in traditional French bakeries, quiche is the first thing that comes to mind. Flaky pastry crust filled with rich unsweetened custard, a little cheese, and a few select vegetables or meats is a pleasing alternative to sweet pastries for breakfast or sandwiches for lunch. At the bakery we make our quiche in mini tart pans (see page 244 for sources), so a whole quiche is an individual serving. Delicious at room temperature, they're handy to carry out and easy to eat, making them a perfect choice for our retail bakery menu. We offer the Ham and Swiss Quiche every day, and we alternate the two vegetable flavors—Spinach and Mushroom, and Roasted Vegetable—so we have two selections available daily.

The crust for a quiche should be more than just a container for the filling. The flavor and texture of the crust should complement and enhance the filling, so that when combined, the two create a totally satisfying eating experience. Here we present the pastry recipes first, followed by the fillings. We tell you which crust and filling combinations we like, but we suggest you try some mixing and matching to discover what pleases your palate.

TIPS and TECHNIQUES

- For best results, the pastry dough for the crust should be well chilled before you start rolling it out. The easiest way to guarantee this is to make the pastry the day before you're going to serve the quiche, so it can rest in the refrigerator overnight. If the dough feels very hard when you remove it from the refrigerator, let it sit at room temperature for 10 to 15 minutes to allow it to soften slightly before you begin rolling it out.

- If you're short of time, the filling for the quiche can be made the day before and refrigerated in an airtight container until you're ready to use it the following day.

- In the bakery's pastry kitchen we use a metal ring that is approximately 6$\frac{1}{8}$ inches in diameter to stamp out pastry rounds to line the mini quiche pans, which are 4$\frac{1}{2}$ inches in diameter. Testing in the kitchen at home, we found a small aluminum pie pan that had a top outside diameter of 6 inches and used that as a guide to cut circles that were slightly larger than 6 inches across.

- To give our quiche a rustic look and allow room for more filling, we leave the edges of the pastry untrimmed and extending about $\frac{1}{4}$ inch above the top of the tart pan.

- We like to bake quiche in tart pans that have had their bottoms removed. The bottomless pastry-filled pans go into the oven placed on a parchment-lined sheet pan. This is a foolproof way to get a nicely browned bottom crust.

- Mr. Coffee–brand 8- to 12-cup paper basket coffee filters are perfect for lining mini 4$\frac{1}{2}$-inch tart shells before filling them with weights for blind baking. We use these at the bakery because it's faster and more cost-efficient than cutting foil or parchment to fit the small pans. The filter papers also won't stick to the crust and damage it.

Basic Quiche Crust

Yield: pastry for six 4½-inch quiches or one 9- or 10-inch quiche

We love this crust with both the Ham and Swiss filling and the Roasted Vegetable filling. Buttery rich, tender, and flaky, it practically melts in your mouth, but it's easy to make in a food processor and sturdy enough to support the quiche fillings even after baking. The fragrance that fills the kitchen when this pastry is baking is indescribable.

Refrigerate the dough for at least 30 minutes before rolling it out. You may also make it the day before and refrigerate it overnight. If there are dough scraps left over, spread them on a parchment-lined baking sheet, sprinkle them generously with sugar and cinnamon, and bake them until they begin to brown. This very special treat transports us back to our childhoods.

INGREDIENTS	GRAMS	OUNCES	VOLUME
Unsalted butter, cut into ½-inch dice	200	7	⅞ cup
Unbleached all-purpose flour	280	9.88	2 cups
Kosher salt	1¾ teaspoons	1¾ teaspoons	1¾ teaspoons
Egg yolks	60	2.12	From 3 large eggs
Ice water	52	1.83	4 tablespoons

1. Freeze the butter for at least 30 minutes.

2. In the bowl of a food processor fitted with the metal blade, combine the flour and salt and process them for 5 seconds until they are just combined. Add the butter cubes from the freezer and process again for 15 seconds, or until the mixture looks like coarse meal. The largest pieces of butter should be about the size of peas. Add the egg yolks and process again for 10 to 12 seconds until the yolks are just incorporated. The mixture should still look like coarse meal, but the crumbs may start to stick together. Transfer the mixture to a large bowl and sprinkle it with the ice water. Using a rubber spatula or a wooden spoon, stir the mixture gently until it begins to form a rough ball of dough. (If you don't have a food processor, mix the dry ingredients in a large bowl with a wire whisk and rub very cold, not frozen, butter into the flour with your fingers until it looks like coarse breadcrumbs. If the butter starts to feel soft, freeze the mixture for 10 minutes before continuing. In a small bowl, whisk together the egg yolks and ice water. Make a well in the center of the flour mixture and pour in the liquid. Using a fork, stir the ingredients together until they start to form a rough ball.)

3. As the ball becomes more defined, use your hands to press it gently together into a single mass of dough. There should not be any pockets of dry crumbs remaining. If necessary, sprinkle in another 1 or 2 teaspoons of ice water. Place the ball of dough on a large piece of plastic wrap, seal the wrap around the dough, and flatten to make a round ¾-inch-thick disk. Refrigerate it for at least 30 minutes before rolling it out. This dough may be kept refrigerated for up to 2 days or frozen for up to 6 months.

Tips *on* lining tart pans *and* blind baking

Rolling out the dough

Remove the chilled pastry from the refrigerator. On a lightly floured surface, roll out the dough to a thickness of ⅛ inch. If the dough starts sticking to the work surface, use a plastic scraper to lift the dough, dust the work surface again with flour, replace the dough with the top side down, and lightly flour the dough before continuing the rolling process. When the dough is the right thickness, cut 6 rounds of pastry 6⅛ inches in diameter. You will probably get only 4 to 5 rounds out of the first rolling. Using a dry pastry brush, brush any excess flour off of the remaining scraps of dough and gently press them together into a cohesive ball. Flatten the ball as much as you can and let it rest for 5 to 10 minutes before you roll it out again. If the dough is still too springy and keeps shrinking back as you roll it, let it rest awhile longer. If the dough seems very warm and soft, wrap it in plastic and put it in the freezer to rest and chill for 10 minutes before rolling it out again.

Lining the tart pans

Remove the bottoms from the pans before filling them with pastry. The bottoms of the crusts brown better in "bottomless" pans. Place all of the mini tart pans, evenly spaced, on a parchment-lined 12 x 17-inch sheet pan. Lay a pastry round gently on top of a tart pan, positioning it so it is centered as evenly as possible. Rotating the pan slowly, work your way around the circle by lifting the edge of the dough and gently pushing it down into the pan, pressing the pastry firmly against the sides, making sure the bottom sits flat in the pan, with no curve where the sides and bottom meet. The dough should extend about ¼ inch above the top of the tart pan. Don't be concerned if the edges are a little uneven; that makes the quiche look rustic.

Blind-baking the crust

Line each pastry-filled tart pan with a Mr. Coffee–brand 8- to 12-cup paper coffee filter. If you don't have coffee filters available, cut six 9-inch circles of parchment paper or aluminum foil to use as liners. Spread ⅓ to ½ cup of uncooked rice, beans, or other pie weights on top of the paper, pressing down gently to be sure the paper is weighted firmly against the sides of the pastry shell. Bake at 400°F for 20 minutes, or until the top edges of the pastry just begin to brown. Remove the paper and the weights, stacking them in an empty bowl to cool, and return the tart shells to the oven. Continue baking for 5 more minutes, or until the shells are lightly browned and the bottoms begin to look a little dry instead of doughy. Remove the pans from the oven and allow them to cool slightly, about 5 minutes, before adding the quiche filling.

Whole Wheat Pastry Crust

Yield: pastry for six 4½-inch quiches or one 9- or 10-inch quiche

The whole wheat flour and cream cheese give this pastry a special flavor and texture that are a perfect complement to our Spinach and Mushroom Quiche filling. This crust is surprisingly light, rich, and tender, so you might want to use the remaining dough scraps to make savory turnovers with any meat and/or vegetable scraps that are hiding in the refrigerator.

INGREDIENTS	GRAMS	OUNCES	VOLUME
Unsalted butter, cut into ¾-inch dice	146	5.15	⅔ cup
Cream cheese, cut into ½-inch dice	112	4.0	⅜ cup + 1 tablespoon
Ice water	52	1.83	4 tablespoons
Apple cider vinegar	2½ teaspoons	2½ teaspoons	2½ teaspoons
Unbleached all-purpose flour	158	5.60	1 cup + 1½ tablespoons
Whole wheat flour	86	3.0	½ cup
Kosher salt	¾ teaspoon	¾ teaspoon	¾ teaspoon
Baking powder	⅛ teaspoon	⅛ teaspoon	⅛ teaspoon

1. Freeze the diced butter and cream cheese for at least 30 minutes. In a small cup or bowl, combine the ice water and the vinegar.

2. In a food processor fitted with the metal blade, combine the 2 flours, salt and baking powder and process them for 5 seconds until they are just combined. Add the frozen chunks of cream cheese and process again for 15 seconds or until the mixture looks like coarse meal. Add the butter chunks and process again for 10 to 15 seconds, until the largest pieces of butter are about the size of peas. Transfer the mixture to a large bowl and sprinkle it with the ice water mixture. (If you don't have a food processor, mix the dry ingredients in a large bowl with a wire whisk and rub very cold, not frozen, cream cheese into the flour with your fingers until it looks like coarse meal. Repeat the process with very cold, not frozen, butter chunks until the largest pieces of butter are about the size of peas. If the butter starts to feel soft, freeze the mixture for 10 minutes before continuing. Sprinkle the ice water mixture over the flour.) Using your hands, stir the mixture, pressing it together firmly until it forms a cohesive ball of dough. There should not be any pockets of dry crumbs remaining. If necessary sprinkle in another 1 or 2 teaspoons of ice water. Place the ball of dough on a large piece of plastic wrap, seal the wrap around the dough, and flatten the ball to make a round ¾-inch-thick disk. Refrigerate for at least 30 minutes before rolling it out. This dough may be kept refrigerated for up to 2 days or frozen for up to 6 months.

Ham and Swiss Quiche

Yield: six 4½-inch mini quiches
Equipment: six 4½ x ¾-inch mini tart pans with removable bottoms;
     one 12 x 17-inch sheet pan

Quiche originated during medieval times, in a German kingdom called Lothringen, which the French later named Lorraine. The word *quiche* is derived from the German word *kuchen*, which means cake. The original "quiche Lorraine" was an open pie with a crust made from bread dough and a filling of eggs, cream, and pieces of smoked bacon. The use of a short pastry crust and the addition of Gruyere cheese came later. Our version of this classic quiche is made with little chunks of ham and shredded Swiss cheese. It may not be historically authentic, but there's no question it's delicious.

INGREDIENTS	GRAMS	OUNCES	VOLUME
Basic Quiche Crust (see page 90)			1 recipe
Cooked ham, cut into ¼-inch dice	150	5.30	1 cup
Swiss cheese, coarsely shredded	100	3.50	1¼ cups
Custard filling			
Half-and-half	240	8.5	1 cup
Eggs	150	5.30	3 large
Kosher salt	½ teaspoon	½ teaspoon	½ teaspoon
Ground cayenne pepper	A pinch	A pinch	A pinch

1. Make one recipe of Basic Quiche Crust and refrigerate the dough for at least 30 minutes. If the pastry was made the day before, remove it from the refrigerator to sit for 10 minutes before rolling it out.

2. Position one rack in the middle of the oven, and preheat the oven to 400°F. Line the 12 x 17-inch sheet pan with baking parchment. Remove the bottoms from the mini tart pans and place the bottomless pans on the prepared sheet pan. Roll out the pastry on a lightly floured surface to a thickness of ⅛ inch. Cut 6 circles of dough, each 6⅛ inches in diameter. Line each tart pan with a dough circle and blind-bake the crusts for 18 to 20 minutes, or until they barely begin to brown. Remove the weights and the paper and continue baking for 4 to 5 more minutes, or until lightly browned and the bottoms are just starting to look a little dry (see page 91 for detailed instructions.) Don't be concerned if the crust bottoms puff up slightly after the weights are removed; they should deflate again when they come out of the oven.

3. While the crusts are baking, combine the diced ham and shredded cheese in a medium bowl, tossing them gently with your hands until they are evenly mixed.

4. To make the custard filling: In a large measuring cup or a 3- to 4-cup container with a pour spout, whisk together the half-and-half, eggs, salt, and cayenne pepper until well combined.

5. Five to 10 minutes after the crusts come out of the oven, with the tart pans still on the baking sheet, spread 40 g/1.4 oz./⅓ cup of the ham and cheese mixture evenly in the bottom of each tart shell. Stir the custard and pour it over the ham mixture, filling each pan to within ⅛ inch of the top edge of the pastry. Don't overfill them, or the custard will run out of the crust during baking. It's not a total disaster if this happens. The quiche will still be edible, but there will be less filling in the shell. Return the pan to the oven and bake for 20 to 25 minutes, or until the edges of the filling begin to puff up and the center still jiggles slightly when you shake the pan. Place the sheet pan on a wire rack to cool. When cool enough to handle, remove the quiche from the pans. Pans with filling that has run over may have to cool longer before you can get the quiche out of the pans. Serve slightly warm or at room temperature. Leftovers may be refrigerated or frozen and reheated in a 400°F oven for 20 minutes, or until heated all the way through.

TIPS *and* TECHNIQUES

For this recipe, coarsely grated cheese is easier to mix with the chunks of ham than finely grated cheese.

To make one large quiche, follow the directions in the Tips and Techniques section for the Spinach Mushroom Quiche on page 96.

Spinach Mushroom Quiche

Yield: six 4½-inch mini quiches

Equipment: six 4½ x ¾-inch mini tart pans with removable bottoms;
one 12 x 17-inch sheet pan

We've always loved the combination of spinach and cheese with eggs, so when we started developing our recipes for quiche fillings, we knew that one of them would have to include spinach. We sautéed some onions with a little garlic, threw in some sliced mushrooms and Monterey Jack cheese, put it all in a flaky whole wheat crust, and came up with a definite winner. Served with a side salad or some fresh fruit, this is a wonderful dish for Sunday brunch.

Before you roll out the pastry dough, drain the spinach and chop all of the vegetables for the filling, so you're ready to sauté them while the pastry shells are baking. It's always best to fill the quiche shells and return them to the oven while they're still warm.

INGREDIENTS	GRAMS	OUNCES	VOLUME
Whole Wheat Pastry Crust (see page 92)			1 recipe
Olive oil	1 tablespoon + ½ teaspoon	1 tablespoon + ½ teaspoon	1 tablespoon + ½ teaspoon
Fresh mushrooms, halved, cut into ⅛-inch slices	231	8.15	One 8-oz. package
Salt and pepper	To taste	To taste	To taste
Onion, finely chopped	106	3.74	¾ cup
Garlic, finely chopped	2½ teaspoons	2½ teaspoons	2½ teaspoons
Frozen chopped spinach, thawed and drained	235	8.30	One 10-oz. package
Monterey Jack cheese, coarsely shredded	72	2.54	1 cup
Custard Filling			
Half-and-half	240	8.5	1 cup
Eggs	150	5.30	3 large
Kosher salt	½ teaspoon	½ teaspoon	½ teaspoon
Ground cayenne pepper	A pinch	A pinch	A pinch

1. Make one recipe of Whole Wheat Pastry Crust, and refrigerate the dough for at least 30 minutes. If the pastry was made the day before, remove it from the refrigerator to sit for 10 minutes before rolling it out.

2. Position one rack in the middle of the oven, and preheat the oven to 400°F. Line the 12 x 17-inch sheet pan with baking parchment. Remove the bottoms from the mini

tart pans and place the bottomless pans on the prepared sheet pan. Roll out the pastry on a lightly floured surface to a thickness of ⅛ inch. Cut 6 circles of dough, each 6⅛ inches in diameter. Line each tart pan with a dough circle and blind-bake the crusts for 20 minutes, or until they barely begin to brown. Remove the weights and the paper and continue baking for 4 to 5 more minutes, until lightly browned and the bottoms are just starting to look a little dry. Don't be concerned if the crust bottoms puff up slightly after the weights are removed; they should deflate again when they come out of the oven.

3. In a medium skillet or sauté pan, heat ½ teaspoon of the olive oil and cook the mushrooms over medium heat with salt and pepper to taste, stirring occasionally, until their water has been released and they start to brown, 6 to 7 minutes. Transfer the mushrooms to a large bowl. Heat 1 tablespoon of the olive oil in the pan and add the onion and garlic with a pinch of salt and pepper to taste and cook, stirring occasionally, until they become translucent, 2 to 3 minutes. Add the spinach to the pan, sprinkle it with salt and pepper to taste, and cook briefly, stirring occasionally, until the spinach is heated through, 1 to 2 minutes. Transfer the spinach mixture to the bowl with the mushrooms and mix it all together with a wooden spoon until everything is evenly distributed. Let cool slightly before mixing in the cheese.

TIPS *and* TECHNIQUES

We've used crimini mushrooms (baby portobellos) in our home tests with excellent results, but at the bakery we use regular white mushrooms.

This filling can be prepared 1 day ahead and refrigerated overnight in an airtight container, but the shredded cheese should not be added until just before you're ready to fill the pastry shells, or it will get soggy.

To make 1 large quiche using a 9- or 10-inch tart pan: roll the pastry as described in the recipe and cut a circle that is 1½ to 2 inches larger than the diameter of your pan. Line the pan with the dough, and trim it so it extends about ¼ inch above the edge of the pan. Blind-bake as described in the recipe, increasing the baking time if necessary. Multiply the ingredient amounts for the custard filling 1½ times. Put all of the vegetable filling in the bottom of the baked pastry shell and fill with custard to within ¼ inch of the top of the pastry. Bake as described, increasing the baking time as necessary, until the center still jiggles slightly when you shake the pan. Cool and serve as described in the recipe.

4. To make the custard filling: In a large measuring cup or a 3- to 4-cup container with a pour spout, whisk together the half-and-half, eggs, salt, and cayenne pepper until well combined.

5. Five to 10 minutes after the crusts come out of the oven, with the tart pans still on the baking sheet, spread 30 g/1.06 oz./⅓ cup of the spinach-and-cheese mixture evenly in the bottom of each tart shell. Stir the custard and pour it over the spinach, filling each pan to within ⅛ inch of the top edge of the pastry. Don't overfill the shells or the custard will run out during baking. It's not a total disaster if this happens. The quiche will still be edible but there will be less filling in the shell. Return the pan to the oven and bake for 20 to 25 minutes, or until the edges of the filling begin to puff up and the center still jiggles slightly when you shake the pan. Place the sheet pan on a wire rack to cool. When cool enough to handle, remove the quiche from the pans. Pans with filling that has run over may have to cool longer before the quiche can be extracted from the pans. Serve slightly warm or at room temperature. Leftovers may be refrigerated or frozen and reheated in a 400°F oven for 20 minutes, or until heated all the way through.

Roasted Vegetable Quiche, Spinach Mushroom Quiche
(page 95), and Ham and Swiss Quiche (page 93)

Roasted Vegetable Quiche

Yield: six 4½-inch mini quiches

Equipment: six 4½ x ¾-inch mini tart pans with removable bottoms;
two 12 x 17-inch sheet pans

Jessica Blank, who is now the facilities manager at our Chelsea Market location, created this wonderful quiche filling with confetti of fresh vegetables when she was the night owl pastry chef at our Hell's Kitchen location. At the bakery, we roast all the vegetables on sheet pans in our convection oven, which is what inspired the recipe's name. For the home kitchen, we still oven-roast the tomatoes, but it's more efficient to prepare the zucchini and peppers in a sauté pan. The essence of the vegetables is enhanced with herbs and a little Parmesan to create a light, refreshing flavor that is a nice counterpoint to the richness of the custard and the crust.

INGREDIENTS	GRAMS	OUNCES	VOLUME
Basic Quiche Crust (see page 90)			1 recipe
Ripe plum tomatoes	240	8.50	2 to 3 medium
Olive oil	1 tablespoon + 2 teaspoons	1 tablespoon + 2 teaspoons	1 tablespoon + 2 teaspoons
Salt and pepper	To taste	To taste	To taste
Zucchini, cut into ¼-inch dice	300	8.15	2⅓ cups
Red bell pepper, cored and cut into ¼-inch dice	180	6.35	1¼ cups
Dried oregano	1¼ teaspoons	1¼ teaspoons	1¼ teaspoons
Dried basil	½ teaspoon	½ teaspoon	½ teaspoon
Parmesan, finely grated	70	2.47	¾ cup
Fresh basil, finely chopped	2 tablespoons	2 tablespoons	2 tablespoons
Custard Filling			
Half-and-half	240	8.5	1 cup
Eggs	150	5.30	3 large
Kosher salt	½ teaspoon	½ teaspoon	½ teaspoon
Ground cayenne pepper	A pinch	A pinch	A pinch

1. Make one recipe of Basic Quiche Crust and refrigerate the dough for at least 30 minutes. If the pastry was made the day before, remove it from the refrigerator to sit for 10 minutes before rolling it out.

2. Position one rack in the middle of the oven, and preheat the oven to 375°F. Line the sheet pans with baking parchment.

TIPS *and* TECHNIQUES

This filling can be prepared one day ahead and refrigerated overnight in an airtight container, but the vegetables may release some of their juices and will need to be stirred gently so the mixture is evenly moistened. The grated Parmesan should not be added to the vegetables until just before you're ready to fill the pastry shells.

To make one large quiche, follow the directions on page 96.

3. To oven-roast the tomatoes: Trim the ends and cut them into ½-inch-thick slices. In a medium bowl, toss the tomato slices with 2 teaspoons of the olive oil and salt and pepper to taste. Place the tomatoes cut side down on one of the prepared sheet pans and bake for 15 minutes, or until the tomatoes have just begun to soften, releasing some of their juice, but still feel firm when touched. Be very careful not to overbake them or they will become mushy and the skin will separate from the slices, making them difficult to chop. Remove the pan from the oven and place it on a wire rack to cool. When the slices have cooled enough to handle, chop them into ½-inch chunks, and put them in a medium large bowl.

4. Increase the oven temperature to 400°F. Remove the bottoms from the mini tart pans and place the bottomless pans on the other clean parchment-lined sheet pan. Roll out the pastry on a lightly floured surface to a thickness of ⅛ inch. Cut 6 circles of dough, each 6⅛ inches in diameter. Line each tart pan with a dough circle and blind-bake the crusts for 20 minutes, or until they barely begin to brown. Remove the weights and the paper and continue baking for 4 to 5 more minutes, until lightly browned and the bottoms are just starting to look a little dry. Don't be concerned if the crust bottoms puff up slightly after the weights are removed; they should deflate again when they come out of the oven.

5. In a large skillet or sauté pan, heat 1 tablespoon of the olive oil and cook the zucchini and bell pepper with the oregano, basil, and salt and pepper to taste, stirring occasionally until they begin to soften but are still firm, 6 to 8 minutes. Transfer the mixture to the bowl containing the roasted tomatoes and mix gently with a wooden spoon until everything is evenly distributed. Let cool slightly before mixing in the Parmesan and basil.

6. To make the custard filling: In a large measuring cup or a 3- to 4-cup container with a pour spout, whisk together the half-and-half, eggs, salt, and cayenne pepper until well combined.

7. Five to 10 minutes after the crusts come out of the oven, with the tart pans still on the baking sheet, spread 50 g/1.76 oz./⅓ cup of the vegetable-and-cheese mixture evenly in the bottom of each tart shell. Stir the custard and pour it over the vegetables, filling each shell to within ⅛ inch of the top edge of the pastry. Don't overfill the shells or the custard will run out of the crust during baking. It's not a total disaster if this happens. The quiche will still be edible but there will be less filling in the shell. Return the pan to the oven and bake for 20 to 25 minutes, or until the edges of the filling begin to puff up and the center still jiggles slightly when you shake the pan. Place the sheet pan on a wire rack to cool. When cool enough to handle, remove the quiche from the pans. Pans with filling that has run over may have to cool longer before the quiche can be extracted from the pans. Serve slightly warm or at room temperature. Leftovers may be refrigerated or frozen and reheated in a 400°F oven for 20 minutes, or until heated all the way through.

Andrew Harriott and Jamie Larsen Thomas

We have so many stories about our customers that we could write a sitcom. Like the story of Andrew Harriott who comes in for his cup of coffee at least once a day—we always ask him, "How do you take that?" knowing his response in advance. "Black and bitter like me," he says with his charming British accent, giving us a huge grin. And we all laugh and enjoy the joke though we've heard it a million times. It's always a pleasure to hear Andrew's deep voice and infectious laughter when we're walking through the café. And then there's Jamie Larsen Thomas (pictured), a friend of Andrew's, who has been a loyal customer in our Hell's Kitchen store for as long as we can remember. He comes in nearly every day and sits at a table to enjoy his scone and coffee while he's writing. We hate to interrupt his train of thought but we love to chat with him and talk about life in the neighborhood. One of Jamie's many talents is writing his own music. He sings and plays the guitar. Some of the songs from Jamie's CD are included in the music list that we play in the Hell's Kitchen café. Andrew and Jamie are such favorite customers that our retail team invited them to our staff holiday party last year. They came and ate and schmoozed, and danced the night away with all of us—they've both got all the moves on the dance floor! Life in a bakery is hard work but when you love what you do there are also many opportunities to have fun.

Cookies

*O*nce we understood that we couldn't have a proper bakery without offering our customers sweets, we decided to add a few cookies to our menu. Though there were still only a handful of us running the bakery, we made time to mix up some cookie dough and squeeze a few sheet pans of cookies into the bread oven at least every other day. We started with the four varieties of cookie everyone knows and loves—Gingersnap, Chocolate Chip, Oatmeal Raisin, and Peanut Butter. We used the recipes we grew up with, those found on the backs of cereal boxes or printed on the chocolate chip bag. And of course our cookies had to be made with real butter. Cookies made with butter don't have as long a shelf life as those made with shortening, but they taste oh so much better. Making products that taste as good as they look has always been our primary goal.

As the years went by, the original recipes were gradually changed to satisfy our more sophisticated taste buds, and the cookie menu was expanded from four varieties to nine. Our cookies have become so popular with our customers that we now have a full-time baker whose only responsibility is to mix cookie dough and bake big, beautiful cookies every day of the week. The cookies we make now are about $4^{1}/_{2}$ to 5 inches in diameter, lightly crisped on the outside, and chewy and tender on the inside.

TIPS and TECHNIQUES

- The "slightly softened" butter used in the recipes should be soft enough to take an imprint of your finger with a bit of pressure but not so soft that it's just on the edge of melting. Sticks of butter left at room temperature for an hour are usually soft enough, unless the room is exceptionally cool or extremely warm. Working with butter that is too soft produces cookie dough that is too soft and cookies that will spread and flatten too much as they bake.

- We used the "dip-and-sweep" method of measuring flour volume when we did our recipe testing. That means you loosen the flour in the bag a little by stirring it with a big spoon, and then dip the measuring cup down into the bag, bring up the overfilled cup, and level off the top with the flat edge of a knife or spatula. Keep in mind that weighing the flour, however, is the most foolproof way to duplicate our recipes.

- We recommend that you use a heavy-duty electric stand mixer, such as a KitchenAid, that has a large bowl and a paddle attachment, to mix the cookie dough. The second best method is to use a portable electric hand mixer with a strong motor, because you can lift it periodically to let the heavy butter and dough that sticks in the beaters spin off into the bowl. A less powerful stand mixer can be used if that's all you have available, but you'll have to fuss with it a lot to clear the beaters of butter and dough.

- At the bakery, we use a metal ice cream scoop to portion the cookie dough. We then weigh the dough on a digital scale and drop it onto a prepared cookie sheet. After years of scooping thousands of cookies, our cookie baker can tell just by looking at the dough if it is the right weight. You can also use a large metal soup spoon, a measuring cup, or your clean hands, moistened with water, to pick up a ball of dough and put it on the scale—or skip the scale entirely and drop the dough directly on the cookie sheet. After the sheet is filled, round off the dough blobs so they're shaped like balls. It's the best way to get nice round, uniformly shaped cookies. If you don't have a scoop, using your hands makes it easier to form a large ball of dough. We've listed the weight of each cookie in the recipes so you can duplicate the size of the big cookies we sell in the bakery, but feel free to make the cookies any size that makes you happy. If your cookies are small, you may have to reduce the baking time by 1 or 2 minutes.

TIPS *and* TECHNIQUES

• Cover the bottom of your cookie sheets with baking parchment for easier cleanup. We recommend using cookie sheets that are 12 x 17 inches, like the ones used in commercial kitchens, because they're heavier, allow for more even heat distribution, and can fit more cookies. These are available now in most good kitchenware stores. Regular home cookie sheets are fine, too, but you'll have to experiment to determine how many large cookies will fit on each sheet without merging into one another. One advantage to using the lighter home cookie sheets is that they cool off faster, so you can use them sooner to pan up more cookies. If you put dough on cookie sheets that are still hot, the dough will start to melt before you get it into the oven, causing the cookies to spread too much and bake unevenly.

• Leave at least 3 inches around the dough balls to allow for spreading. Some cookies spread more than others. Soft cookie dough spreads more than stiff cookie dough. At the bakery, we put 6 of the big cookies on each 12 x 17-inch sheet pan; for the smaller Gingersnaps, for example, it's 12 cookies per pan.

• If possible, use 2 racks in your oven and bake 2 sheets of cookies at a time, turning the pans around and rotating them from top to bottom halfway through the baking time for more even browning.

• Control the texture of your cookies by changing the amount of time you bake them. If you like them crunchy, bake them 2 or 3 minutes longer. If you like them softer, bake them 1 or 2 minutes less. Test a batch using the times shown in the recipe, and then adjust the baking time to suit your taste.

• Cool the cookies for about 5 minutes before moving them off the cookie sheet and onto cooling racks. The cookies continue to bake for several minutes when left on the hot sheet. We call this residual baking. When determining how long to bake a cookie to the desired level of doneness, always take the residual baking time into consideration.

• Let the cookies cool completely before storing them in a container with an air-tight lid. Eat them within three days for optimal flavor and texture.

A Tale about Quality Control

Regular customers are our biggest fans and our harshest critics. We worry constantly about maintaining the quality and consistency of our products, but it's not possible for us to taste-test every single product we make every single day. Fortunately for us, we have regular customers who visit our café every day, sometimes two or three times a day. When their favorite cookie or scone or sandwich or sticky bun doesn't live up to their expectations, they're not shy about letting us know. We always take these customer complaints very seriously and launch an investigation to find out what made the finished product different from usual. Sometimes it happens because we're training a new baker who hasn't quite mastered the necessary techniques, or sometimes an experienced baker has just had a bad day. Sometimes our supplier runs out of our usual brand of flour and sends us a temporary substitution, or the wheat crop gets too much or too little rain, so the quality of our usual flour brand has changed. Sometimes it's something completely unexpected, as the following story illustrates.

One of the wholesale customers who buys a selection of our big home-style cookies mentioned to our Customer Service staff that the Chocolate Chip Cookies had been tasting different lately, as if they were stale. Customer Service sent an e-mail to Toy to let her know there had been a complaint about one of the pastry products. Toy was more than a little surprised, because we bake our cookies fresh every single day, seven days a week, using fresh ingredients of excellent quality, so how could they possibly be stale? She immediately tasted one of the cookies from the Hell's Kitchen retail café, and she also asked our Amy's Bread resident chocolate chip cookie fanatic, David Chaffin, to taste a cookie from the Chelsea Market retail café, where he is daytime production manager. David loves our chocolate chip cookies so much that one year, for his birthday, we made him a gigantic chocolate chip cookie and wrote, "Happy Birthday, David!" on it in chocolate frosting. Both Toy and David agreed that the cookie didn't taste quite right. It didn't have the nuances in flavor that both of them expected. The flavor was flat. Where was that lovely subtle taste of lightly salted, toasted wheat and melted butter mixed with overtones of sugar and semisweet chocolate?

Toy checked with Molly, the daytime pastry chef, and Frank Luca, our full-time cookie baker, to see if they had recently changed anything in the recipe for that cookie. The answer was no. Toy waited for several days, and then she and David did a second taste test. This time the cookies tasted great. Again Toy questioned Frank to see what, if anything, he had done that would have made this difference in taste—how about baking times and temperatures, or the temperature of the dough before baking? After baking, were the cookies being cooled completely before they were packed?

Frank Luca has been part of our baking team for five years and he takes great pride in his work baking cookies for Amy's Bread. When a customer complains about one of his cookies, he takes it very personally. Molly, Frank, and Toy went over the recipe again and discussed the procedure for mixing and baking the Chocolate Chip Cookie dough. Everything seemed to be in order—until they started talking about how many times a week Frank was making the dough. With great pride, Frank said, "I've gotten really efficient mixing my cookie dough by making bigger batches, so I usually have to make it only once a week." Aha! There was the answer to the problem. When the cookie dough was fresh (up to three days after it had been mixed), the cookies tasted fresh. By the end of the week, though, when the dough was stale, the cookies also tasted stale, even though they were "baked fresh" every day. Frank was devastated. His solution for more efficient production times had in fact compromised the quality of his cookies. Now Frank is back to mixing his cookie dough at least twice a week, and there have been no further complaints about his Chocolate Chip Cookies.

Gingersnaps

Yield: 5 dozen small cookies
Equipment: two 12 x 17-inch cookie sheets

Susan Crawford (née Kantor) was an operating room nurse whose specialty was open heart surgery. After years of working under the stress and tension that went with that job, she decided to make a career change. A graduate of the Culinary Institute of America, in Hyde Park, New York, she eventually came to work at Amy's Bread when we were still in our infancy. The focus and discipline she learned in the operating room paid off in spades when she became a professional baker. We've rarely encountered anyone who can bake as accurately and efficiently as Suze. She ran circles around the rest of us and made it look like a walk in the park. Suze baked bread with us, but her first love was really pastry. The Gingersnaps are one of Suze's contributions to the Amy's Bread sweets menu.

This little cookie actually tastes better than it looks. It gets so dark when it's baking that it almost looks like it's burned. About the size of a sand dollar, these crisp, glossy, dark brown wafers melt in your mouth, with a buttery blast of ginger, molasses, and just a touch of black pepper to make them even snappier. They're great with coffee, milk, or tea, or crumbled over a dish of vanilla ice cream.

INGREDIENTS	GRAMS	OUNCES	VOLUME
Unbleached all-purpose flour	250	8.82	1¾ cups
Ground ginger	12	0.42	2 tablespoons
Baking soda	2 teaspoons	2 teaspoons	2 teaspoons
Cinnamon	2 teaspoons	2 teaspoons	2 teaspoons
Allspice	1 teaspoon	1 teaspoon	1 teaspoon
Finely ground black pepper	1 teaspoon	1 teaspoon	1 teaspoon
Kosher salt	½ teaspoon	½ teaspoon	½ teaspoon
Eggs	100	3.50	2 large
Molasses	56	2	Scant ¼ cup
Finely grated lemon rind	8	0.28	1½ teaspoons, firmly packed
Unsalted butter, slightly softened	200	7	⅞ cup
Sugar	112	4	½ cup
Dark brown sugar	112	4	½ cup

1. The day before you plan to bake, sift the flour, ginger, baking soda, cinnamon, allspice, pepper, and salt into a bowl. In a separate bowl, whisk together the eggs, molasses, and lemon rind.

2. Using an electric mixer with a paddle attachment, cream together the butter and the sugars on medium speed for 2 minutes or until light and fluffy, scraping the sides and bottom of the bowl frequently. Gradually add the egg mixture until everything is well combined. The batter may look a little curdled at this point.

3. With the mixer on low speed, add the dry ingredients in stages. Mix only until everything is just combined. Scrape the sides and bottom of the bowl frequently. There should not be any pockets of dry flour left in the dough. Scrape the dough into a container with a tight cover and refrigerate it overnight to make it firm.

4. Before you take the dough out of the refrigerator, preheat the oven to 350°F and line the cookie sheets with baking parchment.

5. Using a 1-inch metal food scoop or 2 small teaspoons, drop up to 12 little balls of dough on each cookie sheet, leaving at least 2 inches around each ball. Do not flatten the ball of dough. Bake the cookies for about 16 minutes, rotating the sheets after the first 8 minutes. These cookies will spread a lot, puff up a little in the beginning of baking, and then flatten out. They should be completely flattened, very dark, and firm to the touch when they're done. If they're still soft, bake them for another 1 or 2 minutes, until they're firm. These cookies are the only ones we make that should be crisp instead of chewy.

6. Cool the cookies on the sheets for 5 minutes, then move them to a rack and cool completely before storing.

TIPS and TECHNIQUES

This dough is very soft because the proportion of flour to butter and sugar is very low for cookie dough. It's best to make the dough the day before you bake the cookies, leaving it in the refrigerator overnight so it gets very firm. Return the dough to the refrigerator between baking batches of cookies to keep it firm.

To make measuring molasses easier, coat your measuring container with vegetable oil first, and the molasses will slip right out.

Use a 1¼-inch-diameter metal food scoop to shape the dough and drop it directly onto the cookie sheet without flattening it, to help minimize spreading during baking. If you don't have a food scoop, use a regular teaspoon to drop balls of dough that are approximately 1¼ inches in diameter onto the prepared sheet.

Nuevo Chocolate Chip Cookies

Yield: 1 dozen large cookies
Equipment: two 12 x 17-inch cookie sheets

Our first chocolate chip cookies were made from the standard recipe found on the back of the semisweet chocolate chip bag, but we omitted the nuts because some of our customers had complained that we used nuts or raisins in too many things. Then one day our daytime pastry chef, Molly, decided she wanted us to have a chocolate chip cookie that had a little more complex flavor than the run-of-the-mill variety. To distinguish the new recipe from the old recipe while she was testing it, she playfully incorporated the word *nuevo* as part of the recipe title because several of our pastry bakers speak Spanish as well as English. Our customers did comment on the change in taste, and for a couple of weeks we thought we might have to go back to the old formula. But gradually the chocolate chip cookie sales increased and then actually exceeded the old levels—a good indication that Molly's *nuevo* version was a keeper. The subtle flavors of slightly salted, toasted wheat, melted butter, and molasses mixed with overtones of sugar and semisweet chocolate make these cookies one of the bakery's biggest sellers.

INGREDIENTS	GRAMS	OUNCES	VOLUME
Unbleached all-purpose flour	288	10.14	2 cups
Baking soda	1¼ teaspoons	1¼ teaspoons	1¼ teaspoons
Kosher salt	½ teaspoon	½ teaspoon	½ teaspoon
Ground ginger	¼ teaspoon	¼ teaspoon	¼ teaspoon
Eggs	50	1.76	1 large
Egg yolk	20	0.70	From 1 large egg
Vanilla extract	1¼ teaspoons	1¼ teaspoons	1¼ teaspoons
Unsalted butter, slightly softened	160	5.70	¾ cup
Light brown sugar	140	5.0	⅔ cup, firmly packed
Sugar	120	4.20	⅔ cup
Molasses	20	0.70	1 tablespoon
Semisweet chocolate chips	214	7.50	1⅛ cups

1. Position one rack in the top third of the oven, one rack in the bottom third of the oven, and preheat the oven to 350°F. Line the cookie sheets with baking parchment.

2. In a bowl, add the flour, baking soda, salt, and ginger and whisk together. In a separate bowl, add the egg, egg yolk, and vanilla and whisk together.

3. In another bowl, using an electric mixer with a paddle attachment, cream together the butter, the sugars, and molasses on medium speed for 2 minutes, or until light and fluffy, scraping the sides and bottom of the bowl frequently. Gradually add the egg mixture until everything is well combined.

4. With the mixer on low speed, add the dry ingredients in stages. Mix only until everything is just combined, scraping the sides and bottom of the bowl frequently. There should not be any pockets of dry flour left in the dough. Add the chocolate chips and continue mixing at low speed until they are evenly distributed. If you're using a mixer with standard beaters instead of a paddle, you may want to use a spatula or a wooden spoon to fold in the chocolate chips by hand. If you're adding nuts (see Tips and Techniques for this recipe), fold them in at this point, too.

5. Using a large soup spoon, a metal ice cream scoop, or your clean hands moistened with water, scoop out big balls of dough, placing 6 balls on each prepared cookie sheet. Each ball of dough should weigh approximately 85 g/3 oz. and be about 2¼ inches in diameter. If you don't have a scale, use a scant ½-cup measuring cup to estimate the size. Do not flatten the dough balls. Bake the cookies for about 18 minutes, rotating the sheets halfway through the baking time. These cookies will spread a lot during baking. They should be golden brown and just set when they're done.

6. Cool the cookies on the sheets for 5 minutes, then move them to a rack and cool completely before storing.

TIPS *and* TECHNIQUES

This dough can be made ahead and refrigerated in an airtight container, but should be taken out to sit at room temperature until it is soft enough to scoop easily for baking.

These cookies are also good with 1¼ cups of coarsely chopped toasted walnuts thrown in for extra flavor and crunch.

Front to back: Oatmeal Raisin
Cookies (page 118), Nutty
Peanut Butter Cookies, and
Nuevo Chocolate Chip Cookies
(page 110)

Nutty Peanut Butter Cookies

Yield: 1 dozen large cookies
Equipment: two 12 x 17-inch cookie sheets

Our first Peanut Butter Cookie recipe came from the original *Fannie Farmer Junior Cookbook*—the first cookbook Toy ever owned. In fact, those were the first cookies Toy ever made, when she was seven years old. Little did she know then that one day she'd be baking cookies for a living. One day Amy decided she'd like our Peanut Butter Cookies to have a salty-sweet taste, reminiscent of a Payday candy bar, so we incorporated salted peanuts into the batter. They add a pleasant crunchiness and a slight saltiness to this chewy, sweet, buttery treat—a peanut lover's delight.

INGREDIENTS	GRAMS	OUNCES	VOLUME
Unbleached all-purpose flour	256	9	1¾ cups
Kosher salt	2 teaspoons	2 teaspoons	2 teaspoons
Baking soda	¾ teaspoon	¾ teaspoon	¾ teaspoon
Eggs	100	3.50	2 large
Vanilla extract	¾ teaspoon	¾ teaspoon	¾ teaspoon
Natural-style smooth peanut butter	173	6.10	⅔ cup
Unsalted butter, slightly softened	164	5.78	¾ cup
Dark brown sugar	164	5.78	⅔ cup, firmly packed
Sugar	128	4.50	⅔ cup
Salted peanuts	180	6.35	1¼ cups

1. Position one rack in the top third of the oven, one rack in the bottom third of the oven, and preheat the oven to 350°F. Line the cookie sheets with baking parchment.

2. In a bowl, add the flour, salt, and baking soda and whisk together. In a separate bowl, add the eggs and vanilla and whisk together.

3. In another bowl, using an electric mixer with a paddle attachment, cream together the peanut butter, butter, and sugars on medium speed for 2 minutes, or until well combined, scraping the sides and bottom of the bowl frequently. Gradually add the egg mixture until everything is well combined.

4. With the mixer on low speed, add the dry ingredients in stages. Mix only until everything is just combined, scraping the sides and bottom of the bowl frequently. There should not be any pockets of dry flour left in the dough. Add the salted peanuts and continue mixing on low speed until the nuts are evenly distributed. If the nuts are very oily, you may have to fold them in to the dough by hand.

5. Using a large soup spoon, a metal ice cream scoop, or your clean hands moistened with water, scoop out big balls of dough, placing 6 balls on each prepared cookie sheet. Each ball of dough should weigh approximately 80 g/2.82 oz. If you don't have a scale, use a scant ½ cup to estimate the size. The dough balls should be about 2¼ inches in diameter. Flatten each ball of dough by pressing the top down firmly with the flat of your hand, then use the tines a fork to make a criss-cross pattern in the center of each cookie. The cookies should be ⅜ to ½ inch thick before they're baked. Bake the cookies for about 17 minutes, rotating the cookie sheets halfway through the baking time. These cookies do not spread very much during baking. They should be golden brown and just set when they're done. Be careful not to underbake them or they'll be doughy and will crumble easily.

6. Cool the cookies on the sheets for 5 minutes, then move them to a rack and cool completely before storing.

TIPS *and* TECHNIQUES

The peanut butter we use at the bakery is made with nothing but ground peanuts. It has a more definitive peanut flavor and gives us more control over the type and the amount of sugar and salt we use in the recipe. When we tested this recipe for the cookbook, we used Smucker's Natural Creamy Peanut Butter, which does contain a little added salt, but the results were delicious.

Lime Cornmeal Cookies

Yield: 1 dozen large cookies
Equipment: two 12 x 17-inch cookie sheets

The inspiration for these luscious cookies happened one day when the roommate of our daytime pastry chef, Molly, brought home a cookie for her to taste—a crisp little cornmeal wafer that had a light coating of lime-flavored glaze on the top. Molly loved how the combination of buttery sweet corn and zesty lime tickled her taste buds. When she worked on the idea in the bakery pastry kitchen, this recipe was the result. Instead of a small crisp wafer, she made a big, soft, voluptuous cookie with crunchy bits of coarse cornmeal and flecks of lime zest scattered throughout. Topping it off is a light glaze made with confectioner's sugar and freshly squeezed lime juice. The whole combination is irresistible. Can you tell this is one of our personal favorites? These are the perfect finish for a meal with a southwestern theme.

INGREDIENTS	GRAMS	OUNCES	VOLUME
Unbleached all-purpose flour	215	7.60	1½ cups
Coarse cornmeal	168	5.90	1 cup
Unbleached bread flour	120	4.23	⅞ cup
Kosher salt	1¾ teaspoons	1¾ teaspoons	1¾ teaspoons
Baking soda	⅞ teaspoon	⅞ teaspoon	⅞ teaspoon
Sugar	250	8.80	1¼ cups
Unsalted butter, slightly softened	243	8.57	1 cup + 1 tablespoon
Lime zest, finely minced	1½ teaspoons	1½ teaspoons	1½ teaspoons
Eggs	100	3.50	2 large
Egg yolks	40	1.40	From 2 large eggs
Confectioner's sugar	227	8	1⅞ cups
Lime juice, strained	45	1.60	3 tablespoons

1. Position one rack in the top third of the oven, one rack in the bottom third of the oven, and preheat the oven to 350°F. Line the cookie sheets with baking parchment.

2. In a bowl, add the all-purpose flour, cornmeal, bread flour, salt, and baking soda and whisk together.

3. In another bowl, using an electric mixer with a paddle attachment, cream the sugar, butter, and lime zest together on medium speed for 2 minutes, or until light and fluffy, scraping the sides and bottom of the bowl frequently. Gradually add the eggs and egg yolks, mixing until everything is well combined.

4. With the mixer on medium-low speed, add the dry ingredients in stages. Mix only until everything is well combined, scraping the sides and bottom of the bowl frequently. There should not be any pockets of dry flour left in the dough.

5. Using a large soup spoon, a metal ice cream scoop, or your clean hands moistened with water, scoop out big balls of dough, placing 6 balls on each prepared cookie sheet. Each ball of dough should weigh approximately 90 g/3.2 oz. If you don't have a scale, use a scant ½ cup to estimate the size. The dough balls should be about 2¼ inches in diameter. This dough will be soft, so don't flatten the dough balls at all before baking. Bake the cookies for about 18 minutes, rotating the cookie sheets halfway through the baking time. The cookies should be lightly browned on the edges and baked all the way into the center. They should be soft, but be careful not to underbake them or the centers will collapse and be doughy.

6. Cool the cookies on the sheets for 5 minutes, then move them to a rack and cool completely before glazing.

7. Whisk together the confectioner's sugar and the lime juice to make a loose glaze. Use a 2-inch pastry brush to frost the top of each cookie, leaving an unfrosted ¼-inch border around the edge. Let the glaze dry completely before storing the cookies in an airtight container.

TIPS and TECHNIQUES

Be sure to use coarse cornmeal. If you can't find it at your regular grocery store, go to a health food store or a natural foods market. Finely ground cornmeal will not work with this recipe. Polenta is a suitable substitute.

In the bakery, we use special all-purpose flour that has a slightly higher protein content than the kind you buy in the grocery store. To get a close approximation of that flour in this recipe, we combine regular all-purpose flour with a little bread flour to increase the protein content. Pillsbury Bread Flour is available in most local grocery stores now. You can also find unbleached bread flour at most natural food and health food stores. That little bit of extra protein is really necessary in these cookies, to give them the proper texture and keep them from being too heavy and doughy.

Oatmeal Raisin Cookies

Yield: 1 dozen large cookies

Equipment: two 12 x 17-inch cookie sheets

Oatmeal cookies are right up there with chocolate chip and peanut butter cookies when it comes to evoking happy childhood memories surrounding cookie baking and eating. So of course we had to have an oatmeal cookie on our menu, and of course it had to have raisins in it. Once again we started with a recipe from a cereal box and tweaked a few things here and there to make it more pleasing to our now-grown-up taste buds. Be sure to use the old-fashioned-style oats, not the quick-cooking or instant variety, for the best flavor and texture. Bake a batch and eat them with a big glass of milk while they're still warm from the oven. You might just feel like a kid again.

INGREDIENTS	GRAMS	OUNCES	VOLUME
Unbleached all-purpose flour	214	7.5	1½ cups
Kosher salt	1½ teaspoons	1½ teaspoons	1½ teaspoons
Baking soda	1 teaspoon	1 teaspoon	1 teaspoon
Cinnamon	⅜ teaspoon	⅜ teaspoon	⅜ teaspoon
Eggs	100	3.5	2 large
Vanilla	1 teaspoon	1 teaspoon	1 teaspoon
Old-fashioned rolled oats	270	9.50	3⅛ cups
Raisins	175	6.17	1¼ cups
Unsalted butter	228	8	1 cup
Dark brown sugar	212	7.50	⅞ cup, firmly packed
Sugar	90	2.55	½ cup

1. Position one rack in the top third of the oven, one rack in the bottom third of the oven, and preheat the oven to 350°F. Line the cookie sheets with baking parchment.

2. In a bowl, add the flour, salt, baking soda, and cinnamon and whisk together. In a separate bowl, whisk together the eggs and vanilla. In a third bowl, mix the oats and raisins.

3. In another bowl, using an electric mixer with a paddle attachment, cream together the butter and sugars on medium speed for 2 minutes, or until light and fluffy, scraping the sides and bottom of the bowl frequently. Gradually add the egg mixture until everything is well combined.

4. With the mixer on low speed, add the flour mixture in stages. Mix only until everything is well combined, scraping the sides and bottom of the bowl frequently. There should not be any pockets of dry flour left in the dough. Then add the oats and raisins and mix again on low speed until everything is evenly distributed.

5. Using a large soup spoon, a metal ice cream scoop, or your clean hands moistened with water, scoop out big balls of dough, placing 6 balls on each prepared cookie sheet. Each ball of dough should weigh approximately 100 g/3.5 oz. If you don't have a scale, use a scant ½ cup to estimate the size. The dough balls should be about 2¼ inches in diameter. Press down on these cookies very lightly, to just barely flatten the tops before they're baked. They will spread a lot during baking. Bake the cookies for about 18 minutes, rotating the cookie sheets halfway through the baking time. They should be golden brown and baked all the way into the center. They should be soft, but be careful not to underbake them or they'll be doughy and fall apart easily.

6. Cool the cookies on the sheets for 5 minutes, then move them to a rack and cool completely before storing.

Double Chocolate Chip Cookies and
White Chocolate Cherry Chunkers (page 123)

Double Chocolate Chip Cookies

Yield: 1 dozen large cookies
Equipment: two 12 x 17-inch cookie sheets

These were the first double chocolate chip cookies we made to sell in our Hell's Kitchen café. Amy tried half a dozen recipes for double chocolate chip cookies, but none of them quite matched the cookie she had in her imagination. So she took the best qualities from each of her tests and finally came up with this winner. Not too sweet, crunchy on the edges, moist and chewy in the middle—this cookie fills your mouth with the flavor of deep dark chocolate, melted butter, and a hint of toasted pecans from the first bite. And the more of it you eat, the better it tastes. This cookie is especially great warm from the oven, when the chocolate chips are still melted. Sadly, we no longer sell double chocolate chip cookies in our cafés. Their delicate texture made them too fragile to transport to our other retail locations safely, so a lot of them were broken when they arrived. (The staff loved this, of course, because they got to eat the broken ones!) We replaced this cookie with a sturdier one, but this one is still our favorite. Many of our customers who lamented the demise of this cookie will be thrilled to see this recipe in print.

INGREDIENTS	GRAMS	OUNCES	VOLUME
Unbleached all-purpose flour	236	8.32	1⅝ cups
Cocoa powder	⅜ cup	⅜ cup	⅜ cup
Baking soda	1¼ teaspoons	1¼ teaspoons	1¼ teaspoons
Kosher salt	⅛ teaspoon	⅛ teaspoon	⅛ teaspoon
Semisweet chocolate chips	390	15	2¼ cups
Unsalted butter, slightly softened	227	8	1 cup
Dark brown sugar	120	4.20	½ cup
Sugar	100	3.5	½ cup
Eggs	100	3.5	2 large
Vanilla extract	1 teaspoon	1 teaspoon	1 teaspoon
Pecans, toasted, chopped (see page 242)	90	3.20	¾ cup

1. Position one rack in the top third of the oven, one rack in the bottom third of the oven, and preheat the oven to 350°F. Line the cookie sheets with baking parchment.

2. In a bowl, add the flour, cocoa powder, baking soda, and salt and whisk together.

3. In a glass bowl, melt 281 g/10 oz./1½ cups of the chocolate chips in a microwave oven at 50 percent power for 3 minutes. Stir them to make them smooth, then set aside to cool.

4. In another bowl, using an electric mixer with a paddle attachment, cream together the butter and sugars on medium speed for 2 minutes, or until light and fluffy, scraping the sides and bottom of the bowl frequently. Pour in the melted chocolate and continue mixing until the mixture is uniform in color. The chocolate should be pourable but not hot, or the butter will melt. Gradually add the eggs and the vanilla, mixing until everything is well combined.

5. With the mixer on low speed, add the dry ingredients in stages. Mix only until everything is well combined. Scrape the sides and bottom of the bowl frequently. There should not be any pockets of dry flour left in the dough. Add the remaining chocolate chips and the pecans and continue mixing at low speed until the chips and nuts are evenly distributed. If you're using a mixer with standard beaters instead of a paddle, you may want to use a spatula or a wooden spoon to fold the chocolate chips and nuts in by hand. Chill the dough in the refrigerator until it is firm but not hard.

6. Using a large soup spoon, a metal ice cream scoop, or your clean hands moistened with water, scoop out big balls of dough, placing 6 balls on each prepared cookie sheet. Each ball of dough should weigh approximately 90 g/3.17 oz. each. If you don't have a scale, use a scant ½ cup to estimate the size. The dough balls should be about 2¼ inches in diameter. Press each ball very lightly on the top, just to level the top of the ball. Do not flatten the ball. Bake the cookies for about 18 to 20 minutes, rotating the cookie sheets halfway through the baking time. These cookies will spread a lot during baking. They should be just set when done.

7. Cool the cookies on the sheets for 5 minutes, then move them to a rack and cool completely before storing.

TIPS and TECHNIQUES

Instead of weighing the cocoa powder for this recipe, we're showing only a volume measurement. The weight of cocoa powders varies so dramatically from one brand to the next that it's safer in this case to use the volume measurement. We tested this recipe using Bensdorp Dutch-processed cocoa powder with delicious results, but any good-quality cocoa powder will do.

White Chocolate Cherry Chunkers

Yield: 1 dozen large cookies
Equipment: two 12 x 17-inch cookie sheets

This delightful combination came about when Amy asked our daytime pastry chef, Molly, to develop a new cookie using white chocolate. Using the Kitchen Sink cookie recipe as a starting point, Molly decided to try a combination of white chocolate and dried cherries. It took a couple of tries to get the balance just right, but the marriage of the two flavors worked to perfection. It's like eating cherries and cream in a cookie, with oatmeal thrown in for some crunch.

INGREDIENTS	GRAMS	OUNCES	VOLUME
Unbleached all-purpose flour	244	8.6	1²/₃ cups
Old-fashioned rolled oats	188	6.60	2¹/₄ cups
Baking soda	1¹/₄ teaspoons	1¹/₄ teaspoons	1¹/₄ teaspoons
Kosher salt	¹/₂ teaspoon	¹/₂ teaspoon	¹/₂ teaspoon
Eggs	100	3.52	2 large
Vanilla extract	1¹/₄ teaspoons	1¹/₄ teaspoons	1¹/₄ teaspoons
Dried tart cherries	170	6	1 cup
White chocolate chunks or chips	125	4.4	³/₄ cup
Unsalted butter, slightly softened	227	8	1 cup
Dark brown sugar	144	5	¹/₂ cup, firmly packed
Sugar	125	4.40	⁵/₈ cup

1. Position one rack in the top third of the oven, one rack in the bottom third of the oven, and preheat the oven to 350°F. Line the cookie sheets with baking parchment.

2. In a bowl, add the flour, oats, baking soda, and salt and whisk together. In a separate small bowl, whisk together the eggs and vanilla. In another larger bowl, add the cherries and white chocolate and toss gently to combine.

3. In another bowl, using an electric mixer with a paddle attachment, cream together the butter and sugars on medium speed for 2 minutes, or until light and fluffy, scraping the sides and bottom of the bowl frequently. Gradually add the egg mixture until everything is well combined.

4. With the mixer on low speed, add the flour mixture in stages. Mix only until everything is well combined, scraping the sides and bottom of the bowl frequently. There should not be any pockets of dry flour left in the dough. Add the cherries and chocolate and mix again on low speed until everything is evenly distributed. If you're

TIPS and TECHNIQUES

Try to find dried cherries that have a sweet-tart flavor. When we were testing this recipe, we found packets of Welch's dried cherries displayed with the raisins in our local super-market. The flavor of these cherries duplicated exactly the ones we have in the bakery. If you can't find dried cherries, Ocean Spray Craisins are a good substitute. Dried blue-berries would be fun, too—for a blueberries-and-cream experience.

As the name implies, we like to use big chunks of white chocolate in these cookies, but white chocolate chips are okay, too, if that's the only white chocolate you can find.

using a mixer that has beaters instead of a paddle, you may want to fold these last ingredients in by hand with a wooden spoon or a rubber spatula.

5. Using a large soup spoon, a metal ice cream scoop, or your clean hands moistened with water, scoop out big balls of dough, placing 6 balls on each prepared cookie sheet. Each ball of dough should weigh approximately 100 g/3.5 oz. If you don't have a scale, use a scant ½ cup to estimate the size. The dough balls should be about 2¼ inches in diameter. Press down on them lightly to flatten them to a thickness of about 2 inches. They will spread a lot during baking. Bake the cookies for about 18 minutes, rotating the cookie sheets halfway through the baking time. They should be golden brown and baked all the way into the center. They should be soft, but be careful not to underbake them or they'll be doughy and will fall apart easily.

6. Cool the cookies on the sheets for 5 minutes, then move them to a rack and cool completely before storing.

Kitchen Sink Cookies

Yield: 2 dozen large cookies
Equipment: two 12 x 17-inch cookie sheets

Yes, these cookies do have just about everything in them but the kitchen sink—two kinds of chocolate, coconut, raisins, pecans, and oatmeal, all rolled into one fabulous treat. At Christmastime we pack five of these big cookies in a festive cellophane bag, tie it with a generous length of ribbon, and sell them for hostess gifts or stocking stuffers.

Try this recipe, then, using your imagination. Mix and match different kinds of chocolate, nuts, and dried fruits to create your own kitchen sink.

INGREDIENTS	GRAMS	OUNCES	VOLUME
Unbleached all-purpose flour	244	8.60	1⅔ cups
Old-fashioned rolled oats	188	6.60	2¼ cups
Baking soda	1¼ teaspoons	1¼ teaspoons	1¼ teaspoons
Kosher salt	¾ teaspoon	¾ teaspoon	¾ teaspoon
Eggs	100	3.50	2 large
Vanilla extract	1¼ teaspoons	1¼ teaspoons	1¼ teaspoons
Semisweet chocolate chips	60	2	⅓ cup
White chocolate chunks or chips	50	1.76	⅓ cup
Raisins	45	1.60	⅓ cup
Pecans, toasted (see page 242), chopped	38	1.34	⅓ cup
Sweetened flaked coconut	34	1.20	¼ cup, firmly packed
Unsalted butter, slightly softened	227	8	1 cup
Dark brown sugar	144	5	½ cup, firmly packed
Sugar	118	4.16	½ cup

1. Position one rack in the top third of the oven, one rack in the bottom third of the oven, and preheat the oven to 350°F. Line the cookie sheets with baking parchment.

2. In a bowl, combine the flour, oats, baking soda, and salt and whisk together. In a small bowl, whisk together the eggs and vanilla. In another larger bowl, add the 2 chocolates, raisins, pecans, and coconut and toss gently to combine.

3. In another bowl, using an electric mixer with a paddle attachment, cream together the butter and sugars on medium speed for 2 minutes, or until light and fluffy, scraping the sides and bottom of the bowl frequently. Add the eggs and vanilla, mixing until everything is well combined.

4. With the mixer on medium-low speed, add the flour mixture in stages. Mix only until everything is well combined, scraping the sides and bottom of the bowl frequently. There should not be any pockets of dry flour left in the dough. This dough will be very stiff. It will be easier at this point to transfer it to a larger mixing bowl, adding the chocolate mixture and folding these last ingredients in by hand with a wooden spoon until they are evenly distributed.

5. Using a large soup spoon, a metal ice cream scoop, or your clean hands moistened with water, scoop out big balls of dough, placing 6 balls on each prepared cookie sheet. Each ball of dough should weigh approximately 100 g/3.5 oz. If you don't have a scale, use a scant ½ cup to estimate the size. Roll the dough into round balls. The balls should be about 2¼ inches in diameter. Press down firmly to flatten them into ¾-inch thick disks. They will spread a moderate amount during baking. Bake the cookies for about 16 minutes, rotating the cookie sheets halfway through the baking time. They should be golden brown and just barely set in the center. They should be soft, but be careful not to underbake them or they'll be doughy and fall apart easily.

6. Cool the cookies on the sheets for 5 minutes, then move them to a rack and cool completely before storing.

TIPS and TECHNIQUES

Be sure to use the old-fashioned-style rolled oats, not the quick-cooking or instant variety.

Because this dough is very stiff we think the easiest way to form the cookies is to use your clean hands, lightly moistened with water, to scoop up a big chunk of dough and roll it into a ball before placing it onto the cookie sheet.

Orange Butter Cookies

Yield: 1 dozen large cookies
Equipment: two 12 x 17-inch cookie sheets

Every good cookie menu should include a variety without any chocolate or nuts. This simple gem is the Amy's Bread version of a basic sugar cookie. Instead of making a standard sugar cookie, we decided to include a little orange zest to perk up the flavor, and a couple of egg yolks to add a touch of richness. These are amazing with a dish of orange or strawberry sorbet.

INGREDIENTS	GRAMS	OUNCES	VOLUME
Unbleached all-purpose flour	260	9.20	1¾ cups
Cake flour	190	6.70	1⅔ cups
Baking soda	½ teaspoon	½ teaspoon	½ teaspoon
Kosher salt	1 teaspoon	1 teaspoon	1 teaspoon
Sugar, plus extra for topping before baking	250	8.80	1¼ cups
Unsalted butter, slightly softened	227	8	1 cup
Orange zest, finely minced	10	0.35	2½ teaspoons, tightly packed
Eggs	50	1.76	1 large
Egg yolks	40	1.40	From 2 large eggs

1. Position one rack in the top third of the oven, one rack in the bottom third of the oven, and preheat the oven to 350°F. Line the cookie sheets with baking parchment.

2. In a bowl, add the all-purpose flour, cake flour, baking soda, and salt and whisk together.

3. In another bowl, using an electric mixer with a paddle attachment, cream together the sugar, butter, and orange zest on medium speed for 2 minutes, or until light and fluffy, scraping the sides and bottom of the bowl frequently. Gradually add the eggs and egg yolks, mixing on medium speed until everything is well combined.

4. With the mixer on low speed, add the dry ingredients in stages. Mix only until everything is well combined, scraping the sides and bottom of the bowl frequently. There should not be any pockets of dry flour left in the dough.

5. Using a large soup spoon, a metal ice cream scoop, or your clean hands moistened with water, scoop out big balls of dough, placing 6 balls on each prepared cookie sheet. Each ball of dough should weigh approximately 85 g/3 oz. If you don't have a scale, use a scant ½ cup to estimate the size. The dough balls should be about 2¼ inches in diameter. Using the three middle fingers of your hand, press firmly on the

top of each ball to flatten it to a thickness of ½ inch. Allow the dough to push up between your fingers so an imprint of valleys and ridges remains. If the dough is sticky, you may have to moisten your fingers slightly with cold water to keep them from sticking to the dough. Sprinkle the tops of the cookies generously with the extra granulated sugar. They will spread a moderate amount during baking. Bake the cookies for about 17 minutes, rotating the cookie sheets halfway through the baking time. The cookies should be pale but baked all the way into the center. They should be soft, but be careful not to underbake them or the centers will be doughy.

6. Cool the cookies on the sheets for 5 minutes, then move them to a rack and cool completely before storing.

TIPS *and* TECHNIQUES

At the bakery, we make these cookies with unbleached pastry flour. Because this is not easy to find in local supermarkets, we've adapted the recipe with a combination of unbleached all-purpose flour and cake flour. If you don't have cake flour on hand, use 100 percent unbleached all-purpose flour, or even 100 percent bleached pre-sifted all-purpose flour. The texture of the cookies may be a little coarse, but they'll still taste delicious.

Biscotti

In Italy, *biscotti,* which means "twice baked," is the name given to all kinds of cookies, but here in America it usually refers to a cookie that has been baked first in a log shape and then sliced and baked again to make it toasty, crunchy, and dry. Biscotti are perfect for dipping into espresso or dessert wine. Ours are made with a lot less butter than regular cookies, so although they're not exactly "diet food," they are a lighter indulgence with plenty of flavor and body—and all that crunching makes them pretty satisfying, too. Over the years we've experimented with several different kinds of biscotti made with different spices, nuts, and grains. As with most of our sweets, the ones our customers request most often have become our daily standards and are always available in our three retail cafés. The three we make cover the range of tastes: one is dark chocolate with hazelnuts and chocolate chips; one is a little spicy, with black pepper and citrus; and the third features the classic pairing of anise and almonds.

TIPS and TECHNIQUES

• Since our biscotti have less butter than regular cookies, we look for a sandy mixture instead of a fluffy mixture when we cream the butter and sugar. Once the eggs have been added, the batter becomes full and fluffy. Although the butter needs to be slightly softened for creaming, it is easier to shape the biscotti dough into logs if all the other ingredients are cool. If the logs are shaped when the dough is warm and soft, the biscotti will spread and become flat. If you like a slightly taller cookie, with a rounded top, keep the dough and your kitchen cool when preparing the biscotti, or place the dough in the refrigerator to cool for 30 minutes after mixing it and before rolling it into logs.

• We suggest slicing the biscotti with a serrated knife. This makes a cleaner slice and helps to prevent the slices from breaking during the cutting process. We suggest times for toasting your biscotti, but the final hardness is a matter of preference. If you like a very hard and crunchy cookie, toast the biscotti for the maximum amount of time. They stay fresh and crisp longer if they are toasted firmly. Some people like a softer cookie that isn't a jaw breaker. If that's the case, then toast the biscotti less. It's hard to tell how crisp they'll be until they cool completely. Right when they come out of the oven they may still feel slightly soft to the touch, but they usually get very crisp when they cool. If they feel firm coming out of they oven, they'll be very hard and crisp when they cool. If they're not as crisp as you like, toast them for a few more minutes.

Toasted Hazelnut Biscotti with Citrus Zest and Pepper

↻ **Yield:** 3 lbs. of biscotti, about 4 dozen pieces
↻ **Equipment:** two 12 x 17-inch cookie sheets

These crunchy and delicious biscotti, fondly known as Pepper Nut at the bakery, make a great snack or an afternoon pick-me-up with coffee. We got the recipe from our good friend Alison Weiss, who makes them regularly for her friends and guests at her summer home. Their base is a simple mixture of flour, sugar, eggs, and butter, with a generous amount of toasted hazelnuts, but these biscotti really come to life with the addition of grated lemon and orange zest, and a dose of ground black pepper. After the initial baking, they are sliced and toasted again. Once they've cooled, they have a long shelf life and can be kept at room temperature in an airtight container for several weeks, or even longer in the freezer. We like to keep a secret stash tucked in our freezer at home, just in case we need a spicy little treat.

INGREDIENTS	GRAMS	OUNCES	VOLUME
Unbleached all-purpose flour	505	17.81	3½ cups
Baking soda	1 teaspoon	1 teaspoon	1 teaspoon
Baking powder	1 teaspoon	1 teaspoon	1 teaspoon
Kosher salt	¾ teaspoon	¾ teaspoon	¾ teaspoon
Ground black pepper	1 tablespoon	1 tablespoon	1 tablespoon
Unsalted butter, slightly softened	170	6	¾ cup
Sugar	400	14.11	2 cups
Eggs	200	7.05	4 large
Lemon zest, grated	2 teaspoons	2 teaspoons	2 teaspoons
Orange zest, grated	12	0.42	2 tablespoons
Vanilla extract	1 tablespoon	1 tablespoon	1 tablespoon
Almond extract	½ teaspoon	½ teaspoon	½ teaspoon
Hazelnuts, with skins, toasted (see page 242)	400	14.11	3 cups
Egg for egg wash	50	1.76	1 large

1. Position one rack in the top third of the oven, one rack in the bottom third of the oven, and preheat the oven to 350°F. Line the cookie sheets with baking parchment.

2. In a medium bowl, add the flour, baking soda, baking powder, salt, and pepper and whisk together.

3. In another bowl with an electric mixer, cream the butter with the sugar for 1 minute or until a sandy mixture has formed. Add the eggs, zests, and extracts and mix until fluffy, about 1 minute more.

4. Add the dry ingredients to the butter mixture and combine well. Add the hazelnuts and fold in with a spatula to distribute the nuts evenly. The dough will be very thick and hard to stir at this point.

5. Divide the dough into four equal portions, about 410 g/14½ oz. each. On a lightly floured counter, roll each portion into a log 9 inches long by 2 inches wide by 1½ inches high. Place 2 logs on each of the prepared cookie sheets with several inches between the logs.

6. In a small bowl, mix 1 egg with 1 teaspoon of water to make an egg wash. Brush each log with egg wash, coating them evenly on the top and sides.

7. Bake for 22 minutes, rotating the cookie sheets from top to bottom halfway through baking. Bake until lightly browned, puffy, and still somewhat soft. Remove from the oven, but leave the oven on.

8. Cool for 30 minutes, then place one log at a time on a cutting board. With a serrated knife, slice each log into individual biscotti by cutting at a slight angle into ¾-inch-thick pieces, keeping the slices in a row. Slide the row of biscotti together, lift and place them back onto the cookie sheets, then separate the slices, leaving ½ inch of space between each one.

9. Bake again for 16 to 20 minutes, rotating once during baking until the biscotti are slightly firm and light brown in color.

10. Cool and eat, or pack in an airtight container to store for up to 6 weeks.

Front to back: Amy's Anise
Almond Biscotti, Chocolate
Hazelnut Biscotti (page 139), and
Toasted Hazelnut Biscotti with
Citrus Zest and Pepper (page 134)

Amy's Anise Almond Biscotti

Yield: 1¾ lbs. biscotti, about 3 dozen
Equipment: one 12 x 17-inch cookie sheet

If you step into a traditional Italian pastry shop, you're sure to find some kind of anise cookie, toast, or biscotti. We love the fragrance and flavor of anise but prefer the smoother flavor of star anise over the sharper flavor of aniseed—the form of anise used in traditional Italian baking. Star anise comes from a completely different plant family than aniseed. The star-shaped seed pod of a small evergreen tree from southwest China, it is widely used in India and China in spice mixes such as Garam Masala and Chinese five-spice powder. When we tried star anise in our biscotti we found the anise flavor to be fragrant yet subtle. When paired with toasted almonds, it makes a simple and satisfying palate cleanser at the end of a meal. It's not always easy to find star anise in the grocery store. Either purchase it where you buy Indian spices or order it by mail or online. See the Tips and Techniques for this recipe for the name of a spice merchant who carries it.

INGREDIENTS	GRAMS	OUNCES	VOLUME
Unsalted butter, slightly softened	57	2	¼ cup
Sugar	227	8	1 cup + 2 tablespoons
Eggs	150	5.29	3 large
Ground star anise	18	0.63	¼ cup
Anise extract	16	0.56	1 tablespoon + 1 teaspoon
Unbleached all-purpose flour	290	10.23	2 cups
Baking soda	1 teaspoon	1 teaspoon	1 teaspoon
Kosher salt	1 teaspoon	1 teaspoon	1 teaspoon
Whole almonds, toasted (see page 242)	290	10.23	2 cups + 1 tablespoon
Egg for egg wash	50	1.76	1 large

1. Position one rack in the middle of the oven, and preheat the oven to 350°F. Line the cookie sheet with parchment paper.

2. In a bowl with an electric mixer, cream the butter with the sugar for 1 minute or until a sandy mixture has formed. Add the eggs and mix on medium speed until fluffy, about 1 minute more.

3. Add the ground star anise and anise extract to the butter mixture and mix to combine.

4. In a medium bowl, add the flour, baking soda, and salt and whisk together. Add to the butter mixture and mix slowly on low speed to incorporate. Fold in the almonds by hand.

5. Divide the biscotti dough into 2 equal pieces, about 510 g/18 oz. each. On a lightly floured counter, roll each piece of dough into a log about 2 inches wide by 14 inches long by 1½ inches high. Place the logs on the prepared cookie sheet with several inches between them.

6. In a small bowl, mix the remaining egg with 1 teaspoon of water to make an egg wash. Brush each log with egg wash, coating it evenly on the top and sides.

7. Bake for 30 minutes rotating the cookie sheet from front to back halfway through baking, until lightly browned and somewhat firm. Remove from the oven and reduce the oven temperature to 300°F. Keep the oven turned on.

8. Cool the logs for 25 minutes, then place on a cutting board. With a serrated knife, slice each log into individual biscotti by cutting on a slight angle into ¾-inch-thick pieces, keeping the slices in a row. Slide the row of biscotti together, lift and place them back onto the cookie sheet, then separate the slices, leaving ½ inch of space between each one.

9. Bake again for 20 to 22 minutes, rotating once during baking until the biscotti are slightly firm and light brown in color.

10. Cool and eat, or pack in an airtight container to store for up to 6 weeks.

TIPS *and* TECHNIQUES

Ground star anise is not easy to find. At the bakery, we order it from Penzey's, a well-established spice merchant. They have a mail-order catalogue (phone number is 800–741–7787), or order it online at www.penzeys.com.

Chocolate Hazelnut Biscotti

Yield: 1¾ lbs. biscotti, about 3 dozen
Equipment: one 12 x 17-inch cookie sheet

Chocolate is a great gift to bakers and eaters alike. In nearly every category of baked goods we make, the products made with chocolate are by far the most popular. That is certainly the case for biscotti. These Chocolate Hazelnut Biscotti sell three to four times faster than any other kind. They are dark and chocolaty, with a deep flavor coming from unsweetened cocoa powder and instant coffee. After the dough is made, chocolate chips and toasted hazelnuts are folded in. The chocolate chips melt, leaving little pockets of soft chocolate to complement the hard, crunchy dark chocolate cookie—and that seems to be the winning combination. If you pick just one recipe to try, this is it!

INGREDIENTS	GRAMS	OUNCES	VOLUME
Unsalted butter, slightly softened	28	1	1 tablespoon
Sugar	212	7.48	1 cup + 1 tablespoon
Eggs	100	3.52	2 large
Vanilla extract	½ teaspoon	½ teaspoon	½ teaspoon
Unbleached all-purpose flour	170	6	1⅛ cup
Unsweetened cocoa powder	52	1.83	½ cup + 2 teaspoons
Instant coffee powder	1 teaspoon	1 teaspoon	1 teaspoon
Baking soda	1 teaspoon	1 teaspoon	1 teaspoon
Cinnamon, ground	¼ teaspoon	¼ teaspoon	¼ teaspoon
Hazelnuts, whole, toasted (see page 242)	227	8	1¾ cups
Semisweet chocolate chips	130	4.59	¾ cup
Egg for egg wash	50	1.76	1 large

1. Position one rack in the middle of the oven, and preheat the oven to 350°F. Line the cookie sheet with parchment paper.

2. In a bowl with an electric mixer, cream the butter with the sugar for 1 minute or until a sandy mixture forms. Add the eggs and vanilla and mix until fluffy and lighter in color, about 1 minute more.

3. In a medium mixing bowl, add the flour, cocoa powder, coffee powder, baking soda, and cinnamon and whisk together. Add to the butter-and-egg mixture in 2 additions, and mix only until combined.

4. Fold the hazelnuts and chocolate chips into the dough, and mix until evenly distributed. The dough will be thick and hard to stir. If it is too sticky, chill briefly.

5. Divide the dough into 2 equal pieces, about 454 g/16 oz. each. On a lightly floured surface, roll each piece of dough into a log about 2 inches wide by 14 inches long by 1½ inches high. Place the logs on the prepared sheet pan with several inches between them.

6. In a small bowl, mix 1 egg with 1 teaspoon of water to make an egg wash. Brush each log with egg wash, coating them evenly on the top and sides.

7. Bake for 27 minutes, rotating the cookie sheet from front to back halfway through baking, until very lightly browned and somewhat firm. Remove from the oven and reduce the oven temperature to 300°F.

8. Cool the logs for 20 minutes, then place them on a cutting board. With a serrated knife, slice each log on a slight angle into ¾-inch-thick pieces, keeping them in a row. Slide the row of biscotti together, lift and place back onto the cookie sheet, then separate the slices, leaving ½ inch of space between each one.

9. Bake again for 9 to 12 minutes, rotating once during baking until the biscotti feel slightly firm.

10. Cool and eat, or pack in an airtight container to store for up to 6 weeks. They freeze well, too—if you have any that don't get eaten right away.

Bars

We love bars, and so do our customers. Although Brownies are our customers' favorite bar, they're followed closely by Coconut Dream Bars, Lemon Bars, and Butterscotch Cashew Bars as the coffee break treats to indulge in. Amy has a particular fondness for bars. The first recipe she learned to bake as a child was Lucy's Lemon Bars, from the *Peanuts Cook Book*. Her mom is a bar specialist if ever there was one. She may have only two or three kinds of cookies in her baking repertoire, but when it comes to bars, she keeps about fifteen different recipes in her rotation of sweets for every occasion.

Bars are easy to make and don't require any special shaping techniques. Once they're mixed, they go right into the pan to be baked. Their shape is square or rectangular, depending on how you cut them from the pan. Bars are often decadent and chewy like candy bars—only better, because they aren't as sweet. They may have a buttery crust on the bottom, topped with a soft or chewy or crunchy topping. Many of our bars contain nuts, some contain chocolate, and they're all made with butter. They can be dressed up for a fancy dessert or make the perfect ending to a casual picnic. We like the fact that they can be made in advance and kept for several days in the refrigerator—and they freeze perfectly. With a few bars tucked away in the freezer, you'll always have something on hand for a quick dessert.

TIPS and TECHNIQUES

• Several of these recipes require the preparation of a bottom crust followed by a topping. The bottom crust will be much more tender and delicious if you don't handle the dough too much. As when making a tender butter cookie or a pie crust, the flour, butter, and sugar are mixed just enough to form a crumbly meal and then pressed into the pan. Handle the crust any further and the bottom of your bars will become tough.

• In some of the bar recipes, we recommend the use of a 12 x 17-inch pan, which is a baking pan with sides that are nearly 1 inch high. When we use the 12 x 17-inch pan at the bakery, we cut each pan of bars into 20 large squares, because our customers want something to sink their teeth into. At home, however, you may choose to cut the bars into much smaller pieces, so your batch goes a little further. Since bars are generally pretty rich, a small square goes a long way to satisfying your sweet tooth.

Award-Winning Brownies

Yield: one 9 x 13-inch pan, 12 large or 24 small bars
Equipment: 9 x 13-inch pan

Are your favorite brownies moist and cakey or thick and fudge-like? Are they full of crunchy nuts or do they have no nuts at all? Our brownies are fudge-like and moist, and they're full of walnuts and chocolate chips. We also make a simple, no-nut version, but the brownies in this recipe are by far our most popular. They're very chocolaty, soft, and tender, and have a deep, rich flavor.

We started to make brownies within the first two years of opening our doors. It seems that a bakery without chocolate treats, especially brownies, just doesn't measure up with its customers. Our brownies were very popular right off the bat.

Many of our customers have told us they're the best brownies in New York. We tend to agree! In fact, a neighborhood organization gave us a "Best Brownie" award the first year we were open. If you want the ultimate decadent treat, top one of these brownies with vanilla ice cream and a little hot fudge. After a few bites, you'll be right in chocolate heaven.

INGREDIENTS	GRAMS	OUNCES	VOLUME
Semisweet chocolate chips	566	20	3⅓ cups
Unsalted butter	227	8	1 cup
Unsweetened chocolate, chopped	85	3	½ cup + 1 tablespoon
Sugar	200	7.05	1 cup
Eggs, lightly beaten	150	5.29	3 large
Vanilla extract	1 tablespoon	1 tablespoon	1 tablespoon
Unbleached all-purpose flour	80	2.82	½ cup + 1 tablespoon
Baking powder	1½ teaspoons	1½ teaspoons	1½ teaspoons
Baking soda	½ teaspoon	½ teaspoon	½ teaspoon
Kosher salt	½ teaspoon	½ teaspoon	½ teaspoon
Walnut pieces, toasted (see page 242)	190	6.7	1¾ cups

1. Position one rack in the middle of the oven, and preheat the oven to 350°F. Grease the pan with softened butter and line the bottom with parchment paper.

2. In a medium bowl set over a pot of simmering water, add the butter, half of the chocolate chips, and the unsweetened chocolate and melt together, stirring occasionally. Set the mixture aside to cool until it's warm, not hot, before adding to the eggs in the next step.

3. While the chocolate is cooling, in a large bowl, whisk together the sugar, eggs, and vanilla until they are just mixed. Fold in the warm chocolate mixture.

4. In a medium bowl, add the flour, baking powder, baking soda, and salt and whisk together. Fold the dry ingredients into the chocolate mixture until just combined. Add the remaining chocolate chips and the walnuts and fold in until just mixed.

5. Pour the batter into the prepared pan and spread to an even thickness. Bake for 32 to 36 minutes. The brownies will puff up during baking and begin to feel slightly firm at the edges, but the center will be soft when they are fully baked. Rotate the pan from front to back halfway through the baking time. Do not overbake.

6. Allow the brownies to cool completely in the pan on a wire rack. We like to chill them to make them firmer before cutting, but if you can't chill them, cut them carefully or they may crumble. We cut the pan into 12 large bars, 3 across by 4 down. Each large bar can be cut in half to make 24 smaller bars. Although these brownies are easier to cut when chilled, they are best served at room temperature. Store the remaining brownies in the refrigerator, tightly covered, for up to 5 days.

TIPS *and* TECHNIQUES

It is tempting to whisk the eggs and sugar until they are light and frothy, but too much whisking will make your brownies very fragile and almost crumbly, so whisk these ingredients only until they are just mixed.

After the chocolate is melted over simmering water, it will be very hot. Be sure to let it cool down before adding it to the eggs.

It may seem hard to tell when the brownies are done, and it's better to underbake than to overbake them. You will see the center puff up a bit during baking. Once the edges feel slightly firm, even though the center is still soft and puffy, the brownies are finished baking.

Butterscotch Cashew Bars

Yield: one 12 x 17-inch pan, 25 bars
Equipment: 12 x 17-inch pan

Butterscotch Cashew Bars were a favorite after-school treat when Amy was growing up, but today our adult customers seem to enjoy them even more than kids do. They're a mix of sweet, salty, nutty, and chewy, and something about them makes us want to go back for more. One secret that makes them especially good is the inclusion of salted, roasted cashews. They bring out the flavor of the butterscotch and make the bars even more appealing. Make sure you choose high-quality butterscotch chips that melt smoothly. And use restraint when it comes to preparing the crust and pressing it into the pan. Just blend or pulse it until it's crumbly like coarse meal, then pat it gently into the bottom and corners of the pan. Less handling makes for a crust that stays tender after baking. Once you pour on the topping and return the pan to the oven, determine whether you want the caramel to be stretchy and chewy or a little firmer. With a couple more minutes of baking time, the topping will go from soft to firm. These bars make a great snack and are fun to share with others at a cookie exchange. They can be made several days in advance, and they freeze well, too.

INGREDIENTS	GRAMS	OUNCES	VOLUME
Crust			
Unbleached all-purpose flour	388	13.68	2²/₃ cups
Kosher salt	2 teaspoons	2 teaspoons	2 teaspoons
Unsalted butter, cold	284	10	1¼ cups
Light brown sugar, packed	250	8.82	1⅛ cups
Topping			
Butterscotch chips	284	10	1²/₃ cups
Light corn syrup	205	7.23	½ cup + 2 tablespoons
Unsalted butter	50	1.76	3½ tablespoons
Water	28	1	2 tablespoons
Kosher salt	¼ teaspoon	¼ teaspoon	¼ teaspoon
Cashew pieces, roasted and salted	256	9.03	2 cups

1. Position one rack in the middle of the oven and preheat the oven to 350°F. Grease a 12 x 17-inch sheet pan lightly with softened butter and line it with aluminum foil, pressing the foil up the sides of the pan and into the corners. Grease the foil with softened butter.

2. To make the crust: In the bowl of a food processor fitted with a metal blade, combine the flour and salt. Dice the butter into 1-inch pieces and place half in the food processor with the flour. Pulse for a few seconds. Add half of the brown sugar and pulse again, and then add the remaining butter and brown sugar and process for 20 to 30 seconds until a coarse meal is formed and the dough is just beginning to gather into a ball. If you don't have a food processor, follow the same procedure but cut the butter into the flour, alternating with the brown sugar, using a pastry blender to form a coarse meal. The dough will be a little crumbly but will almost form a ball.

3. Spread the crust evenly in the bottom of the prepared pan. Pat it gently and evenly into the pan all the way to the corners. Be careful not to pack it down too much or the crust will become tough. Bake it for about 5 minutes, then prick the dough lightly with a fork all over, and return the pan to the oven and bake for about 10 more minutes. The crust should be slightly browned and soft to the touch. Remove from the oven and allow the crust to cool for several minutes. Do not turn off the oven.

4. To make the topping: In a medium saucepan, add the butterscotch chips, corn syrup, butter, water, and salt and cook over medium heat, stirring constantly until the chips have melted completely and the topping has just begun to simmer, about 5 minutes.

5. Stir the cashew pieces into the hot topping and spread it evenly over the baked crust. Try to spread it out to the corners if possible, but the topping will spread into any bare spots during baking.

6. Bake again for 11 to 15 minutes, or until the surface is brown and very bubbly.

7. Allow the bars to cool completely on a wire rack before cutting them into 25 pieces 5 across by 5 down.

TIPS *and* TECHNIQUES

We do not endorse any specific products, but after extensive testing we've found that Hershey's butterscotch chips work best for this recipe because they melt smoothly and have a good flavor. If you can't find Hershey's, Nestlé's butterscotch chips will work well, too.

Zesty Lemon Bars

Yield: one 9 x 13-inch pan, 20 bars
Equipment: 9 x 13-inch pan

When it comes to lemon desserts, we like ours on the tart and tangy side. We think that the flavor of lemon should shine through in perfect harmony with the tender, buttery crust. Our lemon bars are more delicate than some we've tried. They have a melt-in-your-mouth crust and a soft top, and they go perfectly with tea or coffee for an afternoon dessert shared with friends. We can picture the table covered with a floral tablecloth and a gentle breeze blowing through the open window. The pale yellow squares might be served on a pretty china plate with a delicate silver dessert fork. If you love lemon desserts, we think you'll be delighted with these bars.

INGREDIENTS	GRAMS	OUNCES	VOLUME
Crust			
Unbleached all-purpose flour	220	7.76	1½ cups
Confectioner's sugar	63	2.20	½ cup
Cornstarch	25	0.88	3 tablespoons
Kosher salt	1½ teaspoons	1½ teaspoons	1½ teaspoons
Unsalted butter, cold	156	5.5	½ cup + 3 tablespoons
Topping			
Sugar	400	14.10	2 cups
Eggs, slightly beaten	200	7.05	4 large
Unbleached all-purpose flour	25	0.88	3 tablespoons
Lemon juice, freshly squeezed	145	5.11	⅝ cup + ¾ teaspoon
Milk, whole	70	2.47	¼ cup + 1 tablespoon
Kosher salt	¼ teaspoon	¼ teaspoon	¼ teaspoon

1. Position one rack in the middle of the oven, and preheat the oven to 350°F. Grease a 9 x 13-inch pan with softened butter, then line with parchment paper.

2. To make the crust: In the bowl of a food processor fitted with the metal blade, combine the flour, confectioner's sugar, cornstarch, and salt and process them for 5 seconds to combine. Dice the butter into 1-inch pieces and add to them to the flour mixture, processing for 10 seconds, or until the mixture is pale yellow and resembles coarse meal. If you don't have a food processor, work the butter into the flour quickly with a pastry blender or your fingers, being careful not to warm it up.

3. Place the crust mixture in the prepared pan and press it firmly with your fingertips into an even ¼-inch-thick layer over the entire pan bottom and ½ inch up the sides of the pan. Seal the crust to the sides of the pan by pressing firmly at the edges. This will help to prevent the topping from seeping under the crust during baking. If possible, chill the pan in the freezer for 30 minutes, then bake for about 20 minutes, or until light golden brown. Rotate the pan once during baking.

4. Meanwhile, to make the topping: In a bowl, whisk together the sugar, eggs, and flour, then stir in the lemon juice, milk, and salt and blend well. Set aside until the crust is baked.

5. Remove the crust from the oven, stir the topping again to blend, and pour it onto the warm crust. Bake it for 20 minutes, or until the topping is just set and not browned.

6. Allow the bars to cool completely on a wire rack before cutting into 20 pieces, 4 across by 5 down. To store the lemon bars, wrap the pan tightly with plastic film and refrigerate.

TIPS *and* TECHNIQUES

It takes the juice of 4 to 5 lemons to make these lemon bars.

When you are making the crust, we suggest that you pulse the ingredients in a food processor, but if you don't have one, it works fine to cut the butter into the flour by hand with a pastry blender.

We like the lemon topping to be soft. Watch it closely as it bakes so that it doesn't become too firm or too brown.

Gooey Coconut Dream Bars

Yield: one 9 x 13-inch pan, 20 bars

Equipment: 9 x 13-inch pan

Amy's mom is the "queen of bars," and these are another of her favorites to make for friends and family. They show up in the summer at picnics and backyard barbeques, at potluck parties, and even on the sweets platter at Christmastime. In her house, they're known as "Mounds" bars, after the famous candy bar, and they're always made without nuts. They're soft, tender, and buttery, and really satisfy a craving for a sweet treat. If you keep a few simple ingredients on hand, you can whip up these bars in a hurry when you need dessert in a pinch. Although we have seen other versions of these bars in various places, for us they're still "Mom's Homemade."

INGREDIENTS	GRAMS	OUNCES	VOLUME
Crust			
Graham cracker crumbs	312	11	3 cups, about 20 crackers
Unsalted butter, melted	170	6	¾ cup
Kosher salt	¼ teaspoon	¼ teaspoon	¼ teaspoon
Topping			
Semisweet chocolate chips	170	6	1 cup
Sweetened flaked coconut	200	7.05	2 cups
Sweetened condensed milk	600	21.16	2 cups minus 2 tablespoons

1. Position one rack in the middle of the oven, and preheat the oven to 350°F. Grease the bottom and sides of a 9 x 13-inch pan with softened butter, then line with parchment paper.

TIPS and TECHNIQUES

To make graham cracker crumbs from whole crackers, give them a quick spin in the blender or food processor. It saves a lot of time, and the crumbs will be evenly broken up and finer than those crushed by hand.

Our recipe takes about 1½ cans of sweetened condensed milk, unlike other recipes that call for exactly 1 can. We think that the extra milk is a worthwhile addition because it gives these bars the gooey richness that sets them apart from others.

2. To make the crust: In a medium bowl, mix together the graham cracker crumbs, melted butter, and salt. Pat the mixture evenly into the prepared pan.

3. To make the topping: In another medium bowl, mix together the chocolate chips and coconut and sprinkle the mixture evenly over the crust all the way to the edges.

4. Pour the condensed milk evenly over the coconut and chips to cover the entire surface. Bake for 26 to 32 minutes. Rotate the pan from front to back halfway through the baking time. Watch the bars carefully toward the end. The top should not get too brown and the milk should not bubble over the pan.

5. Allow the bars to cool completely on a wire rack before cutting into 20 bars, 4 across by 5 down. To store the bars, wrap tightly in plastic film and refrigerate, or freeze them after they have been tightly wrapped.

Blondies

Yield: one 12 x 17-inch pan, 25 large bars
Equipment: 12 x 17-inch pan

We weren't sure if we should share our recipe for Blondies because we have seen so many of them over the years. But most of those we've tasted have been a bit disappointing. Our Blondies are moist and tender, with just the right amount of chocolate chips and nuts suspended atop the sweet and cakey middle. For sweets lovers who want a dessert that is less chocolaty than a brownie, these are the answer. They're called Blondies because their batter contains no cocoa powder or melted chocolate, so they're light brown in color, unlike their beautiful brunette cousin the brownie. Here's our version of a delicious, sweet, and tender Blondie topped with crunchy walnuts and chocolate chips.

INGREDIENTS	GRAMS	OUNCES	VOLUME
Unbleached all-purpose flour	580	20.46	4 cups
Baking powder	2¼ teaspoons	2¼ teaspoons	2¼ teaspoons
Kosher salt	1 teaspoon	1 teaspoon	1 teaspoon
Unsalted butter, melted	454	16	2 cups
Dark brown sugar	785	27.69	3½ cups
Eggs	200	7.05	4 large
Vanilla extract	1½ teaspoons	1½ teaspoons	1½ teaspoons
Semisweet chocolate chips	360	12.70	2 cups + 2 tablespoons
Walnut pieces, toasted (see page 242)	300	10.58	2¾ cups

1. Position one rack in middle of the oven, and preheat the oven to 350°F. Grease a 12 x 17-inch pan with softened butter, then line the bottom of the pan with parchment paper.

2. In a medium bowl, add the flour, baking powder, and salt and whisk together.

3. In a large mixing bowl, combine the melted butter and brown sugar, stir to combine, then allow the butter to cool slightly before continuing. Whisk in the eggs and vanilla.

4. Fold the flour mixture into the sugar mixture and stir until it is almost combined, then add ¼ of the chocolate chips and walnuts and fold them into the batter.

5. Spread the batter evenly into the prepared pan. Sprinkle the remaining chocolate chips and walnut pieces evenly on top of bars, all the way to the corners. Bake for 10 minutes, then reduce the temperature to 325°F and bake for 16 to 21 more minutes,

rotating the pan from front to back halfway through the baking time. The bars will be golden brown and slightly soft to the touch—not firm.

6. Allow the Blondies to cool completely on a wire rack before cutting into 25 bars, 5 across by 5 down. Wrap the Blondies well with plastic wrap and store them at room temperature for up to 4 days, or freeze them tightly wrapped in plastic, then foil.

Blondies and Award-Winning Brownies (page 144)

Old-Fashioned Layer Cakes

The next two chapters are devoted to our old-fashioned American-style layer cakes and the frostings that go with them. We never wanted to do cakes. Our passion was bread—crusty, dense, chewy, hearth-baked loaves with the sweet, earthy flavor of naturally leavened grains, crackling on the wire racks when you take them from the oven. That's music to a bread baker's ears. And the indescribable aroma of freshly baked bread is perfume of the gods. That's something to be passionate about. But cakes? They were never on any of our product development lists. Our customers had other ideas, though. We got so many calls lamenting the fact that we didn't make cakes, and assuring us that any cake we made would have to be great because everything else we made was so delicious, that we finally capitulated.

We knew we wanted our cakes to be basic old-fashioned layer cakes like the ones our mothers used to make. No fancy buttercream flowers or the intricately piped frosting borders and designs commonly seen on many commercial bakery cakes. No endless combinations of fillings and frostings. No photo transfers or little plastic tchotchkes to satisfy every personal whim. No formal wedding cakes. We would do just a few basic flavors of cake, in a few basic sizes, that would be filled with the same frosting we used to finish the cakes. Simple, but they would have to be delicious.

We've been baking our cakes for more than six years now, and they've become so popular that we actually got a phone call from a customer who wanted to know if we made anything besides cake. We like to joke about changing our name to Amy's Cake. The calls and e-mails we get now are from people begging for copies of our cake recipes. So we're once again fulfilling the wishes of our customers and offering them the recipes for Amy's cakes.

When we began doing recipe development for cakes at the bakery, we started with existing cake recipes, playing around with them until we had achieved the exact tastes and textures that fit the products we'd imagined. We then tweaked the recipes to accommodate large-scale commercial production techniques. What cake batter and frosting go through when we're making enough for one or two cakes is often quite different from what they must endure when we're cranking out twenty times that much in our bakery's pastry kitchen. Developing recipes is what we consider the fun part of our work, because we get to exercise our experience and creativity. Everything has to be taken into consideration. Which flours should we use? Which sugars? What kind of butter, vanilla, and chocolate? What size and kind of cake pan? How thick or thin should the frosting be? How does the cake taste after the first bite? How does it feel in your mouth? How does it taste after the last bite? What size serving  should we sell in our retail cafe? How long is the cake's shelf life and how should it be stored? What's the best way to package and transport it from one location to another? The questions are endless. Who knew that making a simple piece of cake would be so complicated?

We have a much greater appreciation for cakes now than we did before we became "Amy's Cake." We understand, for example, that our customers want cakes to help them celebrate the important events in their lives. When we get special orders for cakes to celebrate birthdays, anniversaries, new babies, Broadway show openings and closings, graduations, and a multitude of other occasions, we've learned that there are complex emotional strings attached to those orders. It's a big responsibility to make sure that every single cake lives up to our customers' expectations. It's a completely different ballgame from selling a loaf of bread. And when we succeed, it's a happy occasion for us and our customers. When we fail, and once in a while we do, it's devastating—for the customer, the retail staffer involved, the manager who has to intercede, and the person in the kitchen or the office who may have made the mistake. Emotional strings are fragile commodities. We never imagined that baking cakes would be like this.

Now, every day, the oven room of our Hell's Kitchen store is filled with the sweet, buttery or chocolaty aromas of freshly baked cakes. Now we hear the clanking of cake pans, the squealing of rolling racks being pushed in and out of the new rack oven, and the alarm on the oven that sounds like a European-style ambulance barging its way through the kitchen. It's a long way from the crackling of cooling bread loaves, but somehow this, too, has become music to our ears.

Molly Killeen, our daytime pastry chef, loves making cakes. Her energy and enthusiasm for our cake project and her ability to develop speedy, foolproof production techniques have been the cornerstones for the success of the Amy's Bread cakes.

When Molly was a student at the California Culinary Academy, she told her chef Instructor, Peter Reinhart, that her dream was to work at Amy's Bread. Before moving to California, Molly had lived in New York City and had solicited bread donations from Amy's Bread for a rehabilitation facility where she worked at the time. She was very impressed with the helpful, enthusiastic service we provided and by the fact that Amy herself actually took the time to give Molly a tour of the bakery when she requested one.

We ran into Peter Reinhart at a bread bakers' event and he mentioned Molly's name to us then. Shortly after graduation, Molly moved back to New York and sent us a copy of her résumé. Remembering her name, we called her in for an interview and a trail (professional kitchen term for an employee tryout) and offered her a job as the daytime sweets baker (we had only one at the time) in our Hell's Kitchen location. Her dream was realized. As our pastry baking team grew, Molly eventually took on the responsibilities of our daytime pastry chef. She's been a valuable member of our team since 1998. Her mom, Susan Wessel, and her aunt, Patricia Callaghan, who live in Missouri, send us their charming hand-quilted pot holders to sell in our Hell's Kitchen retail café, and her husband, Ronan, who is an artist, filmmaker, and photographer, sometimes comes in during the holidays to help turn our decorated cookies into little works of art. Having people like Molly and her family as an integral part of our bakery life is one of the reasons Amy's Bread is a unique and rewarding place to work.

TIPS and *TECHNIQUES*

Making a cake with good flavor and texture can sometimes be complicated, but we don't include a detailed discussion of cake baking techniques in this book because there are other cookbooks available that do a masterful job of teaching technique. Two of our favorites are Rose Levy Beranbaum's *The Cake Bible,* published by William Morrow and Company, and Carole Walter's *Great Cakes,* published by Random House. However, there are a few tips we would like to share that have helped us achieve good volume and texture with our cakes and frostings.

• Be sure that any butter, milk, and eggs in the recipe are at cool room temperature. In the bakery the ideal temperature is 60° to 63°F, but we use powerful, heavy-duty commercial equipment that raises the temperature of the ingredients quickly during mixing. When using home kitchen appliances, the ideal temperature is slightly higher, 63° to 65°F. If you don't have a digital kitchen thermometer to test the temperature of the ingredients, then leave them out in a cool room for about 2 hours before you use them. If the room temperature is very warm, don't leave them out that long. The butter should be firm to the touch but take a slight imprint when pressed with your finger. The eggs should not feel cold. If they do, let them soak for a few minutes in a bowl of very warm (not hot) water.

• We prefer using a paddle attachment instead of a whip or beaters for creaming and mixing our cake ingredients, and our mixing speeds are generally in the low to medium speed range. We found that higher speeds whip too much air into batter and frosting, which results in cakes that are too fragile or have a coarser cell structure than we like, and frostings that have too many little air bubbles in them and separate when they're being spread on the cake.

• We believe it is especially important when making cake to weigh the ingredients whenever possible instead of measuring them by volume with cups. When we were testing these recipes, the weight of a cup of unbleached all-purpose flour varied from 114 g/4 oz. to 158 g/5½ oz., even when we were using the same brand and type of flour and what we thought was a consistent "dip-and-sweep" technique—dipping the cup down into the flour, stirring it around a little bit to fluff the compacted flour, then drawing it up and leveling it off with the flat edge of a knife. In the Ingredients and Equipment section at the back of this book we tell you where you can purchase a reasonably priced digital home kitchen scale if you don't already have one.

• When trying to show volume equivalents for the gram weights in these cake recipes, you will notice that we are somewhat more detailed than we might be with a cookie recipe or a muffin recipe because the proper chemical balance among ingredients for a cake recipe is more critical for a good result.

• When weighing eggs, one large whole egg without the shell weighs about 50 grams. If you need to use less than a whole egg to achieve the weight in a recipe, whip a whole egg with a fork to mix the white and yolk evenly before using a portion of it to get the weight you need.

• The cake pans we use for the double layer cakes are standard 9 x 2-inch round aluminum pans with straight sides. A lot of cake pans made for home bakers are only 1½ inches high and have slightly sloped sides. Most good kitchenware stores have the 2-inch-deep pans. Try not to use nonstick pans or pans that have a dark finish. If you must use pans with a dark finish, lower your oven temperature by 25 degrees to prevent the sides of the cake from overbaking before the center is done.

• The pans we use for the two sheet cake recipes (Apple Walnut Cake and Carrot Cake) are known as "half-sheet pans" in the professional baking industry. They are heavy aluminum pans that have inside dimensions of 12 x 17 x 1 inch (outside top dimensions are 13 x 18 inches); also available in kitchenware stores. Refer to the equipment chapter at the back of this book for more information.

• One of the mistakes most frequently made when making cake is baking it too long. Overbaked cake has a dry crumb, and the flavor is diminished. To avoid overbaking, we recommend removing the cake from the oven when a toothpick inserted in the center comes out with a few moist crumbs sticking to it and the cake is almost ready to start pulling away from the sides of the pan. It should also immediately shrink away from the side of the pan as soon as it's taken out of the oven. Cake that has pulled away from the pan while still in the oven will usually be overbaked. Cake continues to bake for several minutes after being removed from the oven while cooling briefly in the pan. This is called residual baking. When determining how long to bake a cake to achieve the desired level of doneness, we always take the residual baking time into consideration. This is why we like to take cakes out of the oven just before they have completely finished baking.

• During baking, if the sides of the cake pull away from the pan but the center is still too wet, in the future, you may need to start with a lower oven temperature so the sides and the center bake at a more even rate. You may also have to start with a lower oven temperature if the cake layers have pronounced doming and cracking in the center.

• If your oven isn't exactly level, you'll end up with cake layers that are higher on one side than the other. Compensate for this when frosting the cake by making sure the low side of the top layer is lined up with the high side of the bottom layer.

TIPS and TECHNIQUES

• Most of the cake recipes in this book make a standard 9-inch round double-layer cake. In the bakery retail stores, we cut these cakes into 10 large wedges, but as we tell our customers, you can easily get up to 15 satisfying wedge-shaped portions from a cake this size.

• The only cakes that require refrigeration are the Carrot Cake (page 183) and Monkey Cake (page 185), which are frosted with cream cheese icing, and the Coconut Cream Cake (page 189) because the coconut milk, cream cheese, and heavy cream that make up the Coconut Custard Frosting will go sour if left too long at room temperature. These refrigerated cakes taste best at room temperature, however, so they should be taken out of the refrigerator about an hour before serving time. Any leftovers should be returned to the refrigerator for storage. Be sure to store them in an airtight container so the frosting doesn't absorb any other food flavors.

Amy's Bread Red Velvet Cake

Yield: one 9-inch double-layer cake
Equipment: two 9 x 2-inch round cake pans

This is our version of the dramatic red and white cake that is much loved and familiar to anyone who was raised or has lived in the southern United States. When someone asks us to describe how it tastes, we can only say, "It tastes like red velvet cake." It has its own very unique flavor. It doesn't taste at all like chocolate, though it does have a little bit of cocoa in it. We use Swiss Meringue Buttercream Frosting to finish this cake. At the bakery we love to dress this cake up for holidays. We feature it at Christmas by decorating the snow white frosting with green rolled fondant holly leaves, with the holly berries piped on in red frosting. For Valentine's Day we bake thinner layers in a sheet pan and cut out heart shapes with a 5-inch cookie cutter. Then, using a pastry bag with a star tip, we pipe decorative concentric outlines of either pink or white frosting around the top of the heart until it's completely covered with a frilly blanket. For the Fourth of July, we sprinkle it generously with confetti made of little red, white, and blue stars.

INGREDIENTS	GRAMS	OUNCES	VOLUME
Sour cream, full fat	120	4.23	½ cup
Valrhona cocoa powder	12	0.42	2 tablespoons
Baking soda	1 teaspoon	1 teaspoon	1 teaspoon
Christmas Red food coloring	16	0.56	1 tablespoon
Boiling water	226	8	1 cup
Cake flour, sifted	342	12.10	3 cups
Kosher salt	½ teaspoon	½ teaspoon	½ teaspoon
Baking powder	1½ teaspoons	1½ teaspoons	1½ teaspoons
Eggs	250	8.82	5 large
Vanilla extract	1½ teaspoons	1½ teaspoons	1½ teaspoons
Unsalted butter, slightly softened	170	6	¾ cup
Dark brown sugar	542	19.12	2½ cups, firmly packed
Swiss Meringue Buttercream Frosting (see page 198)			1 recipe

1. Preheat the oven to 350°F. Grease the cake pans. Line the bottoms with rounds of baking parchment then dust them lightly with cocoa powder or flour. Shake out the excess. Or use Baker's Joy baking spray that contains both oil and flour so you don't have to flour the pan. With Baker's Joy, put the parchment liner in after you spray the pan.

2. In a large bowl, whisk together the sour cream, cocoa, baking soda, and food color until it is a smooth paste. Very gradually add the boiling water, whisking until it is fully incorporated. In another bowl, combine the cake flour, salt, and baking powder and whisk them gently for even distribution. In a separate small bowl, whisk together the eggs and vanilla.

3. Using an electric mixer, with a paddle attachment, cream the butter and brown sugar on medium speed until it is light and fluffy, about 2 minutes. Add the egg mixture gradually, mixing well after each addition, scraping the sides and bottom of the bowl often.

4. Lower the mixing speed to medium-low and add the flour to the butter in 3 parts, alternating with the liquid mixture, also in 3 parts, beginning with the flour and ending

with the liquid. Mix until it is evenly incorporated. There should not be any lumps or dry pockets of flour remaining. This is a fairly thin cake batter, so there is not much danger of overmixing it, but don't go above medium-high speed.

5. Divide the batter equally between the 2 prepared cake pans. Weighing the batter into the pans is the most accurate way to do this. This ensures that both layers will be uniform in size and will finish baking at the same time. You'll have approximately 820 g/29 oz. of batter per pan. The pans should be about ½ full. Place the pans on the center rack in the preheated oven. Bake them for about 35 minutes or until the cake is almost ready to pull away from the side of the pan and a toothpick inserted into the center of the cake comes out with a few moist crumbs. Rotate the layers carefully from front to back after 20 minutes, for even baking.

6. Cool the pans on a rack for 10 minutes, then invert them onto a wire rack that has been sprayed with cooking spray and lift off the pans. To prevent cracking, carefully right each layer so the top side

is up and the parchment-lined bottom is down. Cool them completely on the rack. Before frosting, be sure to remove the parchment from the bottom of each layer. While the cake layers are cooling, prepare the frosting.

To assemble the cake:

7. Place one layer, top side down, on a flat serving plate. Cut several 4-inch-wide strips of parchment or waxed paper to slide under the edge of the layer to keep the plate clean. Using a thin metal spatula, spread the top of this cake round with a ½-inch-thick layer of frosting, leaving a ¼-inch unfrosted border around the edge. Place the second layer top side up on the first, aligning the layers evenly. Spread a generous layer of frosting around the sides of the cake, rotating the plate as you work so you're not reaching around the cake to frost the other side. Try not to let any loose crumbs get caught in the frosting. If you can, let the frosting extend about ¼ inch above the top of the cake.

8. Starting in the center of the cake, cover the top with a generous layer of frosting, taking it all the way to the edge and merging it with the frosting on the sides. Try to use a forward-moving, circular motion, not a back-and-forth motion, to avoid lifting the top skin of the cake. Rotate the plate as necessary. Use the spatula or a spoon to make decorative swirls. Slide the pieces of parchment paper out from under the edge of the cake and discard them. Store the cake at room temperature, preferably under a cake dome, for up to 3 days.

TIPS and TECHNIQUES

If you can't find Valrhona cocoa powder, try another premium-quality brand, but be sure to use the volume measurement of 2 tablespoons, not the weight. Cocoa powder brands vary dramatically by weight. When we weighed 5 tablespoons of three different brands, the weights we got were 12 g, 20 g, and 30 g, so the safest thing to do is to use the tablespoon measurement for anything other than Valrhona cocoa. This is one of the few times we recommend using a volume measurement instead of a weight.

Be sure to use full-fat sour cream in this recipe, not lowfat or nonfat. Fat is a flavor carrier. Whenever naturally occurring fat is removed from an ingredient, much of the ingredient's flavor is also removed. Fat also is a key factor in the texture of baked goods.

In the bakery, we buy gallons of Christmas Red food coloring. We chose this particular red because the baked cake comes out a nice, dark red color instead of the pale orangey-red that often occurs with other shades of red food coloring. In the Ingredients and Equipment section at the back of this book we tell you where you can purchase Christmas Red food coloring.

Simply Delicious Yellow Cake

Yield: one 9-inch double-layer cake
Equipment: two 9 x 2-inch round cake pans

This is the cake recipe we use for our almost famous Amy's Bread "Pink Cake," a moist vanilla-flavored butter cake inspired by a recipe from one of our favorite baking colleagues, Carole Walter, in her book *Great Cakes*. The delicate flavor and texture of this cake is a perfect match for a heavy, intensely sweet frosting such as a classic confectioner's sugar buttercream—to which we add 1 or 2 drops of rose food coloring to give it a pale pink tint. It's also delicious with chocolate frosting, but bittersweet chocolate tends to overpower the delicate vanilla flavor. At the bakery, we use a more subtle, creamy Milk Chocolate Buttercream Frosting that comes directly from *The Cake Bible,* by Rose Levy Beranbaum, so we can't include that recipe in our frosting chapter. The retail staff and the bakers in the pastry kitchen are always hoping for broken layers or cupcakes because they love to eat this cake without any frosting at all, to savor the sweet warm flavors of butter and vanilla. Try it plain with sliced fresh strawberries or peaches for a sublime summer dessert.

INGREDIENTS	GRAMS	OUNCES	VOLUME
Unbleached all-purpose flour, sifted	420	14.81	3 cups
Baking powder	20	0.71	1 tablespoon + 1 teaspoon
Kosher salt	¾ teaspoon	¾ teaspoon	¾ teaspoon
Milk	340	12	1¼ cups + 3 tablespoons
Vanilla extract	2 teaspoons	2 teaspoons	2 teaspoons
Unsalted butter, slightly softened	320	11.29	1¼ cups + 2 tablespoons
Sugar	560	19.75	2¾ cups + 2 teaspoons
Eggs	260	9.17	5 large
Sweet Pink Buttercream Frosting (see page 201)			1 recipe

1. Preheat the oven to 350°F. Grease the cake pans. Line the bottoms with rounds of baking parchment then dust them lightly with flour. Shake out the excess. Or use Baker's Joy baking spray that contains both oil and flour, so you don't have to flour the pan. With Baker's Joy, put the parchment liner in after you spray the pan.

2. In a large bowl, combine the flour, baking powder, and salt and whisk them gently for even distribution. In a separate bowl combine the milk and vanilla.

3. Using an electric mixer with a paddle attachment, cream the butter and sugar on medium speed until it is light and fluffy, 3 to 4 minutes. Add the eggs gradually, mixing well after each addition, scraping the sides and bottom of the bowl often.

4. Lower the mixing speed to medium-low and add the flour mixture to the butter in 3 parts, alternating with 2 parts of the milk mixture, beginning and ending with the flour. Mix just until it is evenly incorporated. This is a thick, fluffy batter, resembling whipped cream. There should not be any lumps or dry pockets of flour remaining. If the batter has a curdled appearance it has not been mixed enough. Increase the speed to medium and mix for another minute or until it is thick and fluffy.

5. Divide the batter equally between the 2 prepared cake pans. Weighing the batter into the pans is the most accurate way to do this. This ensures that both layers are uniform in size, and finish baking at the same time. You'll have approximately 930 g/32.8 oz. of batter per pan. The pans should be about ⅔ full. Smooth the batter so it fills the pans evenly. Place the pans on the center rack in the preheated oven. Bake them for about 35 to 40 minutes, or until the cake is almost ready to pull away from the side of the pan and a toothpick inserted into the center of the cake comes out with a few moist crumbs. Rotate the layers carefully from front to back after 20 minutes, for even baking.

6. Cool the pans on a rack for 10 minutes, then invert them onto a wire rack that has been sprayed with cooking spray and lift off the pans. To prevent cracking, carefully right each layer so the top side is up and the parchment-lined bottom is down. Cool

While we were in the final development stages on this cake, Molly, our daytime pastry chef, was testing different colors in the frosting to see which one the customers found most appealing. It was a warm summer day in June and she was carrying her latest test cake, with pale pink frosting, from the kitchen in the back of our Hell's Kitchen location out into the retail café to be displayed and served in slices. At the same time, a great bear of a man in construction worker's clothing had just walked through the open front door. When he saw that pink cake, his eyes widened and he said in a voice that was filled with amazement and longing, "Oh my god, that looks just like the cake my mother used to make. I've gotta have a piece of that." We made the frosting pale pink from that day forward. Men love the Pink Cake. For his birthday, Chef Bill Telepan, owner of Manhattan's acclaimed Telepan Restaurant, asks his wife, Beverly, to order "that cake from Amy's that has the pink frosting on it." Bill and Amy have birthdays that are one day apart. In a recent phone conversation right around their birthdays, Amy asked Bill if we could put his name in our new cookbook as a lover of our Pink Cake. His response: "Absolutely. I'm always telling people it's the best cake in New York City." We're happily making this recipe available to the public for all those men who can't make it to Amy's Bread to get a slice of our nostalgia-inducing Pink Cake.

them on the rack completely. Before frosting, be sure to remove the parchment from the bottom of each layer. While the layers are cooling, prepare the frosting.

To assemble the cake:

7. Place one layer, top side down, on a flat serving plate. Cut several 4-inch-wide strips of parchment or waxed paper to slide under the edge of the layer, to keep the plate clean. Using a thin metal spatula, spread the top of this cake round with a ½-inch thick layer of frosting, leaving a ¼-inch unfrosted border around the edge. Place the second layer top side up on the first, aligning the layers evenly. Spread a generous layer of frosting around the sides of the cake, rotating the plate as you work so you're not reaching around the cake to frost the other side. Try not to let any loose crumbs get caught in the frosting. Let the frosting extend about ¼ inch above the top of the cake.

8. Starting in the center of the cake, cover the top with a generous layer of frosting, taking it all the way to the edge and merging it with the frosting on the sides. Try to use a forward-moving, circular motion, not a back-and-forth motion to avoid lifting the top skin of the cake. Rotate the plate as necessary. Use the spatula or a spoon to make decorative swirls. Slide the pieces of paper out from under the edge of the cake and discard them. Store the cake at room temperature, preferably under a cake dome, for up to 3 days.

TIPS and TECHNIQUES

After it's baked, handle this cake carefully, as its delicate texture makes the layers easy to break. Also be careful not to pile the heavy pink frosting on too thickly or it may weigh down the cake, causing it to crack.

Some professional bakers frost cakes by covering the sides first, then covering the top to finish the cake. Others do just the opposite. Either method is fine to use as long as it feels comfortable to you.

Definitely Devil's Food Cake

Yield: one 9-inch double-layer cake
Equipment: two 9 x 2-inch round cake pans

When we finally gave in to the requests of our customers and decided to add cakes to the sweets menu, our first job was to make a list of the cake flavors we wanted to include. Chocolate cake topped the list. However, coming up with what we thought was the perfect chocolate cake recipe was not an easy task. Too often we've been disappointed by chocolate desserts that fail to live up to the promise of their appearance. The challenge was to create a chocolate cake that tasted as good as it looked. If the number of special orders we fill, praise from our customers, and the constant requests we get for this recipe are any indication, we can happily say we've succeeded. Finished with our Chocolate Silk Frosting (see photo on page 205), this dark, moist cake has a bittersweet chocolate flavor that intensifies with every bite. For those who prefer a slightly less intense chocolate experience, we use an untinted white version of our Sweet Pink Buttercream Frosting to make a Black and White Cake, decorated with a pattern of piped chocolate polka dots for a whimsical retro look.

INGREDIENTS	GRAMS	OUNCES	VOLUME
Unsweetened chocolate, coarsely chopped	136	4.80	7/8 cup
Sour cream, full-fat	136	4.80	1/2 cup + 1 tablespoon
Valrhona cocoa powder	30	1	5 tablespoons
Baking soda	2 3/8 teaspoons	2 3/8 teaspoons	2 3/8 teaspoons
Boiling water	340	12	1 1/2 cups
Cake flour, sifted	224	8	2 cups
Kosher salt	5/8 teaspoon	5/8 teaspoon	5/8 teaspoon
Eggs	180	6.35	4 large
Vanilla extract	2 1/2 teaspoons	2 1/2 teaspoons	2 1/2 teaspoons
Unsalted butter, slightly softened	170	6	3/4 cup
Dark brown sugar	432	15.24	1 3/4 cups, firmly packed
Chocolate Silk Frosting (see page 203)			1 recipe

1. Preheat the oven to 350°F. Grease the cake pans. Line the bottoms with rounds of baking parchment then dust them lightly with cocoa powder or flour. Shake out the excess. Or use Baker's Joy baking spray that contains both oil and flour, so you don't have to flour the pan. With Baker's Joy, put the parchment liner in after you spray the pan.

2. Melt the chocolate and set it aside to cool. In a large bowl, whisk together the sour cream, cocoa, and baking soda until it is a smooth paste. Very gradually add the boiling water, whisking until it is fully incorporated. In another separate bowl, combine the cake flour and salt and whisk them together gently for even distribution. In a small bowl, whisk together the eggs and the vanilla.

3. Using an electric mixer, with a paddle attachment, cream the butter and sugar on medium speed until it is light and fluffy, 2 to 3 minutes. Add the melted chocolate, which should be pourable but not too hot. Continue mixing until the chocolate is completely incorporated, scraping the sides and bottom of the bowl as needed. Add the eggs gradually, mixing well after each addition.

4. Lower the mixing speed to medium-low and add the flour to the butter in 3 parts, alternating with the liquid mixture, also in 3 parts, beginning with the flour and ending with the liquid. Mix until it is evenly incorporated. There should not be any lumps or dry pockets of flour remaining. This is a very thin, almost watery, cake batter, so there is not much danger of overmixing it.

TIPS and TECHNIQUES

If you can't find Valrhona cocoa powder, try another premium-quality brand, but be sure to use the volume measurement of 5 tablespoons, not the weight. Cocoa powder brands vary dramatically by weight. When we weighed 5 tablespoons of three different brands, the weights we got were 12 g, 20 g, and 30 g, so the safest thing to do is to use the tablespoon measurement for anything other than Valrhona cocoa. This is one of the few times we recommend using a volume measurement instead of a weight.

The volume of the unsweetened chocolate will vary depending on how coarsely or finely it's chopped. Coarsely chopped chocolate may equal a whole cup; finely chopped may fill only ¾ or ⅔ of a cup. That's one of the reasons we generally prefer weighing ingredients; 136 g of chocolate is 136 g of chocolate regardless of how it's been chopped. The cocoa mentioned here is one of the few exceptions to this rule.

Be sure to use full-fat sour cream in this recipe, not lowfat or nonfat. Fat is a flavor carrier. Whenever naturally occurring fat is removed from an ingredient, much of the ingredient's flavor is also removed. Fat also is a key factor in the texture of baked goods.

Do not refrigerate this cake. If you do, the Chocolate Silk Frosting will turn into a chocolate candy bar and the interior crumb of the cake will have a "frozen" quality. Left at room temperature, the frosting should be soft and creamy and the cake should be moist and tender.

5. Divide the batter equally between the 2 prepared cake pans. Weighing the batter into the pans is the most accurate way to do this. This ensures that both layers are uniform in size, and finish baking at the same time. You'll have approximately 794 g/28 oz. of batter per pan. The pans should be about ½ full. Place the pans on the center rack in the preheated oven. Bake them for about 35 minutes, or until the cake is almost ready to pull away from the side of the pan and a toothpick inserted into the center of the cake comes out with a few moist crumbs. Rotate the layers carefully from front to back after 18 minutes, for even baking.

6. Cool the pans on a rack for 10 minutes, then invert them onto a wire rack that has been sprayed with cooking spray and lift off the pans. To prevent cracking, carefully right each layer so the top side is up and the parchment-lined bottom is down. Cool them completely on the rack. Before frosting, be sure to remove the parchment from the bottom of each layer. While the cake layers are cooling, prepare the frosting.

To assemble the cake:

7. Place one layer, top side down, on a flat serving plate. Cut several 4-inch-wide strips of parchment or waxed paper to slide under the edge of the layer to keep the plate clean. Using a thin metal spatula, spread the top of this cake round with a ½-inch thick layer of frosting, leaving a ¼-inch unfrosted border around the edge. Place the second layer top side up on the first, aligning the layers evenly. Spread a generous layer of frosting around the sides of the cake, rotating the plate as you work so you're not reaching around the cake to frost the other side. Try not to let any loose crumbs get caught in the frosting. Let the frosting extend about ¼ inch above the top of the cake.

8. Starting in the center of the cake, cover the top with a generous layer of frosting, taking it all the way to the edge and merging it with the frosting on the sides. Try to use a forward-moving circular motion, not a back-and-forth motion, to avoid lifting the top skin of the cake. Rotate the plate as necessary. Use the spatula or a spoon to make decorative swirls. Slide the pieces of paper out from under the edge of the cake and discard them. Store the cake at room temperature, preferably under a cake dome, for up to 3 days.

Cupcake Variation

Cupcake papers should be filled halfway or slightly more than halfway. If you're using a scale, fill the first cupcake paper, make note of the weight, and then pour the same amount of batter into each of the other cups. This helps ensure that all of the cupcakes bake in the same amount of time. Bake them at 350°F, until a toothpick inserted in the center comes out with just a few moist crumbs on it. Cool the cupcakes completely before frosting. In the bakery we use a pastry bag with a star tip to pipe a decorative swirl of frosting on the top of each little cake.

Frances Rehfeld

Rumor has it that eating Amy's Definitely Devil's Food Cake may promote longevity. In one recent week we received four special orders to make birthday cakes for people ranging in age from 100 to 103. In every case the cake requested was our Definitely Devil's Food Cake. Is there a secret to be learned here? Frances Rehfeld, one of our favorite regular customers and a neighborhood legend, turned 103 in December of 2007. She still lives independently, and graces our Hell's Kitchen store frequently to enjoy a light lunch or a big piece of our Definitely Devil's Food Cake. We all love when Frances visits. The minute she walks in the door, one of the retail staffers calls back to the office, "Frances is here!" and each of the managers comes out to talk with her. So do customers sitting at nearby tables. Frances always has something interesting to say. It's not often you get to talk to someone who was living in New York City during the Roaring Twenties and the Great Depression. But Frances, a petite woman always elegantly dressed with a stylish hat to match her outfit, doesn't live in the past. She's a modern New York City woman, up to date on world events, politics, and fashion trends.

The bakery's present to Frances on her one hundredth birthday was a triple-layer sheet cake version of her devil's food favorite, one large enough to feed all of the friends and relatives who threw her a party at a neighborhood restaurant. It was quite a bash. Afterward, everyone was invited across the street to Frances's apartment to continue the festivities. That night, Frances, who retired from her last job when she was in her mid-eighties, was still going strong when we finally left the party. Recently we asked her if she thought there was some mystical reason for centenarians' wanting our devil's food cake. She gave a little chuckle and said, "No. It's just a delicious chocolate cake." Her answer is a perfect example of Frances's philosophy of life—just keep it simple; don't get too carried away with things.

Apple Walnut Cake

ꙮ Yield: one 12 x 17-inch sheet cake
ꙮ Equipment: one 12 x 17 x 1-inch sheet pan

When Sean Coyne, one of our former bread bakers, brought this cake to an employee Christmas Party one year, we loved it so much we badgered him constantly until he finally gave us the recipe. It's his mother's legacy to Amy's Bread. We bake this cake in a sheet pan and cut it into squares to sell in our retail café. Dense and chunky, this ultra-moist cake is filled with the homey flavors of apples, walnuts, sweet-tart cherries, and a hint of cinnamon. It reminds us of the cakes our mothers and grandmothers used to make as treats on cold winter days. Topped with a luscious Maple Syrup Buttercream, this cake takes the idea of comfort food to a whole new level.

Make this cake the next time you're asked to bring dessert to a potluck dinner or family gathering. We guarantee you'll get rave reviews.

INGREDIENTS	GRAMS	OUNCES	VOLUME
Granny Smith apples, peeled and cored	585	20.75	4½ large apples
Dried tart cherries	218	7.69	1⅓ cups
Walnuts, toasted, coarsely chopped (see page 242)	180	6.35	1½ cups
Sugar	600	21.16	3 cups
Corn oil	432	15.24	2 cups
Eggs	200	7	4 large
Vanilla extract	1½ teaspoons	1½ teaspoons	1½ teaspoons
Unbleached all-purpose flour	640	22.57	4½ cups
Kosher salt	10	0.35	1 tablespoon + ½ teaspoon
Baking soda	1½ teaspoons	1½ teaspoons	1½ teaspoons
Cinnamon	1½ teaspoons	1½ teaspoons	1½ teaspoons
Maple Syrup Buttercream (see page 206)			1 recipe

1. Place the oven rack in the lower third of the oven and preheat the oven to 350°F. Spray the sides of the sheet pan with cooking spray or Baker's Joy baking spray. Line the bottom with parchment.

2. Cut the apples into 1-inch chunks. Using a food processor with a blade attachment, process the chunks with a pulsing action 3 to 4 times, or until the apple is finely chopped but not mushy. Toss the chopped apples together with the dried cherries and walnuts.

3. In a medium bowl, whisk together the sugar, oil, eggs, and vanilla until they are well combined. In a separate larger bowl, mix together the flour, salt, baking soda, and cinnamon. Add the liquid ingredients to the dry ingredients and stir them together gently by hand with a large wooden spoon until they're almost completely moistened. This batter will be so stiff and heavy at this point that it's almost like dough. It's okay if there's a little bit of dry flour still visible.

4. Fold the apple mixture into the batter just until everything is evenly distributed. As you stir, the apples will begin releasing their juice and the batter will become softer and easier to handle. Pour the batter into the prepared pan, spreading it into an even layer. The pan will be filled to the top. Place the pan in the lower third of the preheated oven, and bake it for about 30 to 35 minutes, or until a toothpick inserted in the center of the cake comes out with a few moist crumbs. Rotate the pan from front to back after 15 minutes, for even baking.

5. Cool the cake completely on a wire rack. While the cake is cooling, prepare the Maple Syrup Buttercream Frosting. When the cake has cooled, leave it in the pan and spread all of the prepared frosting over the top. Cut it into 20 squares to serve it. Store any leftovers covered in the refrigerator, but bring the cake to room temperature before serving.

TIPS and TECHNIQUES

We use corn oil in this recipe because it has a more buttery flavor than canola oil, but any mild-flavored oil will be fine.

Be sure to use dried "tart" cherries, not sweet or Bing cherries, for this recipe. We tested the recipe using Welch's dried tart cherries from our local grocer, and they worked perfectly.

We like to chop the apples in a food processor rather than grating them, to prevent them from releasing too much moisture into the cake batter before they're baked. However, if you don't have a food processor, using the coarse side of a standard grater will be fine.

Carrot Cake

Yield: one 12 x 17-inch sheet cake
Equipment: one 12 x 17 x 1-inch sheet pan

We've been making Carrot Cake at Amy's Bread for many years. Long before we started baking our old-fashioned layer cakes, we offered sheet cake squares of this simple, deliciously moist classic version made with walnuts and Cream Cheese Icing. We bake it only once a week, on Thursdays, so we'll have it to sell in our cafés through the weekend. Barbara, one of our regular customers at the Hell's Kitchen store, calls or comes in almost every Friday or Saturday to reserve at least one "center-cut" slice. We're always happy to oblige her. Now we also offer a layer cake version of our Carrot Cake for birthdays and other special occasions, but these simple squares are still our favorite way to enjoy this cake. This recipe makes a lot of heavy batter, so be sure to use the pan size specified.

INGREDIENTS	GRAMS	OUNCES	VOLUME
Unbleached all-purpose flour	700	24.69	5 cups
Sugar	558	19.68	2¾ cups
Baking soda	22	0.78	1 tablespoon + 1¼ teaspoons
Kosher salt	8	0.28	1 tablespoon
Cinnamon	2¾ teaspoons	2¾ teaspoons	2¾ teaspoons
Canola oil	538	19	2⅓ cups
Eggs	400	14	8 large
Carrots, peeled, coarsely grated	790	28	5¼ cups, lightly packed
Walnuts, toasted, coarsely chopped (see page 242)	170	6	1½ cups
Cream Cheese Icing (see page 207)			1 recipe

1. Place the oven rack in the lower third of the oven and preheat the oven to 350°F. Spray the sides the sheet pan with cooking spray or Baker's Joy baking spray. Line the bottom with parchment.

2. In a large bowl, whisk together the flour, sugar, baking soda, salt, and cinnamon until they are well combined. In a separate bowl, whisk together the eggs and oil. Add the liquid ingredients to the dry ingredients and stir them together gently with a large wooden spoon until they're almost completely moistened. Add the carrots and the walnuts to the batter and fold them in until they're evenly distributed.

3. Pour the batter into the prepared pan, spreading it into an even layer. The pan will be very full. Place the pan in the lower third of the preheated oven and bake for about 30 to 35 minutes, or until a toothpick inserted in the center of the cake comes out clean with a few moist crumbs. Rotate the pan from front to back after 15 minutes, for even baking.

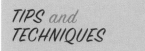

TIPS *and*
TECHNIQUES

This recipe requires approximately 2½ pounds of untrimmed raw carrots.

4. Cool the cake completely on a wire rack. While the cake is cooling, prepare the Cream Cheese Icing. When the cake has cooled, leave it in the pan and spread a ½-inch layer of the prepared icing over the top. Cut the cake into 20 squares to serve it. Store any leftovers covered in the refrigerator, but bring the cake to room temperature before serving.

Monkey Cake

This is the Amy's Bread version of a Hummingbird Cake. We called it a Monkey Cake because we "monkeyed around" with the ingredient proportions and because monkeys love bananas. We know it sounds crazy, but that really is how we came up with the name. This very moist, very dense cake is rich with the fruity sweetness of bananas and pineapple. Toasty chunks of pecan add a nice counterpoint to the soft texture of this cake. Topped with Cream Cheese Icing, it's one of Amy's personal favorites.

INGREDIENTS	GRAMS	OUNCES	VOLUME
Unbleached all-purpose flour	390	13.76	2¾ cups
Kosher salt	2 teaspoons	2 teaspoons	2 teaspoons
Baking soda	1 teaspoon	1 teaspoon	1 teaspoon
Cinnamon	1 teaspoon	1 teaspoon	1 teaspoon
Sugar	350	12.34	1¾ cups
Canola oil	268	9.45	1¼ cups
Eggs	150	5.30	3 large
Vanilla extract	1½ teaspoons	1½ teaspoons	1½ teaspoons
Bananas, ripe, mashed, with chunks remaining	436	15.38	2 cups
Crushed pineapple, with juice	228	8	1 cup
Pecans, toasted, coarsely chopped (see page 242)	114	4	1 cup
Cream Cheese Icing (see page 207)			1 recipe

1. Preheat the oven to 350°F. Grease the cake pans. Line the bottoms with rounds of baking parchment then dust them lightly with flour. Shake out the excess. Or use Baker's Joy baking spray that contains both oil and flour, so you don't have to flour the pan. With Baker's Joy, put the parchment liner in after you spray the pan.

2. In the bowl of an electric mixer with a paddle attachment, combine the flour, salt, baking soda, and cinnamon and stir briefly on medium-low speed, to distribute the ingredients. In a separate bowl, whisk together the sugar, oil, eggs, and vanilla until they are well combined. Add the liquid ingredients to the dry ingredients and mix on medium low speed, just until all the flour has been moistened. This takes less than 20 seconds.

3. Add the bananas and pineapple and stir briefly, 20 seconds, on low speed to distribute them evenly. Then add the pecans and mix again on low speed until just combined, scraping the sides and bottom of the bowl as needed. Do not overmix this batter or your cake will be tough.

4. Divide the batter equally between the 2 prepared cake pans. Weighing the batter into the pans is the most accurate way to do this. This ensures that both layers will be uniform in size and will finish baking at the same time. You'll have approximately 945.0 g/33.3 oz. of batter per pan. The pans should be about ½ full. Place the pans on the center rack in the preheated oven. Bake them for 35 to 38 minutes, or until the cake is almost ready to pull away from the sides of the pan and a toothpick inserted into the center of the cake comes out with a few moist crumbs. The cakes should be uniformly dark golden brown. Rotate the layers carefully from front to back after 20 minutes, for even baking.

5. Cool the pans on a rack for 10 minutes, then invert them onto a wire rack that has been sprayed with cooking spray and lift off the pans. To prevent cracking, carefully right each layer so the top side is up and the parchment-lined bottom is down. Cool them completely on the rack. Before frosting, be sure to remove the parchment from the bottom of each layer. While the cake layers are cooling, prepare the Cream Cheese Icing. Keep the icing refrigerated until you are ready to use it.

TIPS and TECHNIQUES

Be sure to use ripe bananas for maximum flavor and moisture, and leave them a little chunky when you mash them.

Use crushed pineapple packed in juice, not syrup, and include the juice along with the pineapple when weighing or measuring it.

This cake can be mixed easily by hand if you don't have an electric mixer.

To assemble the cake:

6. Place one layer, top side down, on a flat serving plate. Cut several 4-inch-wide strips of parchment or waxed paper to slide under the edge of the layer to keep the plate clean. Using a thin metal spatula, spread the top of this cake round with a ½-inch-thick layer of frosting, leaving a ¼-inch unfrosted border around the edge. Place the second layer top side up on the first, aligning the layers evenly. Spread a generous layer of frosting around the sides of the cake, rotating the plate as you work so you're not reaching around the cake to frost the other side. Try not to let any loose crumbs get caught in the frosting. Let the frosting extend about ¼ inch above the top of the cake.

7. Starting in the center of the cake, cover the top with a generous layer of frosting, taking it all the way to the edge and merging it with the frosting on the sides. Try to use a forward-moving circular motion, not a back-and-forth motion, to avoid lifting the top skin of the cake. Rotate the plate as necessary. Use the spatula or a spoon to make decorative swirls. Slide the pieces of paper out from under the edge of the cake and discard them. Store the cake in an airtight container in the refrigerator, but allow it to sit at room temperature for about an hour before serving.

Coconut Cream Cake

Inspired by Toy's childhood memories of a favorite Hawaiian luau dessert, this light-textured yellow cake is not too sweet and has a subtle coconut flavor that comes from real coconut milk not coconut extract. This white beauty, finished with a rich, creamy Coconut Custard Frosting and a generous sprinkling of shredded coconut, will transport you to the islands with the very first bite. Because the Coconut Custard Frosting will sour if left too long at room temperature, once frosted, this cake must be kept refrigerated. Be sure to remove it from the refrigerator about an hour before serving, as the delicate texture and flavor of the cake are best when enjoyed at room temperature.

Make the custard base for the Coconut Custard Frosting one day ahead so it can be refrigerated overnight. The next day, before you start making the cake, fold the whipped cream into the custard base and return it to the refrigerator to chill thoroughly while you are mixing, baking, and cooling the cake layers.

INGREDIENTS	GRAMS	OUNCES	VOLUME
Cake flour, sifted	440	15.52	3¾ cups
Baking powder	16	0.56	1 tablespoon + ¼ teaspoon
Baking soda	½ teaspoon	½ teaspoon	½ teaspoon
Kosher salt	¼ teaspoon	¼ teaspoon	¼ teaspoon
Buttermilk	240	8.50	1 cup
Coconut milk	120	4.23	½ cup
Vanilla extract	1 teaspoon	1 teaspoon	1 teaspoon
Unsalted butter, slightly softened	180	6.35	¾ cup
Sugar	400	14	2 cups
Eggs	200	7	4 large
Coconut Custard Frosting (see page 211)			1 recipe
Sweetened flaked coconut	150	5.25	2 cups, loosely packed

1. Preheat the oven to 350°F. Grease the cake pans. Line the bottoms with rounds of baking parchment then dust them lightly with flour. Shake out the excess. Or use Baker's Joy baking spray that contains both oil and flour, so you don't have to flour the pan. With Baker's Joy, put the parchment liner in after you spray the pan. Spray the parchment liner with Bakery's Joy after you put it into the pan.

2. In a large bowl, whisk together the cake flour, baking powder, baking soda, and salt until they are well combined. In a separate bowl, whisk together the buttermilk, coconut milk, and vanilla.

3. Using an electric mixer with a paddle attachment, cream the butter and sugar on medium speed until it is light and fluffy, 3 minutes. Add the eggs gradually, mixing well after each addition, scraping the sides and bottom of the bowl often.

4. Lower the mixing speed to medium-low and add the flour mixture to the butter in 3 parts, alternating with 2 parts of the buttermilk mixture, beginning and ending with the flour. Mix just until it is evenly incorporated. This is a thick, fluffy batter. There should not be any lumps or dry pockets of flour remaining, but be careful not to overmix this batter or the cake texture will be tough instead of tender.

5. Divide the batter equally between the 2 prepared cake pans. Weighing the batter into the pans is the most accurate way to do this. This ensures that both layers are uniform in size, and finish baking at the same time. You'll have approximately 775 g/28.3 oz. of batter per pan. The pans should be about ⅔ full. Place the pans on the center rack in the preheated oven. Bake them for about 40 minutes, or until the cake is almost ready to pull away from the sides of the pan and a toothpick inserted into the center of the cake comes out with a few moist crumbs. Rotate the layers carefully from front to back after 20 minutes, for even baking.

6. Cool the pans on a rack for 10 minutes, then invert them onto a wire rack that has been sprayed with cooking spray and lift off the pans. To prevent cracking, carefully right each layer so the top side is up and the parchment-lined bottom is down. Cool them completely on the rack. Before frosting, be sure to remove the parchment from the bottom of each layer. The Coconut Custard Frosting should already be made and chilled in the refrigerator.

To assemble the cake:

7. Place one layer, top side down, on a flat serving plate. Cut several 4-inch-wide strips of parchment or waxed paper to slide under the edge of the layer to keep the plate clean. Using a thin metal spatula, spread the top of this cake round with a ½-inch-thick layer of frosting, leaving a ¼-inch unfrosted border around the edge. Place the second layer top side up on the first, aligning the layers evenly. Spread a layer of frosting around the sides of the cake, rotating the plate as you work so you're not reaching around the cake to frost the other side. Try not to let any loose crumbs get caught in the frosting. Let the frosting extend about ¼ inch above the top of the cake.

8. Starting in the center of the cake, cover the top with a layer of frosting, taking it all the way to the edge and merging it with the frosting on the sides. Try to use a forward-moving circular motion, not a back-and-forth motion, to avoid lifting the top skin of the cake. Rotate the plate as necessary. When the whole cake is frosted, gently smooth the top and sides with the flat side of the metal spatula. Then take a handful of the coconut and gently press it on the sides of the cake. Continue doing this until the sides have been completely covered. Finally, sprinkle coconut flakes to cover the top of the cake. Slide the pieces of paper out from under the edge of the cake and discard them. Store the cake in the refrigerator, covered if possible, until about an hour before serving. Any leftovers should be returned to the refrigerator. This cake should be eaten within 3 days. The custard frosting may turn sour after that. Always taste the cake to be sure it's still fresh.

TIPS and TECHNIQUES

Make sure you purchase canned coconut milk—not cream of coconut, which has sugar added to it. Do not use lowfat coconut milk for this recipe. The cake batter may be too runny, and the subtle coconut flavor will be diminished. Fat is a flavor carrier. Whenever naturally occurring fat is removed from an ingredient, much of the ingredient's flavor is also removed. Fat also is a key factor in the texture of baked goods. Be sure to shake the can or stir the coconut milk until it is smooth and homogenous before weighing or measuring it out for the recipe.

We sprinkle flakes of sweetened coconut on the top and press them to the sides of this cake to give it a festive finish. Commercial-grade sweetened coconut has nice separate flakes that are easy to sprinkle. The Baker's Angel Flake Coconut (available from the local grocer) that we used for testing this recipe had delicious flavor but was so moist the flakes stuck together in clumps and did not lend themselves to sprinkling. If you're using this kind of very moist coconut, spend a little time rubbing it gently with your fingers to separate the flakes before you apply them to the cake.

When refrigerating the cake, be sure to keep it covered to prevent it from absorbing any off-flavors from other foods in the refrigerator.

German Chocolate Cake

꧁ Yield: one 9-inch triple-layer cake
꧂ Equipment: three 9 x 2-inch round cake pans

We had so many requests from our own bakery employees for a German Chocolate Cake that we created this one especially for them—but our customers love it, too. Remembering the delicious recipe on the inside of the Baker's German Chocolate wrappers from childhood, we ran out and bought a bar to see if the recipe was still there. Indeed it was, but somehow the resulting cake just didn't live up to our expectations. We wanted our German Chocolate Cake to have a subtle chocolate flavor reminiscent of smooth milk chocolate and buttery caramel melting together on your tongue. And we wanted its texture to be very moist but slightly dense, similar to fudgey brownies. One of the great things about working in a professional kitchen is having access to an unbelievable array of different brands and formulations of chocolate. We mixed and matched a lot of them before we found the taste we'd imagined. Here's the recipe that finally made us happy. Three luscious layers sandwiched together with a classic Coconut Pecan Topping.

In this recipe we specify a particular brand of chocolate to help you achieve the same flavor nuances we get in the German Chocolate Cake we make at the bakery.

INGREDIENTS	GRAMS	OUNCES	VOLUME
Semisweet chocolate chips	88	3.10	½ cup
Valrhona Guanaja chocolate, 70% cacao, finely chopped	50	1.76	⅓ cup
Water	140	5	⅝ cup
Cake flour, sifted	190	6.70	1⅔ cups
Unbleached all-purpose flour, sifted	160	5.64	1⅛ cups
Baking soda	1¼ teaspoons	1¼ teaspoons	1¼ teaspoons
Kosher salt	1¼ teaspoons	1¼ teaspoons	1¼ teaspoons
Unsalted butter, slightly softened	300	10.58	1⅓ cups
Sugar	450	15.76	2¼ cups
Egg yolks	120	4.23	From 6 large eggs
Vanilla extract	1⅛ teaspoons	1⅛ teaspoons	1⅛ teaspoons
Buttermilk	325	11.46	1⅓ cups
Egg whites	178	6.28	From 6 large eggs
Coconut Pecan Topping (see page 213)			1 recipe

1. Position one rack in the top third of the oven, one rack in the bottom third of the oven, and preheat the oven to 350°F. Generously grease the cake pans, put a parchment liner in the bottom of each pan, spray the liner, then dust the pans lightly with cocoa powder. Shake out the excess. Or use Baker's Joy baking spray that contains both oil and flour, so you don't have to use cocoa on the pans. Spray the parchment liner with Bakery's Joy after you put it into the pan.

2. In a small saucepan over low heat, melt the 2 chocolates with the water, stirring until smooth. Set it aside to cool. In a separate bowl, whisk together the 2 sifted flours, baking soda, and salt.

3. Using an electric mixer with a paddle attachment, cream the butter and 400 g/14 oz./2 cups of the sugar on medium speed until it is light and fluffy, 3 minutes. Add the egg yolks gradually, mixing well after each addition. Add the cooled chocolate and the vanilla. Continue mixing on medium speed until the chocolate is completely incorporated, scraping the sides and bottom of the bowl as needed.

4. Lower the mixing speed to medium-low and add the flour mixture to the butter in 3 parts, alternating with the buttermilk in 2 parts, beginning and ending with the flour. Mix just until it is evenly incorporated. Transfer the batter to a large, clean mixing bowl. Wash the dirty bowl and dry it thoroughly so it can be used to whip the egg whites.

5. With the mixer on medium-high speed, using the whip attachment, whip the egg whites for 1 minute, or until they are foamy but still loose. Add the remaining 50 g/1.76 oz./¼ cup of the sugar. Increase the speed to high and whip just until stiff but not dry peaks form, 30 seconds to 1 minute. Using a rubber spatula, fold ⅓ of the whites into the batter until just incorporated, to lighten the texture of the batter. Add the remaining whipped whites and continue folding them gently into the batter just until there are no visible lumps of egg white remaining. Be careful not to overmix the batter at this point or the cake layers will not have good volume.

6. Divide the batter equally among the three prepared cake pans. Weighing the batter into the pans is the most accurate way to do this. This ensures that all the layers are uniform in size, and finish baking at the same time. You'll have approximately 645 g/22.7 oz. of batter per pan. The pans should be about ½ full. Place 1 pan on the top rack and 2 on the bottom rack of the preheated oven. Rotate the pans from top to bottom after the first 15 minutes of baking time. Bake them for a total of 26 to 28 minutes, or until a toothpick inserted into the center of the cake comes out with a few moist crumbs.

7. Cool the pans on a rack for 10 minutes, then invert them onto a wire rack that has been sprayed with cooking spray and lift off the pans. Gently peel off the parchment liners from the bottom of the layers. To prevent cracking, carefully right each layer so the top side is up and the bottom is down. Cool them completely on the rack. This cake is exceptionally fragile and delicate, so be sure the whole layer is well supported each time you turn it over, to avoid breaking the cake.

8. While the cake layers are cooling, prepare the Coconut Pecan Filling. It should be cooled completely or until it is thick enough to spread before using it on the cake.

To assemble the cake:

9. Place one layer, top side down, on a flat serving plate. Using a thin metal spatula, spread about ⅓ of the Coconut Pecan mixture on the top of this layer, taking it all the way out to the edge of the cake. Place a second layer top side down on the first, aligning the layers evenly. Repeat the process, using ½ of the remaining topping. Put the final layer top side down on the second layer, aligning it evenly again. Cover the top with the remaining portion of the Coconut Pecan mixture once again, taking it all the way to the edges of the cake. Don't frost the sides of this cake. Store the cake at room temperature, under a cake dome, for up to 3 days. It's especially important to keep this cake covered or the sides of the cake will dry out quickly, as they're not protected by frosting.

TIPS and TECHNIQUES

If you can't find Valrhona Guanaja chocolate, substitute another brand of 70 percent cacao chocolate, or the highest percentage cacao chocolate you can find. If the chocolate available to you doesn't list a cocoa percentage, then substitute any good-quality bittersweet chocolate.

With this cake, it's especially important to weigh the egg yolks and whites if at all possible. Yolks add fat to the cake, making the texture more tender and the flavor of the cake richer. The egg whites add volume to the cake, but they can also dry the cake out if you use too many. Generally a whole egg without the shell weighs 50 g; the yolk weighs about 20 g; the white, about 30 g. By those estimates, for the amounts in this recipe you would need to separate about 6 large eggs. However, when we were testing, the large eggs we used had small yolks and larger whites. We needed almost 8 yolks to get 120 g, discarding the extra whites. If we had used just 6 separated eggs, the cake texture would have been drier and less tender than expected.

To avoid having cake layers with sloped sides, we found that we had to spray the parchment liners in the bottoms of the cake pans with Baker's Joy or cooking spray. The texture of this cake is so delicate that it shrinks dramatically from the sides of the pan when it comes out of the oven. If the parchment liner isn't sprayed, the cake sticks too firmly to the paper, which prevents the bottom of the layer from shrinking at the same rate as the top, creating a cake with sloped sides. Removing the parchment after the first 10 minutes of cooling also helps prevent sloping sides.

Handle these German Chocolate layers very gently and support the entire surface of the layers when you move them or your cake layers will break.

Manufacturers of premium mass-market chocolate bars almost always display the cacao (yes, this is the correct spelling) percentage as part of the description on the product's packaging. Cacao is the industry term for the raw chocolate solids that come from the processing of cacao beans. The percentages refer to the ratio of cacao to sugar, so a 70% chocolate would have seven parts cacao to three parts sugar. Chocolate with a lower percentage of cacao has more sugar in it and is therefore generally sweeter. In addition, the cacao portion of chocolate is made up of cocoa butter and cocoa solids, and the ratio between these two ingredients varies in each brand's formulation as well. More cocoa butter produces chocolate with a smoother texture. More cocoa solids will produce a stronger chocolate taste. There are many other factors, such as geography, growing methods, and manufacturing processes, that influence the flavor of chocolate, but these are too complex to include here. This simplified discussion provides at least a little insight into why when developing a new product that contains chocolate, professional bakers and chefs often test with many different brands and formulations of chocolate to achieve exactly the taste and texture they are seeking.

Cake Frostings and Toppings

More than once we've walked through the retail café and seen a customer happily eating all the frosting off of their cake slice. It's the little child in all of us who sees a beautifully frosted cake or cupcake and yearns to reach out, grab a big finger full of frosting, pop it directly into her mouth, and savor the intense gooey sweetness of it as it melts on the tongue. That same little child remembers so well licking frosting off the beaters of Mom's electric mixer, or reaching into a tub of pre-made frosting with her finger or a spoon to sneak a yummy bite when Mom wasn't looking. For many adults as well as children, frosting is the ultimate treat.

We love frosting, too, but we believe the cake is just as important as the frosting. When choosing the topping to go with each of our cakes, we wanted to satisfy both our sense memories from childhood and the more sophisticated taste/texture palates we've acquired in our growth as professional chefs. We wanted the cake and the frosting to complement each other so perfectly that the resulting creation would be superior to that of either item eaten alone. It was a totally sensory experience that took into consideration not only the taste but also the texture and appearance of the finished product.

Every day, customers tell us how much they love our cakes and cupcakes. We feel a great sense of pleasure and accomplishment when we hear those words of praise, and we hope that you, too, will find joy from the praise you hear when you make these cakes in your own kitchen.

TIPS and TECHNIQUES

• Be sure that any butter in the recipe is at cool room temperature. The ideal temperature is 63° to 65°F. If you don't want to bother testing it with a digital kitchen thermometer, leave it out in a cool room for about 2 hours before you use it. If the room temperature is very warm, don't leave it out that long. The butter should be firm to the touch and barely take an imprint when you press it with your finger. We believe working with cooler butter makes frosting that has superior texture, especially when you're incorporating lukewarm syrup or melted chocolate.

• Using a stand mixer with a paddle attachment makes it very easy to reproduce the frostings we make in the bakery. We prefer to use a paddle attachment instead of a whip for creaming and mixing, and use mixing speeds in the low to medium speed range. We found that higher speeds have a tendency to whip too much air into the frosting, which creates too many little air bubbles that can cause the frosting to separate when being spread on the cake.

• If you don't have a stand mixer, using a hand mixer with a powerful motor is the next best thing.

Swiss Meringue Buttercream Frosting

Yield: enough to fill and finish one 9-inch two-layer cake

This elegant buttercream is the frosting we chose for our Red Velvet Cake (see page 165) because it reminds Toy of the fluffy white frosting on the Red Velvet Cake she ate as a child. The small amount of shortening in this recipe is just enough to stabilize the frosting so it can be left at room temperature indefinitely without melting. It's not as sweet as a traditional confectioner's sugar buttercream, and it has a softer, smoother texture that won't develop a thin sugar crust. This smooth texture makes it a perfect frosting to use with a pastry bag and tip to pipe swirls on top of cupcakes or Red Velvet Cake hearts.

Some of our customers like to request this frosting on the Definitely Devil's Food Cake too (see page 175).

INGREDIENTS	GRAMS	OUNCES	VOLUME
Unsalted butter, slightly softened	312	11	1⅜ cups
Shortening	84	3	⅓ cup + 1 tablespoon
Sugar	300	10.58	1½ cups
Egg whites	150	5.30	From 5 large eggs
Light corn syrup	40	1.40	2 tablespoons
Kosher salt	¼ teaspoon	¼ teaspoon	¼ teaspoon
Vanilla extract	1¼ teaspoons	1¼ teaspoons	1¼ teaspoons

1. In a mixing bowl, using an electric mixer with a paddle attachment, cream the butter and shortening together for 1 to 2 minutes, until they are light in color and texture but not too soft. Scrape this mixture into a different bowl and set it aside to use later. Clean the mixing bowl to use for the egg whites.

TIPS and TECHNIQUES

You will need to have a candy thermometer or a digital kitchen thermometer to measure the temperature of the egg whites and sugar as they're being heated.

2. Combine the sugar, egg whites, corn syrup, and salt in the top pan of a double boiler. Heat over simmering water, stirring frequently, until the sugar granules have dissolved and the temperature on a food thermometer registers 140°F. Transfer the whites to the clean mixing bowl. Using an electric mixer with a whip attachment, whip the whites on medium to medium-high speed until the mixing bowl feels just cool to the touch, 10 to 12 minutes. The mixture should be white and fluffy and very thick.

3. Add the butter mixture and the vanilla to the egg white mixture and whip again, on medium speed, until the frosting has a smooth, creamy, spreadable texture, almost like stiff whipped cream, 1 to 2 minutes.

4. The frosting can be used immediately or stored in an airtight container at room temperature, but it should be used within 3 days. You may have to stir it briskly to re-fluff it if it's been sitting for a long time.

Sweet Pink Buttercream Frosting

Yield: enough to fill and finish one 9-inch two-layer cake

This is what makes the famous Amy's Bread Pink Cake (page 169) pink. It's essentially the same frosting recipe that's found on the confectioner's sugar boxes from the grocery store, but we add a pinch of salt to mellow out the intense sweetness of the sugar and a dab of poured fondant to give it a smoother texture and make it easier to spread on the cake. To get the pink tint, we use Baker's Rose liquid food coloring instead of red, because we like the particular shade of pink we get with the rose coloring. But 1 or 2 drops of any red food coloring will be fine. This is a very sweet, heavy, stiff frosting, but you can adjust the spreading consistency by holding back a little of the sugar or adding a few extra drops of milk. Be careful not to make it too soft, or the weight of the frosting will cause it to slip down the sides of the cake and pool around the bottom.

We use this same frosting without the rose coloring on our Definitely Devil's Food Cake (see page 175), to make the Amy's Bread Black and White Cake. Piping a few scattered dots of chocolate frosting on the top and side of the Black and White Cake gives it a whimsical retro look that our customers love.

INGREDIENTS	GRAMS	OUNCES	VOLUME
Confectioner's sugar	845	29.80	7½ cups
Unsalted butter, slightly softened	300	10.56	1⅓ cups
Poured fondant (see page 209)	138	4.87	Generous ⅓ cup
Milk, whole	62	2.19	¼ cup
Vanilla extract	13	0.46	1 tablespoon + ¼ teaspoon
Kosher salt	⅛ teaspoon	⅛ teaspoon	⅛ teaspoon
Red food coloring	1 to 2 drops	1 to 2 drops	1 to 2 drops

1. In a mixing bowl, using an electric mixer with the paddle attachment, beat 600 g/21 oz./5½ cups of the confectioner's sugar, the butter, fondant, milk, vanilla, and salt in the bowl until they are smooth and creamy, 2 to 3 minutes; start out at low speed and increase the speed to medium when the powdery sugar has been moistened. Gradually add the remaining sugar 1 cup at a time until the frosting is of good spreading consistency, scraping the sides and bottom of the bowl often. You may not need to use all of the sugar. The frosting should be stiff enough to hold its shape but not so stiff that you'll be unable to spread it easily on the cake. Add 1 or 2 small drops of red food coloring and continue beating the frosting on medium-low speed until

you have a uniform pale pink color. This frosting is heavy but it should still have a fluffy quality.

2. The frosting can be used immediately or stored in an airtight container at room temperature, but it should be used within 3 days. You may have to stir it briskly to re-fluff it if it's been sitting for a long time.

TIPS and TECHNIQUES

If you can't make or find poured fondant, increase the confectioner's sugar to 1100 g/38.8 oz./9¾ cups, the milk to 100 g/3½ oz./⅓ cup + 2 tablespoons, and the Kosher salt to ¼ tsp.

You may not need to use all of the sugar to get a good spreading consistency. When we tested this recipe, we had 60 g/2 oz./½ cup of sugar left over.

To be sure you don't add too much food coloring, add it one drop at a time and mix it into the frosting completely before adding another drop. Depending on what kind of food coloring you're using, one drop can often create dramatic results.

This frosting quickly develops a thin sugar crust when it sits uncovered. On a finished cake it can be pleasurable to cut through the thin, crisp crust to discover the soft frosting beneath, but keep the cake covered with plastic wrap or in an airtight container prior to frosting it or you'll have crusty lumps in the smooth frosting.

Chocolate Silk Frosting

Two kinds of chocolate plus butter, sugar, vanilla, and salt are all you need to make a little bit of heaven. This dark, rich, not-too-sweet frosting is the perfect match for our Definitely Devil's Food Cake (see page 175). We call it Chocolate Silk because when it's made well, it has a silky smooth texture that melts on your tongue and sends your taste buds on a trip to Nirvana. Because this frosting is made with a high percentage of solid chocolate, cakes finished with it are best kept at warm room temperature. If refrigerated, this frosting turns back into a hard candy bar. Even in a cool room, the texture of the frosting will start to stiffen, but don't be concerned. The flavor will still be divine.

INGREDIENTS	GRAMS	OUNCES	VOLUME
Semisweet chocolate chips	505	17.81	3 cups
Confectioner's sugar	160	5.64	1⅜ cups
Valrhona cocoa powder	75	2.65	¾ cup
Unsalted butter, slightly softened	454	16	2 cups
Vanilla extract	1 teaspoon	1 teaspoon	1 teaspoon
Kosher salt	⅛ teaspoon	⅛ teaspoon	⅛ teaspoon

1. Melt the chocolate chips in the top pan of a double boiler and set it aside to cool. In a separate bowl, sift together the confectioner's sugar and cocoa powder.

2. In a mixing bowl, using an electric mixer with a paddle attachment, cream the butter at medium speed until it's very light but not too soft, about 2 minutes. Add

TIPS and TECHNIQUES

It's especially important to make sure that your softened butter is still very cool and firm. If the butter is too soft in the beginning, when the melted chocolate is incorporated the finished frosting will be too loose to stay on the cake.

If this frosting has been sitting in a cool room for a day or two before being used, it may take on a matte finish and be too stiff to spread. Try stirring it briskly with a spatula or a wooden spoon to warm and soften it again. If that fails, melt a very small amount of the frosting (1 to 2 Tbs.), let it cool slightly, then stir it briskly back into the remaining cooler frosting until it softens enough to spread easily. The high percentage of butter and solid chocolate in this recipe makes this frosting sensitive to temperature extremes, causing it to melt easily if it gets too warm or solidify if it gets too cold.

the sugar mixture and continue to mix on low to medium-low speed until the sugar and cocoa have been well incorporated. Add the melted chocolate, vanilla, and salt and mix again on medium speed until everything is incorporated and the frosting is smooth and has a good spreading consistency, 1 to 2 minutes. Be careful not to over-mix it or the frosting will get too warm and runny. It should be smooth, glossy, and soft enough to spread but still hold a stiff peak.

3. The frosting can be used immediately or stored in an airtight container at room temperature, but it should be used within 3 days.

Maple Syrup Buttercream

✧ Yield: enough to top a 12 x 17-inch sheet cake

Just the thought of maple syrup conjures up cozy feelings of warmth and comfort. That's one of the reasons we made this Maple Syrup Buttercream to go with our Apple Walnut Cake (see page 180). The other reason is that its simple maple flavor and light texture are a perfect complement to the heavier, more complex character of the cake. The secret ingredient in this buttercream is instant coffee, which enhances the color and the flavor of the maple syrup.

INGREDIENTS	GRAMS	OUNCES	VOLUME
Maple syrup	292	10.30	1 cup
Instant coffee	1 teaspoon	1 teaspoon	1 teaspoon
Kosher salt	¼ teaspoon	¼ teaspoon	¼ teaspoon
Water	2 teaspoons	2 teaspoons	2 teaspoons
Unsalted butter, slightly softened	408	14.39	1¾ cups
Confectioner's sugar	288	10.16	2½ cups, lightly spooned

TIPS and TECHNIQUES

It's especially important to make sure that your softened butter is still very cool and firm. If the butter is too soft in the beginning, when the maple syrup is incorporated the finished frosting will be too soft.

1. Add the syrup to a small saucepan. In a small bowl, mix the coffee and salt with the water and add it to the maple syrup. Stir well, bring the syrup to a boil, lower the heat just enough so the syrup doesn't boil over, and continue boiling it for 10 minutes. Remove from the heat and let cool completely.

2. In a mixing bowl, using an electric mixer with a paddle attachment, cream the butter with the confectioner's sugar, starting on low speed and increasing the speed to medium as the sugar starts to moisten, 1 to 2 minutes. It should be light-colored and smooth but not too soft. Gradually add the cooled syrup, whipping the frosting on medium speed until it is thick and fluffy, another 1 to 2 minutes.

3. The frosting can be used immediately or stored in an airtight container in the refrigerator, but it solidifies because of the high butter content. When you're ready to use it, you'll have to leave it at room temperature for 1 to 2 hours to soften it enough to make it easy to spread, and you may have to whip it again slightly to recreate the fluffy texture.

Cream Cheese Icing

Yield: enough to top a 12 x 17-inch sheet cake, or fill and finish one 9-inch two-layer cake

This Cream Cheese Icing is in a class by itself. The reason it's so special is because it's made with poured fondant instead of confectioner's sugar. The fondant gives this icing a smooth, fluffy, very spreadable texture, a silky feel in the mouth, excellent flavor (because the cooked sugar doesn't mask the flavor of the cream cheese and butter the way that confectioner's sugar does), and more stability at room temperature. It's the most delicious and foolproof cream cheese icing recipe we've ever made. Our customers love it, and so do we.

INGREDIENTS	GRAMS	OUNCES	VOLUME
Unsalted butter, directly from the refrigerator	136	4.8	⅝ cup
Poured Fondant (see page 209), at room temperature	270	9.52	¾ cup
Cream cheese, directly from the refrigerator	816	28.78	3½ 8-oz. packages

1. Cut the butter into 1-inch chunks and put them in the mixing bowl of a stand mixer with the paddle attachment. Mix on medium speed until the butter is malleable and spreads on the sides of the bowl, 2 to 3 minutes. Add the fondant all at once, in three or four lumps, and continue mixing on medium to medium-high speed until the mixture is completely smooth, 2 to 3 more minutes, scraping the sides and bottom of the bowl as needed. There should be no visible lumps of fondant remaining.

2. Cut each package of cream cheese into four chunks. Add them gradually in three additions and continue mixing at medium speed until the icing is completely smooth

TIPS and TECHNIQUES

An electric stand mixer with a paddle attachment is required to make this icing. The cold, heavy ingredients and the lengthy mixing time do not lend themselves readily to mixers that use standard beater attachments.

The butter and cream cheese in this recipe should be used cold directly from the refrigerator. Only the poured fondant should be at room temperature.

Cakes finished with this icing should be kept refrigerated until 30 minutes to an hour before serving time. Be sure to cover the cake once the icing has set or the icing will develop an off-flavor from absorbing the aromas of other foods in the refrigerator.

The finished cake can sit out for 2 to 3 hours if the room isn't extremely warm, but leftovers should be stored in the refrigerator.

and has a thick, fluffy texture similar to that of thick whipped cream, 5 to 6 minutes, scraping the sides and bottom of the bowl as needed. There should be no lumps of cream cheese visible.

3. The frosting can be used immediately or stored in an airtight container in the refrigerator until you're ready to use it. If it seems too stiff to spread, let it soften slightly at room temperature and stir it again to create a texture that will spread easily on the cake.

Food Processor Poured Fondant

Yield: about 650 g/22.9 oz.

At the bakery, we use poured fondant as one of the key ingredients in our Sweet Pink Buttercream Frosting (see page 201) and our Cream Cheese Icing (page 207). This one unique ingredient is responsible for elevating these two fairly common frostings to a higher level of quality.

Poured fondant is concentrated cooked sugar syrup that has been cooled and kneaded vigorously so the sugar re-crystalizes, creating a heavy, doughy consistency. Stored in an airtight container, it can be kept in the refrigerator for up to 6 months. When melted to a more liquid state and/or thinned slightly with citrus juice or syrup, it can be used to glaze petits fours, cookies, and cakes. At the bakery, we use it to make the glaze for our Lime Cornmeal Cookies (see page 115).

Making fondant from scratch using traditional techniques requires a lot of time and labor and is hardly worth the effort, especially if you use it only infrequently and in small amounts. Even at the bakery it's much easier and more efficient for us to purchase large plastic tubs of ready-made fondant from our wholesale supplier. If you want to purchase fondant, you will have to go to a store that specializes in cake decorating supplies, or call a friendly local bakery and ask if you can buy a small amount from them. Be sure you ask for "poured" fondant, not "rolled" fondant.

If you have a food processor and an accurately calibrated digital kitchen thermometer, making your own fondant can be a simple, fairly painless process. The recipe here first appeared in Helen Fletcher's book *The New Pastry Cook,* which is now out of print. Helen, whose bakery *Truffes,* in St. Louis, Missouri, sells amazingly beautiful pastries, has generously given us permission to use her recipe here.

INGREDIENTS	GRAMS	OUNCES	VOLUME
Sugar	500	17.64	2½ cups
Water	114	4	½ cup
Light corn syrup	82	2.88	¼ cup

1. In a medium-size heavy saucepan, bring the sugar, water, and corn syrup to a boil, stirring constantly. As soon it boils, stop stirring. Cook the syrup to a temperature of 238°F (soft ball stage). Immediately pour the hot syrup into a food processor fitted with a steel blade. Wash the thermometer well and put back into the syrup. Let the syrup cool undisturbed to 140°F, 25 to 30 minutes.

2. Remove the thermometer and turn the food processor on to process the syrup continuously until it completely converts from a glassy syrup to an opaque paste, 2 to 3 minutes. Pour it into a heatproof container, cover it loosely, and let it cool. When it has cooled completely, seal the container and store the fondant at room temperature for 24 hours before using it. It can be stored like this for up to 6 days, and in the refrigerator for up to 6 months.

TIPS and TECHNIQUES

Plan on making this recipe at least 2 days before you want to use it. It can be stored at room temperature for 5 or 6 days before it has to be refrigerated.

Correct temperatures are very important in this process, so be sure you calibrate your thermometer, or at least know how far off the mark it is, so you can judge when the proper temperature has been reached. In a pan of boiling water, the thermometer should register 212°F.

Once the sugar has come to a boil, stop stirring it to prevent premature re-crystallization.

Be sure to wash the thermometer thoroughly each time you take it out of the boiling syrup and before you reinsert it into the syrup, to avoid premature re-crystallization of the sugar.

If the fondant has been stored in the refrigerator, let it come to room temperature before using it to make frosting.

It helps to handle the fondant with slightly moistened hands.

Coconut Custard Frosting

Coconut milk, cream cheese, white chocolate, and whipped cream blended into a smooth, subtly sweet custard make an extraordinary filling and topping for our Coconut Cream Cake (see page 189). Some of our customers love this topping so much they'd like to just skip the cake and eat the frosting by itself with a spoon, like an exotic coconut pudding. The secret to making this frosting successfully is to cook the custard until it is very thick, otherwise it won't have enough body once the whipped cream is added to have a good spreading consistency. Cook the custard the day before you want to frost your cake, so it can be refrigerated overnight to chill completely before you fold in the whipped cream. After you spread it on the cake, add a sprinkle of sweetened coconut flakes for a snowy finish. This cake looks as beautiful as it tastes.

INGREDIENTS	GRAMS	OUNCES	VOLUME
Coconut milk, full-fat	540	19.05	2¼ cups
Sugar	112	4.0	½ cup + 1 tablespoon
Cornstarch	50	1.76	⅓ cup + 1 tablespoon
Cream cheese, cut into ½-inch cubes	172	6.0	¾ of an 8-oz. package
White chocolate, chopped	85	3.0	Generous ⅓ cup
Vanilla extract	¾ teaspoon	¾ teaspoon	¾ teaspoon
Kosher salt	¼ teaspoon	¼ teaspoon	¼ teaspoon
Heavy cream	360	12.70	1½ cups
Sweetened flaked coconut, for decoration	225	8	3 cups, loosely packed

1. Combine 360 g/12.70 oz. of the coconut milk and the sugar in a medium-size heavy saucepan. Bring it to a boil over moderate heat, stirring it with a wooden spoon or a heatproof spatula until the sugar dissolves completely. Mix the remaining 180 g/6.35 oz. coconut milk with the cornstarch until smooth. Whisk this mixture into the boiling coconut milk, and cook over moderate heat, whisking vigorously until very thick, 2 to 3 minutes.

2. Remove the custard from the heat and whisk in the cream cheese, white chocolate, vanilla, and salt, stirring until it is completely incorporated and smooth. If the saucepan is too small to hold all the ingredients, you may have to transfer them to a larger bowl to whisk them together easily. Pour the custard into a clean bowl, press a piece of plastic wrap directly on the surface of the pudding to keep a skin from forming, and refrigerate it overnight.

3. The next day, remove the custard from the refrigerator. Stir the cold custard vigorously with a whisk just until it's smooth and creamy. In another bowl, whip the heavy cream until it is stiff but not grainy. Whisk ¼ of the whipped cream into the cold coconut custard until it is smooth and well blended. This lightens the custard a little so the rest of the whipped cream can be more easily incorporated. Whisk in the remaining whipped cream until it is well combined and the frosting is thick and fluffy.

4. At this point, if the frosting is nice and thick and of good spreading consistency, it can be used to finish the cake. If it seems too soft, chill it again to thicken it before using it. This custard-type frosting cannot be applied as thickly as a more traditional frosting. It will probably be only about ½ inch thick.

5. Decorate the cake by sprinkling the sweetened coconut flakes on the top and patting them gently onto the sides. Store the finished cake covered in the refrigerator until about an hour before serving. Refrigerate any leftovers. This frosting is highly perishable and will sour after 3 days.

TIPS *and* TECHNIQUES

Do not use lowfat coconut milk for this recipe. The consistency of the frosting may be too runny and the subtle coconut flavor will be diminished. Fat is a flavor carrier. Whenever naturally occurring fat is removed from an ingredient, much of the ingredient's flavor is also removed. Fat also is a key factor in the texture of foods.

The coconut milk in this recipe is divided into 2 portions; one is combined with the sugar, the other with the cornstarch. Be sure to shake the can or stir the coconut milk well before you measure it out.

Use any good-quality white chocolate for this recipe. If the chocolate is already in chips or chunks, it won't be necessary to chop it.

Coconut Pecan Topping

Yield: enough to fill and top one 9-inch three-layer cake

This is the classic topping for the German Chocolate Cake (page 192) we remember from our childhood years. With the richness of evaporated milk, butter, sugar, and egg yolks, and the crunchiness of toasted pecans and coconut, it's another frosting we'd love to eat with a spoon. Be sure to cook it until it's thick and golden so it will hold onto the nuts and coconut when the cake is sliced for serving, and will have the caramel flavor we love so much. Don't try to frost the sides of the cake with this sticky, crumbly topping. Just spread it generously between the layers and on the top. If it's a little uneven and some of it drips down the sides, don't worry. Those drips will only make it look even more appealing.

INGREDIENTS	GRAMS	OUNCES	VOLUME
Evaporated milk	370	13	1½ cups
Sugar	196	7	1 cup
Egg yolks	92	3.24	From 5 large eggs
Kosher salt	¼ teaspoon	¼ teaspoon	¼ teaspoon
Unsalted butter, cut into ½ inch cubes	150	5.29	⅔ cup
Vanilla extract	1½ teaspoons	1½ teaspoons	1½ teaspoons
Sweetened flaked coconut	200	7	2⅓ cups
Pecan pieces, toasted (see page 242), finely chopped	180	6.35	1½ cups

1. Mix the evaporated milk, sugar, egg yolks, and salt in the top part of a double boiler. Cook over medium heat just until the mixture has thickened, 20 to 25 minutes, stirring very frequently. Remove the pan from the heat. Whisk in the butter and vanilla until they're completely incorporated. Add the coconut and pecans and mix with a wooden spoon or a heatproof spatula until they are well distributed.

2. Cool the topping to room temperature, or until it reaches a good spreading consistency. It thickens more as it cools. The topping should have a glossy finish and a lovely light golden color. As soon as it's thick enough, use it to fill and top the German Chocolate Cake layers (see page 192). Store the finished cake covered at room temperature.

TIPS and TECHNIQUES

Be sure you use evaporated milk, not sweetened condensed milk, for this recipe.

It's important to cook this filling long enough to achieve the correct flavor and texture.

It's best to use this topping the day it's made. Refrigerating it makes it turn cloudy. It still tastes fine but it doesn't look as appealing. Let it sit at room temperature for a couple of hours before using it to finish the cake.

Special Seasonal Desserts

When summer finally arrives and we have the chance to walk through one of the many local farmers markets around New York City, we are inspired to make our special desserts once again. These recipes were developed to channel our creativity and satisfy our desire to bake with the best local and seasonal ingredients. When we find the little boxes of fragrant ripe red strawberries, the bushel baskets of fresh golden peaches with their rosy blush, the pint containers of perfect blueberries, and the fascinating selection of fresh plums in shades of purple, red, yellow, and green, our excitement is kindled to start baking our favorite seasonal creations. Of course we enjoy baking the daily bread and pastries our customers love so much, but what really motivates us is the chance to make special desserts. For many years we just didn't have time to bake anything but our regular breads and sweets. But now we make Strawberry Shortcakes in June, Mini Peach Pies and Blueberry Treats in July and August, Upside-Down Cake whenever the mood strikes, and our fragrant Gingerbread Cake and Whole Lemon Pie throughout the winter.

No one knows exactly which days to expect our seasonal desserts, because they're not listed on our menu. But we try to bake them as often as possible, because we know our customers will be as excited about them as we are. We love baking these special desserts and hope you will add them to your file of favorite recipes.

TIPS and TECHNIQUES

- Most of these recipes call for fresh seasonal fruit. Try to find fruit at a local farmers market, if you have one. The desserts taste so much better with exceptional tree- or vine-ripened fruit.

- The recipes in this chapter are fairly simple and don't require any special equipment. These are rustic desserts that won't take a long time to make. If you don't have a specific pan, substitute another. Just try the recipes, have some fun, and enjoy the results.

Amy's Mom's Whole Lemon Pie

Yield: one 9-inch pie
Equipment: one 9-inch glass or metal pie pan

This unique lemon pie is one of the simplest desserts you can make. The recipe was born of necessity, and shared by neighbors with an abundance of lemons. Amy's parents spend the winter in Arizona and are fortunate enough to have a neighbor with a gorgeous and very prolific lemon tree. It provides baskets of the biggest, juiciest lemons you have ever seen to whoever is willing to use them. Just take one of these beauties, trim and seed it, grind it up in the blender with butter, eggs, and sugar, and pour it into an unbaked pie shell. Place it in the oven for less than an hour, and out comes a sweet, tart, custard-rich pie. Since the zest from the whole lemon is in the pie, the lemon flavor really intensifies by the second day. For those of you who don't have a beautiful lemon tree in your backyard, choose a

large, very fresh-looking, thin-skinned lemon at the market. The shiniest lemons are usually the ones with the thinnest skins. If you're lucky enough to find Meyer lemons when they're in season (December through April), you'll be rewarded with a pie of exceptional flavor. The Meyer lemon has a sweeter, less acidic flavor than the more common lemon, and a fragrant edible skin. If you can't find a large lemon, two small ones will do. This pie is a quick and easy crowd-pleaser—the perfect "fast food" dessert to make for a potluck or family get-together.

We have included our recipe for a simple pie crust, but a pre-made crust works well, too. If you make your own crust, make the pie crust dough at least 1 hour before you plan to bake. It must chill for an hour before you can roll it and place it in the pie pan. If you want to save time, use any good-quality pre-made, unsweetened pie crust, including frozen or refrigerated crusts that you buy in the supermarket. Letting someone else prepare the crust makes the whole process much faster and easier.

INGREDIENTS	GRAMS	OUNCES	VOLUME
Pie Crust			
Unsalted butter, cold, cut into ½-inch dice	85	3	6 tablespoons
Unbleached all-purpose flour	181	6.38	1¼ cups
Kosher salt	⅜ teaspoon	⅜ teaspoon	⅜ teaspoon
Cold water	42 to 71	1.5 to 2.5	3 to 5 tablespoons
Shortening	36	1.27	3 tablespoons
Pie Filling			
Lemon, Meyer if available	165	5.82	1 large
Sugar	300	10.58	1½ cups
Eggs	200	7.05	4 large
Unsalted butter, softened	114	4	½ cup (1 stick)
Vanilla extract	1 teaspoon	1 teaspoon	1 teaspoon

1. Prepare the pie crust: Freeze the diced butter for at least 15 minutes. In a large bowl, add the flour and salt and whisk together. Place the cold water in a measuring cup with several ice cubes to chill.

2. Add the diced butter to the flour mixture and toss it quickly to separate the pieces and coat them with flour. Add the shortening to the bowl and toss it with flour. With a pastry blender or 2 knives, quickly cut the butter and shortening into the flour until the fat is in pea-size pieces. Keep the mixture as cold as possible. Add 3 tablespoons of the ice water and try to gather the dough together. If it is too dry, add ice water 1 tablespoon at a time until the mixture is moist enough to gather into a ball. As the ball becomes more defined, use your hands to press it gently together into a single cohesive mass of dough. There should not be any pockets of dry crumbs remaining. Place the ball of dough on a large piece of plastic wrap, seal the wrap around the dough, and flatten the ball to make a ¾-inch-thick disk. If you plan to make the pie in the next hour, place the disk in the freezer to chill. Otherwise, place the pie dough into the refrigerator to firm up before rolling. It can be kept in the refrigerator for up to 2 days before use.

3. Preheat the oven to 350°F. On a lightly floured surface, roll the pie dough into a 12-inch circle. Place it in the pie pan, fold over any excess dough, and crimp the edges around the pan. Place it in the refrigerator to keep it cool.

4. Prepare the pie filling: Wash the lemon, trim off the ends, and cut it into 8 wedges. Remove any seeds and trim off any thick pith or connective membrane. Place the lemon, rind included, in a blender. Puree on high speed for 2 minutes, or until the lemon is very finely pulverized. Add the sugar and eggs and blend again for 2 minutes.

Add the soft butter and vanilla extract and blend again for 1 minute, or until everything is fully combined and smooth.

5. Pour the filling into the prepared pie crust. Bake the pie in the center of the oven for 35 to 40 minutes or until the center is set but still slightly soft. Place the pie on a wire rack to cool completely before serving.

6. Serve the pie on the first day it's baked for a mild lemon flavor, or cover the pie with plastic wrap and keep it at room temperature and serve it the next day, for a fuller flavor. On the second day, the flavor of the zest really permeates the pie and adds a whole new dimension.

TIPS and TECHNIQUES

Whole books have been written about making pie crust, and there are lots of techniques that contribute to a perfect crust. Keep the butter and shortening as cold as possible. Use the lowest-protein flour you have. Some all-purpose flours have less protein than others. We suggest flour with protein of 11.3 percent or less, for the tenderest crust. (See flour protein information, page 239.) Don't work the dough after you have added water or it will become tough. Keep it cool when rolling it out and don't use too much flour on the table. You can substitute all butter for the shortening in the crust, but the crust will become a little chewier on the second day.

To make the pie crust in a food processor, place the flour and salt in the bowl fitted with a metal blade and pulse for 2 seconds. Add the diced cold butter and shortening to the bowl and toss gently with the flour, taking care not to touch the blade with your fingers. Process the mixture for a several seconds until the fat is in pea-size pieces. Add 4 tablespoons of water all at once and process to bring the dough together. If it is still too dry, add 1 tablespoon water and pulse briefly. Don't process the dough anymore—just until the flour is moistened. Gather the dough into a ball, place it on a sheet of plastic wrap, wrap it tightly, and flatten the ball to make a ¾-inch-thick disk. Chill the dough until you are ready to roll it out.

When you are blending the lemon, be sure it is very finely ground. A blender works much better than a food processor to break down the lemon rind. If the rind is left in small bits, the pie will be overwhelmed with the flavor of lemon zest.

Rustic Mini Peach Pies

Yield: 6 rustic mini peach pies
Equipment: two 12 x 17-inch sheet pans

In New York City we are lucky enough to be close to the Garden State of New Jersey, the lush orchards of Pennsylvania, and the rich farming regions of New York State. They are all home to orchards growing gorgeous fresh peaches from July through September. These peaches arrive at farmers markets all over the five boroughs of New York City, and they beckon to be made into pretty little pies. Amy has always felt strongly about buying local fruit. For the past five years she has gone to the farmers market every Wednesday to pay the peach farmer, and then has sent one of our delivery drivers to pick up a crate of peaches for our pies. Now we've found a farm that delivers fresh local peaches to our kitchen along with plums, apricots, currants, and zucchini, all freshly picked. Golden, juicy, and wonderful, fresh peaches are a real treat. We make them into individual pies that are baked free-form on a baking sheet. Just roll out the dough, cut it into disks, top it with fruit, and gather up the crust around the edges. After they are baked, these mini peach pies look very rustic and very tempting—and they taste as good as they look.

INGREDIENTS	GRAMS	OUNCES	VOLUME
Pie Crust			
Unsalted butter, cut into 1/2-inch dice	170	6	3/4 cup
Unbleached all-purpose flour	326	11.5	2 1/4 cups
Sugar	28	1	2 tablespoons
Kosher salt	3/4 teaspoon	3/4 teaspoon	3/4 teaspoon
Cold water	85 to 113	3 to 4	6 to 8 tablespoons
Vegetable shortening	95	3.3	1/2 cup
Pie Filling			
Peaches, fresh, ripe, whole	750	26.45	4 to 5 medium
Light brown sugar	65	2.29	1/3 cup
Cornstarch	22	0.70	2 tablespoons
Cinnamon, ground	1/2 teaspoon	1/2 teaspoon	1/2 teaspoon
Lemon juice	1/2 teaspoon	1/2 teaspoon	1/2 teaspoon
Lemon zest, grated	1/4 teaspoon	1/4 teaspoon	1/4 teaspoon
Kosher salt	1/8 teaspoon	1/8 teaspoon	1/8 teaspoon
Sugar	1 tablespoon	1 tablespoon	1 tablespoon

Rustic Mini Peach Pies (*continued*)

TIPS *and* TECHNIQUES

The pie crust dough must chill for at least 1 hour before you roll it out, but you can make it up to 2 days in advance, and store the dough in the refrigerator until you are ready to use it. See our Tips and Techniques for pie crust on page 219 in the recipe for Whole Lemon Pie.

Make sure to use ripe peaches, or they will be crunchy and lack flavor, even after baking. Don't bother to peel the peaches. The pies look nicer with the beautiful rosy-colored skins on each slice.

1. Prepare the pie crust: Freeze the diced butter for at least 15 minutes. In a large bowl add the flour, sugar, and salt and whisk together. Place the cold water in a measuring cup with several ice cubes to chill.

2. Add the diced butter to the flour mixture and toss quickly to separate the pieces and coat with flour. Add the shortening to the bowl and toss it with flour. With a pastry blender or 2 knives, quickly cut the butter and shortening into the flour until the fat is in pea-size pieces. Keep the mixture as cold as possible. Add 6 tablespoons of the ice water and try to gather the dough together. If it is too dry, add ice water 1 tablespoon at a time until the mixture is moist enough to gather into a ball. As the ball becomes more defined, use your hands to press it gently together into a single cohesive mass of dough. There should not be any pockets of dry crumbs remaining. Place the ball of dough on a large piece of plastic wrap, seal the wrap around the dough, and flatten the ball to make a ¾-inch-thick disk. If you plan to make the pie in the next hour, place the disk in the freezer to chill. Otherwise, place the pie dough into the refrigerator to firm up before rolling. It can be kept in the refrigerator for up to 2 days before use.

3. Preheat the oven to 450°F and position 2 racks in the upper half of the oven. Line the sheet pans with baking parchment.

4. Wash the peaches, cut in half and remove the pits, then cut each half into 4 wedges. In a medium bowl, add the brown sugar, cornstarch, cinnamon, lemon juice, zest, and salt, and whisk together. Add the peaches to the sugar mixture and stir gently to combine. Let the mixture stand for 10 minutes.

5. On a lightly floured surface, roll the pie crust dough into a large free-form oval about 20 inches long and 12 inches wide, and between ⅛ and ¼ inch thick. Use a 6-inch template, such as a small plate or container lid, to cut out 6 circles of dough with a paring knife. Try to keep the circles close together so you don't have much scrap. If you don't have enough dough for 6 circles, roll the scraps and cut out the remaining circles. Gently lift the circles of dough and place 3 on each prepared sheet pan, leaving several inches around each one.

6. Sprinkle each dough circle very lightly with sugar, then place ⅙ of the filling in the center of each one, leaving a 1½-inch border around the fruit. There should be 5 to 6 slices of peach on each pie. Fold the dough border up over the peaches and press it lightly around the fruit. Press down gently on the dough around the edge of each pie, making sure it is sealed tightly to the pan.

7. Bake for 14 minutes, rotate the pans from top to bottom, then reduce the oven temperature to 350°F and bake for 11 to 14 more minutes, or until the crust is golden brown and the filling is thick and bubbly. Watch the bottoms carefully so they do not get too dark.

8. Place the pies on a wire rack to cool before serving. They are delicious warm from the oven, served with a scoop of vanilla ice cream. These pies are best eaten the day they are baked. Store any extras at room temperature covered with foil, and heat in the oven for 8 to 10 minutes at 350°F before serving.

Amy's Secret for Perfect Pie Crust

Amy's Grandma Scherber was an accomplished pie baker. In fact, she won the Minnesota Pie Baking Contest in 1944, for the Best Apple Pie in the state. She was the wife of a farmer and rarely had the chance to show off her baking skills outside the home. At the contest, she was so nervous that she sprinkled salt—instead of sugar—on the top crust of her pie. She immediately recognized her mistake, and the judges were kind enough to give her a second try. Her hands were shaking as she rolled out another circle of crust, but she was able to put her pie together and won the contest.

Maybe one of the secrets to her success was using her trusty rolling pin, one carved by her husband from a single piece of wood. This beautiful handmade pin has perfect balance and heft. Amy knows this because she used it to roll out the pie crusts for this book. Several years ago, her godmother and aunt, Kay Schirmers, gave Amy this beautiful rolling pin so she could carry on the family tradition of making prize-winning homemade pies.

A Helper in the Kitchen

Baking with children can be a great pleasure. Their enthusiasm and observations add a whole new dimension to the process—as long as that process doesn't take too long. Amy's son, Harry, turned three while she was working on these recipes for the cookbook. He loved helping out in the kitchen, especially with the recipes for desserts. Each time they were ready to bake, he put on his pint-size apron, pulled over his sturdy little wooden chair, and stood on the arms of the chair to get a bird's-eye view into the mixer bowl.

He was especially helpful zeroing out the scale, even in the middle of weighing

ingredients which meant Mommy had to weigh everything again! He enjoyed using a pen to scribble on the recipes, making circles and squiggles all over the laser-printed pages. He learned to crack eggs, one by one, sticking his little thumbs into the crack to pull the two sides apart, leaving a little shell in the bowl with each one. He also enjoyed dumping the dry ingredients into the bowl, even though a little flour fell onto the floor every time. But the most fun was pushing the buttons on the mixer to increase the speed. Faster, faster, FASTER!

One day he and his mother were mixing butter and sugar together with the mixer.

After the mixture became light and fluffy, Harry exclaimed loudly and excitedly, *"Mommy, it's starting to look like cake!"* He was becoming an expert already. Even though watching the batter come together was interesting, the most satisfying part of the process was tasting a little of the batter when it was fully mixed. The gingerbread cake was the most delicious. Harry was so enthusiastic about it that he licked the mixer attachments, the spatula, the measuring cup, even a few drips on the side of the mixer and the counter, until his lips and cheeks were totally brown, covered in batter. What could be better than being a kid in the kitchen—except being his mom, enjoying sharing the fun?

Gingerbread Cakes with Lemon Sauce

Yield: 6 individual mini Bundt cakes or one 9-inch square pan of cake
Equipment: 2 mini Bundt pans (6 "cups" each)

The spicy smell of gingerbread cake during the winter months transports Amy back to her mom's kitchen when she was growing up. One of the things her mom loved to bake was gingerbread cake. In Amy's memory, it was sweet, spicy, moist, and tender, served with a tangy lemon sauce and a dollop of barely sweetened whipped cream. To re-create this taste memory, Amy tried lots of recipes, but all of these were either too sweet, not spicy enough, or tasted too strong of molasses. After much testing, Amy came up with this version, which balances sweet, spicy, and fragrant in one delicate cake. It can be baked in one pan and served in squares, or for individual servings and a nicer presentation, it can be baked in mini Bundt pans. When the lemon sauce is drizzled over the ridges of each individual Bundt and the cake is topped with whipped cream, it looks like a fancy dessert. Be careful not to overbake this cake. It is better when it's almost gooey and sticky, and tastes great warm from the oven.

INGREDIENTS	GRAMS	OUNCES	VOLUME
Gingerbread Cakes			
Unbleached all-purpose flour	290	10.23	2 cups
Ginger, ground	2¼ teaspoons	2¼ teaspoons	2¼ teaspoons
Baking soda	1½ teaspoons	1½ teaspoons	1½ teaspoons
Cinnamon, ground	½ teaspoon	½ teaspoon	½ teaspoon
Cloves, ground	¼ teaspoon	¼ teaspoon	¼ teaspoon
Kosher salt	¼ teaspoon	¼ teaspoon	¼ teaspoon
Unsalted butter, softened	71	2.5	¼ cup + 1 tablespoon
Sugar	50	1.76	¼ cup
Eggs	50	1.76	1 large
Molasses, dark	255	9	¾ cup
Water, hot	170	6	¾ cup
Lemon Sauce			
Sugar	125	4.4	⅝ cup
Eggs	50	1.76	1 large
Lemon juice	42	1.5	Juice of 1 large lemon
Water, boiling	42	1.5	3 tablespoons
Lemon zest, grated	1½ teaspoons	1½ teaspoons	1½ teaspoons
Unsalted butter, cold	113	4	½ cup (1 stick)
Whipped Cream			
Heavy cream, cold	116	4.09	½ cup
Sugar	2 teaspoons	2 teaspoons	2 teaspoons

1. Prepare the Gingerbread Cakes: Preheat the oven to 350°F. Grease the pans with softened butter, or spray with nonstick spray.

2. Sift the flour, ginger, baking soda, cinnamon, cloves, and salt onto a sheet of parchment paper.

3. In a small bowl with an electric mixer, beat the butter for 1 minute or until light and fluffy. Add the sugar, and beat again for 1 minute or until light in color. Add the egg and beat the mixture for another minute until it's well combined, scraping down the sides and bottom of the bowl. Pour the molasses into the bowl slowly, beating all the while.

4. Add half of the dry ingredients and fold together with a spatula. Add the remaining dry ingredients and fold together again. Pour in the hot water and fold gently just until the water is well incorporated and there are no more thick lumps of batter.

5. Divide the batter evenly among the pans. A heaping ½-cup measure will fill each mold almost to the top. Bake for about 16 to 17 minutes, until a toothpick inserted in the center of the cakes comes out clean. Cool the individual cakes in the pan for 5 minutes, then tip out onto a wire rack to finish cooling. The cakes are delicious served slightly warm from the oven.

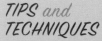

TIPS and TECHNIQUES

To bake the batter in a 9-inch square pan, grease the pan, then pour the prepared batter into the pan. Bake for 20 to 24 minutes, or until a thin bladed knife poked into the center of the cake comes out clean. Place the pan on a wire rack to cool before serving. Cut the cake into 9 squares, 3 x 3.

6. While the cakes are baking, prepare the Lemon Sauce: In a small bowl add the sugar, egg, lemon juice, the boiling water, and the zest, and whisk together. Cook the mixture over a pan of simmering water at medium-low heat for 15 minutes, or until the sauce coats the back of a spoon, whisking often. Strain the sauce to remove the lemon zest. After the sauce has cooled slightly, whisk in pieces of the diced cold butter to thicken it. If you make the sauce before you are ready to use it, place plastic wrap directly on the surface to keep a skin from forming. Leftovers can be chilled and stored in the refrigerator for up to 2 weeks.

7. Prepare the Whipped Cream: In a medium bowl combine the cold heavy cream and 2 teaspoons of sugar. With an electric mixer, whip the cream until soft peaks form. Do not overwhip. Keep the cream chilled until ready to serve.

8. To serve, place a little gingerbread Bundt cake on a dessert plate. Spoon the lemon sauce over the top of the cake so it drips down both sides of the ring and onto the plate. Top with a dollop of whipped cream and serve. This makes a great winter dessert. Store any leftover cake at room temperature, wrapped tightly in plastic.

Plum Upside-Down Cake

Yield: one 9 x 13-inch upside-down cake
Equipment: one 9 x 13-inch metal baking pan

Upside-down cake makes an impressive showing at any time and place. The caramelized fruit looks beautiful over the top of the cake. During the summer months we use black plums to top our cake. We think these plums are especially nice because their skins are deep purple and their flesh is orange. Baking enhances their dramatic color. The tangy sourness of the plums is offset by the sweetness of the brown sugar topping. Combine that with the moist, golden cake, and you have a winning dessert.

INGREDIENTS	GRAMS	OUNCES	VOLUME
Light brown sugar	150	5.29	¾ cup
Unsalted butter	57	2	¼ cup
Black plums, fresh, whole with pits	420	14.81	6 to 8 small plums
Unbleached all-purpose flour	218	7.69	1½ cups
Cornmeal	32	1.13	3 tablespoons
Baking powder	1½ teaspoons	1½ teaspoons	1½ teaspoons
Kosher salt	1 teaspoon	1 teaspoon	1 teaspoon
Unsalted butter, softened	113	4	½ cup
Sugar	200	7.05	1 cup
Eggs, separated	200	7.05	4 large
Vanilla extract	1½ teaspoons	1½ teaspoons	1½ teaspoons
Milk, whole	151	5.33	⅔ cup
Sugar	28	1	2 tablespoons

1. Preheat the oven to 350°F. Grease the pan.

2. In a small saucepan melt the brown sugar and first measure of butter over low heat, whisking constantly, until the mixture becomes lighter in color and slightly foamy, 1 to 2 minutes. Pour the topping into the prepared pan and spread it evenly over the bottom. Wash the plums, cut in half and remove the pits, and cut each half into 4 wedges. Casually arrange the sliced fruit on top of the topping, placing the cut side down on the topping. Set the pan with fruit aside.

3. In a medium bowl, add the flour, cornmeal, baking powder, and salt and whisk together.

4. In a small bowl with an electric mixer, cream the second measure of butter for 1 minute, or until light and fluffy. Add the first measure of sugar and continue beating

for 1½ minutes, or until fluffy. Add the egg yolks and vanilla and mix 1 minute more. Move the batter to a large mixing bowl.

5. Add half the flour mixture to the batter and mix briefly, then add half the milk and mix again. Add the remaining flour and mix, then the remaining milk and mix until it is just incorporated. Set aside.

6. In a small bowl, add the egg whites and beat on low speed for 1 to 2 minutes, until frothy. Increase the speed to medium and continue beating for 3 minutes, or until soft peaks form. Gradually add the second measure of sugar and beat until stiff (not dry) peaks form, 4 to 5 minutes. Fold ¼ of the whites into the batter to lighten it. Gently fold in the remaining whites, just until completely incorporated.

7. Pour the batter into the prepared baking pan and spread it evenly over the topping. Place the pan in the center of the oven and bake for 30 to 33 minutes, until a thin-bladed knife inserted into the center of the cake below the crusty surface comes out almost clean. It's hard to tell when the cake is done baking, but it is better to take it out a little too early than to overbake it. If it is just about fully set, remove it from the oven. It will continue to firm up when it is out of the oven.

8. Let the cake rest on a wire rack to cool for 5 to 10 minutes, and then run a thin-bladed knife around the sides of the pan to release. Unmold it onto a rectangular plate or tray to cool completely.

TIPS and TECHNIQUES

We prefer to make this cake in a metal baking pan because it's easier to release it from the pan when you turn it upside down.

When preparing the brown sugar topping, don't overheat it or cook it too long, or the topping will crystallize. When arranging the plums on the cake, place them in rows to make a fancier presentation. At the bakery we just scatter them over the topping with the cut side down to make a more rustic-looking cake.

It is hard to tell when the cake is done, but be careful not to overbake it.

This cake makes a beautiful addition to a holiday table. To enjoy the cake year round, change the fruit to 1 can of drained, unsweetened pineapple rings or 2 mangoes cut in slices.

Blueberry Almond Treats

Yield: one 9 x 13-inch pan cut into 15 squares
Equipment: one 9 x 13-inch baking pan

These delicious fruit squares are the result of our effort to make a simple dessert that uses the fresh berries of the season. We call them "treats" because it's a treat to eat one as a sweet snack in the afternoon, or as a light dessert at the end of a meal. We make a traditional frangipane (almond filling) and fold in whatever fresh fruit is available. At the bakery we bake the treats in decorative round paper molds as individual servings. Here we've made them into a pan of bars that can be cut into squares. We've added a tender, buttery crust that's topped with the fruit-studded filling. Our favorite fruit addition is fresh New Jersey blueberries. The sweet, juicy berries look beautiful suspended in the golden brown topping, and they provide a nice contrast to the treat's richness. These treats are not overly sweet, so you can taste all the elements within, and not just the sugar. Keep this recipe in your repertoire all year round by substituting fresh raspberries, thinly sliced apples, or fresh cranberries in the autumn.

INGREDIENTS	GRAMS	OUNCES	VOLUME
Crust			
Unbleached all-purpose flour	220	7.76	1½ cups
Unsalted butter, cold, cut into ½-inch dice	140	4.94	½ cup + 2 tablespoons
Sugar	36	1.27	3 tablespoons
Kosher salt	½ teaspoon	½ teaspoon	½ teaspoon
Egg yolk	20	0.70	1 large
Topping			
Unsalted butter, high-fat such as Plugra, softened	150	5.29	½ cup + 3 tablespoons
Sugar	200	7.05	1 cup
Eggs	200	7.05	4 large
Lemon juice	2½ teaspoons	2½ teaspoons	2½ teaspoons
Lemon zest, grated	1 teaspoon	1 teaspoon	1 teaspoon
Vanilla extract	1 teaspoon	1 teaspoon	1 teaspoon
Ground almond meal	186	6.56	1½ cups + 1 tablespoon
Unbleached all-purpose flour	50	1.76	⅓ cup
Kosher salt	½ teaspoon	½ teaspoon	½ teaspoon
Blueberries, fresh	300	10.58	2 cups

1. Preheat the oven to 350°F. Grease the baking pan with softened butter.

2. Prepare the crust: in a small bowl add the flour, diced cold butter, sugar, and salt and toss with your fingers to coat the butter with flour. With a pastry blender or 2 knives, cut the butter into the dry ingredients until small peas form. Add the egg yolk and mix the dough together with your fingers until it gathers into a ball. Pat the crust gently into the prepared baking pan and bake for 10 minutes.

3. While the crust is baking, make the filling: in a medium bowl with an electric mixer, cream the butter and sugar for 2 minutes, or until light and fluffy. Add the eggs, lemon juice, lemon zest, and vanilla and mix again, about 1 minute. In a small bowl, add the almond meal, flour, and salt and whisk together. Fold the almond mixture into the batter and mix until just combined. Add the blueberries and gently fold them in until just combined.

4. Pour the batter onto the crust and spread it evenly into the corners. Bake for 25 to 28 minutes, until the top is light golden brown and slightly firm. A toothpick inserted in the center should come out clean.

5. Place the pan on a wire rack to cool before cutting into 15 squares, 3 x 5. They can be served warm or fully cooled, and can be stored at room temperature covered with plastic wrap for 2 to 3 days.

TIPS and TECHNIQUES

Ground almond meal is simply blanched almonds that have been very finely ground. It can be found in specialty food stores and health food stores with other flours and grains. Store any extra almond meal in the freezer to keep it from turning rancid.

We recommend using high-fat butter (such as Plugra or Lurpak) to make this recipe. It makes the bars richer and very tender. If you can't find it, you can substitute regular unsalted butter in the same quantity.

To make the filling with other seasonal fruits, use 2 cups of any fresh berry such as blackberries, raspberries or cranberries, or firm fruit like apples, which should be peeled and thinly sliced before adding. If you're using fresh cranberries, toss them with 2 tablespoons of sugar before folding them into the filling.

Strawberry Shortcake

Yield: 6 shortcakes with strawberry sauce and whipped cream
Equipment: one 12 x 17-inch sheet pan

The first berries of summer are fresh strawberries, and when they arrive we make our homemade shortcakes. Strawberry "shortcakes" take many forms across the United States, from sponge cake with strawberries, to sweet and chewy biscuits, to what we think are the most authentic: tender, delicate, melt-in-your mouth shortcakes like those we make at Amy's Bread. The word *shortcake* defines a cake that is high in fat and very tender, or "short." The secret to good shortcake is to work quickly when making the dough, to keep your ingredients cold, and to include heavy cream and butter in your dough to add richness to the final biscuit. Our shortcakes are not very sweet and present the perfect canvas for full-flavored fresh strawberries. We try to buy berries from the farmers market when they're available. The deep red color and intense flavor of the fresh local berries make this dessert irresistible.

INGREDIENTS	GRAMS	OUNCES	VOLUME
Unbleached all-purpose flour	260	9.17	1¾ cups + 1 tablespoon
Sugar	43	1.5	3 tablespoons
Baking powder	1 tablespoon	1 tablespoon	1 tablespoon
Kosher salt	1 teaspoon	1 teaspoon	1 teaspoon
Baking soda	½ teaspoon	½ teaspoon	½ teaspoon
Unsalted butter, cold, cut into ½-inch dice	85	3	6 tablespoons
Eggs, separated	100	3.53	2 large
Heavy cream, cold	116	4.09	½ cup
Milk, whole, cold	58	2.04	¼ cup
Sugar, for sprinkling on biscuits	1 tablespoon	1 tablespoon	1 tablespoon
Strawberry Sauce			
Fresh strawberries	680	24	1½ quarts
Sugar	1 tablespoon + 1 teaspoon	1 tablespoon + 1 teaspoon	1 tablespoon + 1 teaspoon
Lemon juice	To taste	To taste	To taste
Whipped Cream			
Heavy cream, cold	116	4.09	½ cup
Sugar	1 teaspoon	1 teaspoon	1 teaspoon

1. Preheat the oven to 375°F. Line the sheet pan with baking parchment.

2. In a large bowl add the flour, sugar, baking powder, salt, and baking soda, and whisk together. Add the cold butter to the dry ingredients and toss with your fingers to coat the butter with flour. With a pastry blender or 2 knives, cut the butter into the dry ingredients until small peas form.

3. In a small bowl, add the egg yolks, heavy cream, and milk and whisk together. Add the liquids to the flour mixture and stir briefly until the dough becomes fully moistened and gathers together. Reserve the bowl from the liquids, including any cream residue in it.

4. Quickly dump the dough onto a lightly floured surface and pat it gently into a ¾-inch-thick disk, trying not to work it at all. Using a 2¾-inch biscuit cutter, cut out 6 biscuits as close together as possible, leaving a minimal amount of scraps. Gently press the scraps together and cut the dough to get a total of 6 biscuits.

5. Mix together the egg whites and the cream residue left in the mixing bowl. Brush a little onto each biscuit and sprinkle each one lightly with sugar. Place the biscuits on the prepared sheet pan and bake for 5 minutes, then reduce the oven temperature to 350°F and bake for 16 to 18 more minutes, until they are golden brown and slightly firm. Cool the biscuits on a wire rack before serving.

6. Prepare the strawberry sauce by washing, stemming, and trimming the berries. Cut them into pieces and sprinkle the sugar over them, then mash about half of the berries with a fork. Stir the berries gently, taste them, and add a little lemon juice to brighten up their flavor if needed. Chill the sauce until ready to use.

7. Prepare the whipped cream: In a small bowl combine the heavy cream and the sugar. With an electric mixer, whip the cream until soft peaks form. Do not overwhip. Keep the cream chilled until ready to serve.

8. To assemble the shortcakes, cut a biscuit in half and place the bottom half on a serving plate. Top that with ½ cup of the strawberry sauce and a spoonful of whipped cream. Place the top of the biscuit slightly off to the side on the whipped cream and serve immediately. Unused biscuits can be wrapped tightly and stored at room temperature for up to 2 days, or frozen. Reheat the biscuits in a toaster oven before serving.

TIPS *and* TECHNIQUES

While making the biscuits, handle the dough gently, keep it cold, and try not to overwork it or the biscuits will become tough. To get the best rise out of your biscuits, don't twist the biscuit cutter as you are cutting out each biscuit. Doing so will seal the edges and keep the biscuit from rising properly.

When selecting fresh strawberries, look for a farmers market that has fresh local berries. Small berries that are deep red in color will have the fullest flavor. Make the strawberry sauce at least one hour in advance, to allow the berries to macerate in the sugar and develop their best flavor.

Ingredients and Equipment

INGREDIENTS

Most of the ingredients we use in our recipes are familiar and easy to find at your local supermarkets and health food stores. Some of those we list in this section may be unfamiliar or difficult to find, or have a major influence on the success or failure of a recipe, and we feel they bear a little discussion.

Flour and Grains

Protein content in flour is the one factor that differentiates one flour from another. Even when using unbleached all-purpose flour, we pay attention to the protein content, as it can vary from one brand to the next. Even a few percentage points can dramatically change the amount of liquid needed in a recipe. Protein absorbs water, so higher-protein flours require more liquid. For the recipes in this book we specify the type of flour to be used. When testing, we used the flour that was available at our local supermarkets and health food stores, national brands that are available in all regions of the country. To help you make more informed flour choices, we include a chart (see page 241) showing the protein content of the unbleached flours and whole wheat flour that we found in our local stores. This information did not come off the flour package. We found it on company websites and by making phone calls to the technical people at some of the companies. Some companies never got back to us. This is not easy information to acquire, but it's beginning to become more available as more professional bakers and avid home bakers request it. *The Baker's Catalogue* put out by the King Arthur Flour company lists the protein content for their flours because they understand how important that information is to a good baker.

Cake flour

This type of flour is made from soft wheat, has a protein content of 6 to 8 percent, and is chlorinated (bleached) to further break down the strength of the protein and give the flour a velvety texture. We use cake flour or a combination of cake flour and unbleached all-purpose flour in some of our cake recipes.

Cornmeal

Our recipes require the coarse-textured, bright yellow, stone-ground variety of cornmeal rather than the finer, pale, more flourlike cornmeal found in supermarkets. Look for it in natural food stores. If you can't find it, dried polenta is a suitable substitute, as long as the granules are not too large. There is a brand of organic polenta—de la Estancia, available at Whole Foods—that is very close to the coarse cornmeal we use in the bakery. Bob's Red Mill makes a coarse cornmeal, too. They also make medium and fine cornmeal, so be sure you buy the coarsely ground version.

Pastry flour

This type of flour is made from soft wheat but has not been bleached, so it has a creamy color, and the protein content is usually 8 to 10 percent. Whole wheat pastry flour is milled using the whole kernel of soft wheat, so the bran and germ are included. We use whole wheat pastry flour in some of our breakfast pastries, to give them a finer texture and a nuttier flavor.

Unbleached all-purpose flour

When using "white" flour, we prefer it unbleached because we appreciate the fact that no chemicals have been used to whiten it, and we think that's better for your body. All-purpose flour is made from a combination of hard and soft wheat, so it can be used for a variety of different baking jobs. The protein content varies from brand to brand, but for common national brands, it is generally 11.0 to 11.8 percent. In some regions of the country, unbleached all-purpose flour can have a protein content as low as 8 percent, which puts it in the same category as pastry flour. So you will be more likely to have success using our recipes if you choose nationally distributed flour brands.

Unbleached bread flour

This type of flour is made from hard wheat, so it has a higher protein content. Protein in flour forms gluten when water is added and the dough is mixed or kneaded, forming a springy web to trap gases caused by yeast fermentation so the bread can rise. Most bread flour has 12 to 14 percent protein.

Whole wheat flour

This type of flour is milled using the whole kernel of grain, so it contains the hull and the germ as well as the white endosperm, making it rich in nutrients and fiber. Whole wheat flour can be very high in protein, but the sharp particles of bran will cut many of the gluten strands that form in dough, reducing the effectiveness of the protein. The protein content for whole wheat flours is often in the 13 to 14 percent range.

Flour Protein Comparison Chart

FLOUR BRAND	FLOUR TYPE	PROTEIN PERCENTAGE
Arrowhead Mills	Enriched Unbleached White Flour	11.7
Hecker's/Ceresota	Unbleached All-Purpose Flour	11.8
Gold Medal	Unbleached All-Purpose Flour	11.0
Gold Medal	Harvest King	12.0
King Arthur	Organic Select Artisan All-Purpose Flour	11.3
King Arthur	Unbleached All-Purpose Flour	11.7
King Arthur	Unbleached Bread Flour	12.7
King Arthur	Traditional Whole Wheat Flour	14.0
King Arthur	Organic Whole Wheat Flour	13.0
North Dakota Mill	Dakota Maid Bread Flour	12.0
Pillsbury	SoftAsSilk Cake Flour	6.0 to 8.0
Pillsbury	Unbleached All Purpose Flour	10.5
Pillsbury	Unbleached Bread Flour	12.0
Swans Down	Cake Flour	6.0 to 8.0
Whole Foods 365	Organic Unbleached All-Purpose Flour	11.5
Whole Foods 365	Organic Whole Wheat Flour	13.0 to 14.0

Food Coloring

In the Sweet Pink Buttercream Frosting (see page 201), we use Baker's brand rose food coloring, and in the Red Velvet Cake (see page 165), we use Christmas Red food coloring. In the bakery, we use liquid gel colors. They're thicker and more concentrated than the food coloring that comes from the supermarket. Be aware that red food coloring sometimes gives food a bitter aftertaste. If you experience that from the food coloring you use, use the liquid gel color called Tulip Red or No Taste Red, which will leave no aftertaste. The liquid gel colors are sold at stores that specialize in cake decorating supplies. You can also buy them online at www.kitchenkrafts.com or mail-order them from New York Cake and Baking Supply. This company will take orders only by phone or by fax: telephone (800) 942–2539 or (212) 675–2253; fax (212) 675–7099.

Leaveners

Leaveners are the ingredients that make baked goods rise. Cookies, cakes, muffins, scones, and quickbreads all use chemical leaveners. Leavened bread uses some form of yeast to make it rise. It's especially important to test your leaveners before baking with them, to be sure they're still potent.

Baking powder

This has limited shelf life and should be replaced after a year. Test its strength by sprinkling it on hot water. If it fizzes a lot, it's fine.

Baking soda

This can have an indefinite shelf life if properly stored. To test it, put ½ teaspoon of baking soda in ¼ cup of vinegar. If it bubbles up dramatically, it's still good.

Active dry yeast

We use this type of yeast in the recipes in this book because it's the easiest to find. Be sure to check the expiration date stamped on the back of the package. Don't buy it if it has expired. Yeast retains its potency longer if stored in an airtight package in the freezer. For the recipes in this book, we give the yeast a "head start" by dissolving it in a little very warm water and letting it sit for a few minutes. If you're dubious about the potency of your yeast, add a pinch of sugar to yeast that's been dissolved in warm water and let it sit for 10 minutes. If the yeast is nice and bubbly after ten minutes, you can use it with confidence.

Nuts

To toast nuts: Preheat the oven to 350°F. Spread the nuts evenly on a 12 x 17-inch sheet pan and toast them for 5 to 8 minutes, until the nuts begin to brown and smell fragrant. Watch them carefully. The nuts around the edges of the sheet pan may toast more quickly, and it's very easy to burn them.

Poured Fondant

See page 209 in the Frostings chapter for a description and details.

Sugar and Other Sweeteners

Turbinado sugar

This is often sold under the brand name Sugar In The Raw. It is raw sugar that has not had all of the molasses refined out of it, so the crystals have a light golden color. The crystals are larger than those of regular granulated sugar, so we like to sprinkle them over the tops of some of our scones and muffins before putting them in the oven.

EQUIPMENT

You don't need a lot of fancy, complicated tools and equipment to make the recipes in this book. In fact, our general motto at the bakery is "keep it simple." In this section we list only equipment that may be difficult to find or that we believe has a major influence on your being able to duplicate our recipes successfully.

Kitchen Scale

If you don't already own a digital kitchen scale, we urge you to buy one. We firmly believe, and know from experience, that the best way to guarantee consistent results from a baking recipe is to weigh the ingredients instead of using measuring cups and spoons. Baking is a science that requires accurate measurements to achieve predictable results. Weights in grams are much more precise than weights in ounces, but ounces are fine if you feel more comfortable using them. At the bakery, all of our recipes are expressed in gram weights. In an effort to represent our bakery recipes as accurately as possible, we list the ingredient amounts for the recipes in this book in grams first. Once you get used to using grams, everything else will seem cumbersome. You will have the most success using the recipes in this book to duplicate the products we make in the bakery if you weigh the ingredients.

Good electronic digital kitchen scales are available in all kitchenware stores and from online retailers that specialize in kitchenware. We don't usually recommend specific brands, but we're so eager to encourage you to purchase a scale that we recommend the very dependable inexpensive scale we found while we were testing recipes for this book. We both used the little Escali Primo scale, which has a maximum capacity of 5 kilos (11 pounds) and uses two AA batteries that last for a very long time. This scale was very accurate and dependable, and it stood up to very heavy use. The cover on the battery compartment does like to fall off, but a piece of tape solves that problem. The scale is available at many kitchenware stores and online at www.amazon.com, www.kingarthurflour.com, and www.target.com.

Mini Bundt Cake Pans

We mention these here because some manufacturers have stopped making them, and they're getting hard to find. We use these little pans for the Lowfat Applesauce Doughnuts (page 53), the Not Lowfat Chocolate Doughnuts (page 56), and the Gingerbread Cakes (page 226). Each pan has 6 cups, so 2 pans are necessary for each recipe. These pans can sometimes still be found at kitchenware stores or purchased online at www.amazon.com (called "Wilton mini-fluted pan") or at www.bakedeco.com (under Bakeware/Molds; select "Bundt pans" and go to page 4).

Sheet Pans

In the recipes in this book, we recommend using 12 x 17-inch sheet pans, called half-sheet pans by professional bakers, to bake cookies, sheet cakes, breakfast pastries, quiche, and bars, and for oven-drying tomatoes and proofing shaped bread. These pans are made from aluminum-coated steel with a rolled edge surrounded by bead wire, so they're heavier than ordinary baking sheets made for the home kitchen. They heat quickly and evenly for more uniform baking, and they won't warp in the oven. They also last forever. The outside top dimensions of the pan are actually 13 x 18 inches. The pans have straight sides and are called "jelly roll pans" at most retailers, though that term is rarely used in professional kitchens. If you don't have them already, we recommend you add two of them to your collection of baking pans. Once you bake with them, you won't want to use anything else. They're usually available in most good kitchenware stores and from online retailers specializing in kitchenware.

Tart/Quiche Pans

The pans we use to make quiche (see page 88) are 4¾ inches in diameter by ¾ inch deep and have removable bottoms. We like the ones made in France by a company named Gobel, which have a nonstick finish. These pans are not much in demand for home baking, so it's unlikely you'll find them in a regular kitchenware store, but it wouldn't hurt to look. The best sources sell to both the commercial baking industry and avid home bakers. To purchase these pans online, go to www.bakedeco.com

(under Bakeware/Molds, select "Tart/Quiche Pans"). Our other source for these pans is New York Cake and Baking Supply. You can see the pans on their website at www. nycake.com. Their 4½-inch size is really 4¾ inches. This company takes orders only by phone or fax: telephone (800) 942–2539 or (212) 675–2253; fax (212) 675–7099. These are great little pans.

Thermometer

We believe an instant-read stem thermometer is one of the most important tools you can have in your kitchen. It's a must for making any of our bread recipes or Poured Fondant (see page 209). They are available at kitchenware stores and online at popular websites that sell kitchenware.

Giampietro (Jack) Mo

Giampietro (Jack) Mo makes Toy laugh. Whenever he's around, the day is a little brighter. A native of Italy, Jack has passion and a personality that reflect all the best qualities of the country in which he was born. If you call one of our retail locations and someone answers the phone with "Amy's Bread. Buon giorno!" you know Jack is on the line. For more than six years he's been our operations manager in the Hell's Kitchen store. He takes care of the facility, ordering ingredients and paper products, and purchasing and maintaining all of the equipment and fixtures. He is great at keeping track of all our special ingredients and sourcing any special equipment we need to make our pastries, using his masterful negotiating skills to ensure we get the best value for our bakery dollars. He also helps manage the retail store, running around the place at a brisk pace like the passionate marathoner and tri-athlete he is. In late summer, when the store is full of European tourists eating breakfast or lunch at the café tables, Jack is happily in his element chatting with the guests, making espresso, and keeping the staff and customers in stitches with his antics. It's not unusual for our European visitors to return on successive trips to New York to spend time again and again at *Amy's Bread* to see their old friend Jack Mo.

Index